The Worst of
the IT Skeptic

from the notorious blog

by

Rob England

Two Hills
Sensible business practices

Created by Two Hills Ltd

letterbox@twohills.co.nz

www.twohills.co.nz

PO Box 57-150, Mana
Porirua 5247
New Zealand

Published by Two Hills
First published 2009

ISBN: 144147837X
EAN-13: 978-1441478375

Cover: Kapiti Island, Pukerua Bay, New Zealand.
Photos by the author.

ITIL® is a Registered Trade Mark and a Registered Community Trade Mark of the UK Office of Government Commerce ("OGC"). ITIL® is registered in the U.S. Patent and Trademark Office.

This book is neither part of nor associated with the IT Infrastructure Library®.

This book and its author are neither associated with nor endorsed by the OGC or any other organisation.

Dedicated to my endlessly supportive wife Vee who helped me break loose from the corporate cocoon.

Mahal kita.

Contents

Part 2: ITIL and CMDB

Part 3: The IT Industry 249

Preface

I strongly urge everyone to do amateur acting classes even if, like me, you never tread the boards. One of the most important things you learn is mask work. It is enlightening to see how a mask transforms your personality as you put it on.

The IT Skeptic didn't set out to be a journalist but that is what he has become. Journalists are a contemptible breed (except of course any reviewing this book). I don't much like most that I have met. But the IT Skeptic performs a useful function in the IT industry, asking hard questions that needed to be asked, especially to put a brake on the wild exuberance that is sweeping the ITIL industry away.

In order to fulfil their function, journalists must be read by many readers. To be successful - to survive - journalists must serve the market. They write what the market wants to read, and the market likes a little titillation with their content.

I can't say I entirely like the IT Skeptic, but I like what he does and I hope he continues to do it. In the end, I have come to terms with him because he is me.

Rob England

Pukerua Bay

February 2009

Introduction

The IT Skeptic is a commentator on IT's sillier moments, especially those related to ITSM in general and ITIL in particular. This is not because the IT Skeptic wishes to focus on ITIL - it is just that ITIL and itSMF provide such great material for a skeptic. If you are reading this you have probably already seen the blog, *the IT Skeptic*, but in case you haven't, it is at www.itskeptic.org.

This book is a collection of selected extracts from the blog, some of them direct quotes and others merged, revised and edited. The line had to be drawn somewhere so it stops at the end of 2008. A few other pieces come from the blog's newsletter *The Skeptical Informer*, articles by the author[1], and the author's other books *Introduction to Real ITSM* and *Owning ITIL®*. Note: Real ITSM is satire, OK? Any part of this book talking about realitsm is a spoof. See www.realitsm.com. Please don't take it seriously and write me any more abusive emails.

One likes to think one's writing comes from a consistent and cohesive set of ideas, but of course it doesn't, especially when written over a three year period. As you read this book you might enjoy spotting errors, rip-offs, re-cycled jokes, contradictions, total back-flips, and inconsistencies. There is a competition for the best ones found, at http://www.itskeptic.org/pulling-apart-it-skeptic.

Commentary written for this book is shaded like this, and content from the original sources looks like...

I'm not sure this was ever a "classy place" but I aint gonna edit no posts just cos they aint got class.

---

[1] See www.twohills.co.nz/portfolio for all articles, books, websites and papers by the author.

A comment on comments

The blog attracted comments from early on. The reason we never had a dedicated forum on the blog was because comments worked so well.

I would love to include the comments in this book but it would soon be a thousand pages and then where would my profits be? And the comments are of such a high standard that selecting and editing would be impossible.

So it is with the greatest reluctance that I have decided to stick to my own content. It was a tough call. Please go browse the comments on the site sometime: they are a rich source of knowledge and stimulation.

So good in fact that we are considering another book: *The Best (Threads) of the IT Skeptic*.

A reference to references

We've inserted key references to other sources as a footnote, and the links will be listed on the website at www.itskeptic.org/worst, but we chose not to link every extract in the book back to the original blog or book entries. If you want to find the original text, Google it.

Part 1:
the Blog and
its Range

The IT Skeptic

The IT Skeptic is a notorious blog. It has attracted unflattering descriptions of the IT Skeptic; strained (but I hope not broken) a few friendships; annoyed one or two people that I am happy to have annoyed; and killed the conversation at parties. On the other hand it has generated writing work for me; got me invited to speaking gigs in exciting countries, some of which I actually went to (the rest I couldn't afford - I didn't say *paying* gigs); and been an awful lot of fun for me and many others.

I write for me – what I would like to read. The blog grew, so it seems a few thousand readers found it interesting. I do try to be an engaging writer. Read this book and judge for yourself. If you don't think it was worth reading, please contact the IT Skeptic at skeptic@itskeptic.org.

Most of all I like to think the blog made a small difference in the ITSM world. Some friends tell me it had more than a small impact but they are just making me feel better about the site being valued for $4000 after a thousand hours of work. This blog takes a lot of time for little return. Costs have been in six figures, counting opportunity costs, and returns have barely made four figures. Of course this book hopes to change that.

This first section introduces the blog and its main characters, and gives you a sample of how widely the IT Skeptic wanders.

First post

On the 16th of May 2006 the IT Skeptic blog went live with the following post...

Now that ITIL is the de facto standard for IT operations, the time is ripe for a more objective evaluation of ITIL's merits and caveats. Let's do that on this website. In the ITIL world it is still spring or summer. This blog seeks to balance that with an icy blast of winter through the techniques of the skeptic – consider the observable facts and question the underlying assumptions – as well as applying that other great Litmus test: common sense (Common sense is something that used to be common, hence the name. You youngsters look it up on Wikipedia).

The IT world is traditionally split into development and operations halves. In the operations hemisphere, ITIL has been the centre of attention for most of this century. If you have anything to do with running computers and you haven't heard of ITIL, you should read up on it, if only to be in the know at those awful parties where IT people talk their own language like some secret society.

Gartner have a most useful model for considering the waves of irrational exuberance that regularly sweep across the IT industry: the hype cycle[1]. ITIL is somewhere around the peak, though it varies around the world. I think it is not in the trough yet anywhere: it is still greeted with acclaim and enthusiasm and often inflated expectations. But progress down the slippery slope is beginning. Hopefully a little objectivity now can reduce the height of the peak and the depth of the trough, and ease the transition into a more stable maturity.

...With that post, the first shot was fired. The IT Skeptic arrived to rattle the walls of Castle ITIL.

Or so people may think, but in fact the blog was never meant to be anything radical. I just wanted to learn how the Web works. I needed a reason for a website so I could learn the LAMP stack (Linux Apache MySQL and PHP) and Content Management Systems and eCommerce.

I had in my head some interesting skeptical questions about ITIL, triggered by my friend Alan Mayo (a New Zealand enterprise architect) who challenged my assumptions when I tried to sell him ITIL. Challenged? He blew me apart. And I am a bona fide paid-up Skeptic

---

[1] http://www.gartner.com/teleconferences/attributes/attr_129930_115.pdf

(www.skeptics.org.nz) but he out-skepticked me. So the blog was born, with an intended lifetime of six months or a year and an expected audience of about none...

Since the IT Skeptic is banging on about transparency, I thought a disclosure of this site's motivations might be in order. There is an agenda here which, whilst not hidden, has not been discussed. I want to be an internet entrepreneur. In the past 18 months I have been on a tremendous learning curve to acquire all the social, business and technical knowledge and skills required to do this. This site is in fact a learning experiment for me, a sandbox, a pilot. Or at any rate that is how it started out: to get my views out there and to learn how to build and run a blog in the process.

Along the way this site has acquired considerably more momentum than I anticipated. It has become more work and responsibility than I planned. In return it has taught me a lot more than I imagined, introduced me to lots of people, opened several unexpected avenues for me, and proved to be loads of fun. So if odd things come and go on the site, things change, even ... gulp ... break occasionally, it is because I am experimenting, learning, getting ready for That Which Comes After, various sites which are aggressively commercial. Sorry if that makes you feel like guinea pigs. But you are. If it is any compensation so am I - I'm part of the experiment - and I'm the one running the treadmill.

Some people believe that skepticism is the rejection of new ideas, or worse, they confuse "skeptic" with "cynic" and think that skeptics are a bunch of grumpy curmudgeons unwilling to accept any claim that challenges the status quo. This is wrong. Skepticism is a provisional approach to claims. It is the application of reason to any and all ideas — no sacred cows allowed. In other words, skepticism is a method, not a position. Ideally, skeptics do not go into an investigation closed to the possibility that a phenomenon might be real or that a claim might be true. When we say we are "skeptical," we mean that we must see compelling evidence before we believe.

Skeptics Society
http://www.skeptic.com/about_us/discover_skepticism.html

Having recently become an author I am learning just how bloody hard it is. My humble efforts in no way compare to what the ITIL V3 authors produced. Although they had a lot more help than me, their products were much bigger, more complex, more closely scrutinised and of course much more significant.

At this time of year [Christmas] I like to remind readers, especially those on the receiving end of the blog, that it isn't personal. I like and respect just about everyone I have met in the ITSM world. There have to be one or two exceptions, or we wouldn't be human, but equally I hope I can count one or two as friends. And I profoundly respect what the Architect and Authors achieved, and all those who helped to bring ITIL V3 to fruition. I respect it even more so now my own humble effort is out the door. So to all the authors and vendors and trainers and consultants and analysts, to all at OGC and itSMF and APMG and TSO, and most of all to you my readers I wish each and every one of you a very merry Christmas and a most happy New Year.

Like all bad ideas, this one [the book *Introduction to Real ITSM*] started out small and just grew. Originally this was going to be a small book run quickly through the on-demand publishing system to learn some of the pitfalls before publishing That Which Comes After, The Book About ITIL [*Owning ITIL*]. That way I would only make new mistakes on the second book.

But this book developed a life of its own, with a related website (www.realitsm.com) and a club (EgoITSM), and silly illustrations.

A word about those illustrations: there is a story that Neil Young only played guitar and never sang because he was too embarrassed about his voice, until one day he heard Bob Dylan. I felt the same way about my drawing when I saw Scott Adams' *Dilbert*. Unfortunately, Neil Young sings better than I draw.

Anonymity

At first the IT Skeptic was anonymous. Being the newsletter editor for itSMF New Zealand it seemed like a good idea to avoid embarrassment for the Committee.

But everybody locally was supportive and I started to have ideological problems with anonymity, so I "came out"...

The IT Skeptic has decided to abandon anonymity on this blog.

Why did the IT Skeptic choose to be anonymous?

1) I can comment without restraints that might be imposed by other roles I perform in my profession

2) I can avoid nasty emails and heated debates at conferences and meetings. I imagine my physical safety could be an issue with a few of the comments I have made

3) it's fun

A fourth reason, related to the first, was to avoid any embarrassment to colleagues on the committee of itSMFnz. I was concerned that some overseas itSMF people might not appreciate the itSMFnz newsletter editor giving them stick, and they might make life difficult for the New Zealand executive.

(The New Zealand committee have always been in the know, and unanimously supportive).

In the early days of the blog this was probably the right decision: it saved hassles and it made the blog a bit more interesting.

As time has passed, anonymity has become increasingly farcical. All the people who might make waves know exactly who the IT Skeptic is, along with a tribe of others in the know.

I hope the probability of anyone objecting has declined as the blog established credibility and a track record for fairness (or at least even-handed unfairness), and for moderation of comments. In addition the itSMFnz editorials have been written by my "regular" self demonstrably free of Skeptic subversion – well at least no more than any good editor would exhibit. Readers can judge for yourselves[1].

---

[1] www.itsmf.org.nz/index.php?option=com_docman&task=cat_view&gid=55&Itemid=254

Furthermore this blog spends a fair amount of time campaigning for transparency and community involvement in itSMF and other ITIL bodies. Any attempt to stifle debate now would just be grist for the mill.

These are considerations, but the main reasons to drop anonymity are more fundamental ones.

First, even though I strived to establish as much credibility as possible, reading comments on the blog and other websites showed that anonymous writing in general suffers from diminished integrity.

There are some distasteful corners of the internet, where people air opinions and attack others in a manner they simply would not be able to before the emergence of the internet. There are forums and sites that are no better than scribblings on toilet walls, or the malicious gossip whispered amongst a bitchy few. But now this rubbish is broadcast to the planet. The IT Skeptic has no desire to be associated with this kind of social deviancy.

Second, there is a fundamental inconsistency in an anonymous blogger advocating transparency and disclosure. And I was unable to challenge anonymous commenters on my blog to identify themselves when they made attacks on other people.

I conclude that anonymity has its place:

- In the early days of a blog

- Where employers and associates might object or feel uncomfortable

- Where the physical security of the blogger and family might be compromised

But in general blogalistic integrity is (hopefully) enhanced by standing behind one's remarks, and a more wholesome blog environment can be encouraged.

...So far so good. The cat has been out of the bag for two years now. One very senior ex-member of Castle ITIL didn't want to talk to me, but otherwise everyone has been very civil and the house is unburnt.

Early on, pre-coming-out, a convention speaking invitation came to nothing when the convention itself folded. It was shame because I had been looking forward to speaking in a burkha.

Dropping anonymity has not prevented me from generating an alter ego...

The IT Swami

The IT Swami is the IT Skeptic's alter-ego. While the IT Skeptic uses known facts to draw inference or predict outcome, the IT Swami is not so constrained. He uses instinct, second sight, crystals and patchouli to wildly speculate on the present and future.

The IT Swami first appeared on the blog in January 2007 to give us his New Year predictions...

The IT Skeptic takes the day off, doing what skeptics do for fun (don't ask). In his place we have his alter-ego the IT Swami kicking off the New Year with some predictions for IT in the coming twelve months.

In Service Management:

The itSMF, EXIN and ASEB – all snubbed by OGC - will drive the new ISO20000 industry. [Wrong. The ISO20000 industry continued to be moribund]

The ITIL 3 books will be good. Sales will be brisk. They will be greeted with acclaim in most quarters and criticism in a few (including this site, you can bet). One country in Europe will be less enthusiastic. [Correct]

There will be legal wrangling over rights to parts of ITIL 3 or its ancillaries. [Wrong, but watch 2009]

The feverish sheep-dipping industry (ITIL Foundation training) will cool as APMG brings it to heel by taking their tithe. Many small players will drop out. [Wrong. The industry drove it to ever greater frenzies]

A consulting industry will spring up around ITIL 2 to ITIL 3 "transitions" or "upgrades" or "refresher training" or "re-certification". Is a "process factory" possible? If so, look for them to arise in India. [Wrong. Not enough organisations went to ITIL V3]

Aggressive price wars will break out in the service desk software market as people realise that they all work, pretty much. [Partly right??]

Fortunes will be squandered trying to implement CMDB. Several organisations will actually succeed: we will hear about them everywhere (but not how much they spent). The noises about vendor collaboration on CMDB will remain just that. [Correct]

Look for the continuing trend to adopt process methodologies from other areas of business, primarily manufacturing, in a continuing drive to increase IT operations efficiency (read: less people and less investment). [Correct: "lean" and "green"]

OGC will launch a participatory, wiki- and forum-based online community for ITIL contributions and feedback. No... wait... that was just a smudge on the crystal ball. They won't. [Correct: they didn't. The forum finally arrived in 2008]

And wider afield:

Web 2 will cease to have any meaning at all as it gets applied to everything from Ajax to tags. Forrester will do a white paper on Web 3. Gartner will present a keynote on Web Extended Edition at a major conference. [Correct about 2.0 being slapped on everything from Enterprise 2.0 to – in 2009 – Sales 2.0]

Neural learning and/or evolutionary software will be used in website design to optimise consumer appeal. [Not yet?]

Google, Microsoft and Yahoo will continue to expand, acquire and mimic - consolidating the internet industry. More and more bit players will get swallowed or crushed. A challenger will emerge. [Correct about the swallowing. Is Amazon a challenger?]

Servers will finally catch up with mainframes and the distinction will disappear (perhaps it already has). [Yes it already has, except for the price tags]

3G phones will remain a plaything of teenagers and geeks (especially teenage geeks). The bulk of the public will stubbornly refuse to want to watch TV on 300x200 pixels. When they want to find a restaurant they will ask someone. [Correct]

Look for a fusion of game machine and internet-based TV to challenge cable: Microsoft or Sony, your pick. In a similar vein, look out for the virtual (i.e. hosted) home PC using the same game machines and a VirtualPC server farm. Why pay a couple of thousand for a PC and monitor when you already have an Xbox and a TV? Just a little more bandwidth for a little less cost... [Wrong: still waiting]

The inflatable PC will be announced, using roll-up screen and virtual keyboard. [Nearly there]

The growth of YouTube and wannabes will start to peak as all the adolescents and other exhibitionists have too many online profiles to manage, and the female ones start to be driven off by online perverts. [Wrong: the perverts are having a field day. You should see Second Life.]

Eastern bloc spammers and pornographers will start getting disappeared by mysterious assassins. The US will announce generous funding for eastern bloc internet connectivity. (Think about what spam costs the US economy each year. Then ponder where many of the spammers are, and what it costs to get someone rubbed out in those places. Then imagine a CIA man with a suitcase full of dollars being fed tip-offs from Echelon. And you heard it from a skeptic blog.) [Wrong. I wish. Spammers remain a pest on the blog despite aggressive response.]

A new internet craze will emerge involving real-time phone video and a body part or function. [Wrong. The craze was to beat people up and film it.]

Microsoft will apply for a patent on the binary number system. [Pretty much everything else]

Britney Spears will get arrested for gross indecency. [Partly correct. January 2008 and not for indecency. In February 2007 a satirist pinched the idea and claimed she was.]

These prognostications are offered for entertainment purposes only. Any conclusions or actions derived from them are the reader's sole responsibility. The IT Swami will not be responsible for any loss or ritual humiliation resulting from their use. And anyone who believes someone else can see the future gets what they deserve.

...Then a few months later on a freezing Southern midwinter solstice night in June 2007, beside a driftwood bonfire on wild Pukerua Bay beach, New Zealand, the IT Swami gazed into the future to give us his "Southern New Year" predictions for the IT Infrastructure Library. We cover these on page 147. He disappeared until early 2008 when...

Several readers of The IT Skeptic have asked where is the IT Swami and in particular where were his New Year's predictions for 2008? Now we can reveal all.

The current New Zealand government achieved notoriety by funding a $26,000 cultural fact-finding tour overseas which turned out to be studying hip-hop as a key element of contemporary indigenous culture. (It was not by any means their best effort). This is the equivalent of the US government paying some gangstas to check out the dance moves in Europe as a contribution to the cultural development of the USA.

In the resulting climate of closer scrutiny of arts grants, more money is now being channelled to scientific research. As a result, in 2007 the IT Swami succeeded in his application for a grant to travel to the Netherlands for "Investigation of Psychotropic Prognostication Techniques for Forecasting in the IT Service Management Industry". This was in recognition of his previous work, "VISIONS OF THE FUTURE: the IT Swami's seven visions of the future of ITIL".

This two week study tour in December last year turned into a three month trip from which the IT Swami has only recently returned, apparently with the encouragement of the Dutch authorities and the assistance of the New Zealand Embassy in Amsterdam.

Like all government-funded research, a report was required on the results of the IT Swami's trip. We will not post the whole 126-page document here as it is extremely technical and quite heavy going, but in summary the IT Swami has revised his Seventh Vision of the Future of ITIL.

In the original Vision he said:

> There are three castors, yes, three castors and The ...Three ...Castors ...Of ...The ...Seat ...Of ...IT's ...Future ...are ...are ...Governance, Service and Compliance!!

Now as a result of his latest research, he has apparently "dissipated the clouds of uncertainly discombobulating my prognostications" and can now say "most certainly indeed, my goodness" that the Three Castors Of The Seat Of IT's Future are Governance, Service and **Assurance**.

He concludes: "Readers will I'm sure agree that the staggering profundity of this extensive revision to the Vision patently justifies the money and time spent in Holland and represents an excellent return on investment on the Government's $53,000."

...There followed another long break until January 2009...

Late last night as I worked at my computer, I looked up at a sound in the normally quiet cul-de-sac that houses Two Hills World Headquarters Tower. From the back door of a police car tumbled the IT Swami, closely followed by his swag, which appeared to have been hurled rather than just fell. The police car then drove off while he picked himself up and examined himself for broken bones, or perhaps it was just some exotic late-night yoga - he does subscribe to strange practices. In a familiar routine, I raced downstairs to hide the good whisky and cognac before he got to the doorbell. I slipped the smaller ornaments into a cupboard and put the kettle on. I knew he would need a coffee to sober him up.

It has been some time since I saw the IT Swami. Last heard of, there was an incident involving a free-love commune in the north of Queensland. Something to do with a mayor's daughter. Before that he wrote to me to solicit funds for an organic textile-fibre-growing operation in Takaka[1]. I got confused reports about the outcome of that one but I gather much of the stock was damaged by fire. Some angry emails I was copied on suggest he is or was the architect for a software product out of San Francisco that delivers service catalogues on Twitter. I believe he is also involved in an internet-based religion built on meditation using party pills. Long-term readers will recall the government-funded psychotropic tour of the Netherlands which resulted in the vision that "The three castors of the seat of IT's future are Governance, Service and Assurance".

He was most distressed to hear that the Labour government is out on its ear and the new one is highly unlikely to fund similar "cultural" activities. But I'm getting ahead of myself. I told him of recent developments in our country during an all-night conversation over large mugs of what my late father called the "cooking whisky" (Grants). That conversation followed only after I helped him up the steps and ordered him into the shower before the smell woke my wife. It was a relief not to have to search him for illegal contraband for once - I figured that was unnecessary so soon after his ejection from a New Zealand police car.

Aaaaanyways, somewhere around 3am, we got onto IT Service Management, once we had run out of other topics. (I would love to tell you about some of the other stuff we covered but I can't). I asked him if he had thought any more about ITSM since the three-castor thing. He looked surprised and said he hadn't other than to use the new OGC logo [see p300] as part of tantric sex meditation.

I said he was long over-due for predicting ITSM's future, so we tumbled out the front door (I repaired it today) and wobbled off up the track in the dark to his favourite trance rock. After the rest of the Grants, and an Indonesian cloves cigarette (or so he told me) which he had left under the rock from last time, and some delicious cookies he found in his jacket, he squinted out over the ocean and began to speak. And this is what he told me. Actually it is merely the bit I recall with any clarity. There was much more but I seem to have forgotten most of it. I vaguely recall - I think - stuff about a COBIT-vs-ITIL price war, the itSMFUK chair, an ATO mutiny, an ITIL-based ISO9000 compliance certification, ITIL Live™

---

[1] An infamous marijuana-growing area in New Zealand

closing down, the runaway success of Novell's myCMDB, CA being acquired... many things which I can't be sure of.

Apparently, ITIL is now hurtling down the other side of the Gartner hype curve into the trough of disillusionment. Questions will be asked. Heretics will speak up. There will be sporadic lynching of vendors.

We will also see the start of a search for "better than ITIL" and "less than ITIL". The herd will fragment as some come to see ITIL as only for the great unwashed and others see it as high-fallutin' overkill for fancy folks. As a result we will see more attention on alternatives: COBIT, ITSM Library, FITS, MOF...

ITIL projects will be cancelled all over the place as the recession bites, but just as many will be spawned as part of efficiency drives, as CIOs madly spend money to be seen to be doing something about cost cutting. (Maybe all the recently-unemployed Kiwi consultants can then bugger off back to London and Sydney and give me my consulting market back).

The ITSM philosophers, "the intellectual masturbators like the IT Skeptic" as he put it, will see ITSM as so Noughties and turn to other topics like Governance and Lean and Assurance and Professionalism for the coming decade.

Come the end of 2009, everyone will still be arguing about the ITIL V3 certification scheme, ITIL V2 will still be adopted as often as V3, and there still won't be any central register of itSMF membership or ITIL certification. Two new books will have rounded out COBIT as a complete BOK equivalent to ITIL, and a thousand people worldwide will know what DSDM Atern is. One vendor will have filed for bankruptcy, and the IT Skeptic will have actually published *Owning ITIL*.

This afternoon after we got up the IT Swami took three hundred bucks that I apparently owed him since 1997, and borrowed my new copy of The Guide to the Universal Service Management Body of Knowledge (an emerging BOK that I only recently managed to scam for free from the author, Ian Clayton). He was last seen slumped on his swag out on the highway hitching north. There is a New Age Crystals and CMDBs Festival he hopes to set up a stall for if he can find it in time.

Annual Awards

Each year, the IT Skeptic is pleased to announce our annual New Year's awards. These awards are presented to deserving figures and organisations in the IT industry in general and the ITSM industry in particular.

2006[1]

The Stallman Award for Most Outstanding Contribution to the Documentation of ITIL Best Practice goes to those tireless volunteers who are building the Wikipedia ITIL entry(s). Runners up were the other open websites such as OpenITIL, the ITIL Open Guide and the ITIL Wiki.

The Platinum Microscope for the Finest Hair Split goes to Pink Elephant for assuring the world that PinkVerify does not certify ITIL compliance. Assessment, validation, verification, certification, compatibility, comparison against criteria, explicit demonstration of commitment, reassurance, diligence, support for definition and requirements, and guidance met ... but not compliance.

The Trump Medal for Most Inappropriate Empire Building goes to the executive of itSMF International for attempting to get control of ITIL through the CAR tendering and now attempting to get control of ISO20000 certification. The itSMF exists as a volunteer organisation to further ITSM professionalism and best practice, whatever flavour. These commercial and political manoeuvrings are unbecoming.

The Gold Finger for Megalomania goes to Microsoft for trying to patent everything.

The Engelbert Humperdink Memorial Codpiece for Worst Change of Name goes to OGC for publishing the updated "ITIL in SITU" [Small IT Units] as "ITIL Small-scale Implementation". How could they lose such a clever name?

The Tolstoy Championship for Forum Contributions Above and Beyond goes to Frank Guerino, founder and CEO of TraverseIT, whose forum posts and comments invariably extend to several screensful of content that ranges from the astute to the fixated, but always passionate and nearly always managing to mention his product.

---

[1] http://www.itskeptic.org/node/89

The Terminological Debasement Cup goes to Dennis Drogseth of EMA for trying to redefine CMDB as a process not a thing.

The Gartner Ribbon for Most Preposterous Statistic goes to ... who else ... Gartner for assuring us that ITIL reduces costs by up to 48%. Not 50% Not 45% Exactly 48%

The Hussein Trophy for Most Hypocritical Protestations goes to those members of the itSMF who howled about letting CAR contracts to a privately owned company (APMG) and the sale of TSO when their own private companies are doing so nicely out of contractual links with ITIL.

The Andrés Escobar Memorial Shield for Best Own Goal goes to itSMF USA for publishing the research result that "A staggering 72 percent felt unable to acknowledge any linkage at all between process maturity and performance improvement"

The Caterpillar Cup for the Most Outstanding Contribution to ITIL Case Studies goes to Pink Elephant for finally giving us some names to add to the thoroughly worn-out Proctor and Gamble, Caterpillar and Ontario Justice.

The Kim Il-sung Memorial Vase for Keeping It In The Family goes to the OGC committee awarding ITIL 3 refresh authoring contracts, for ensuring all contributors came from the Western corporate ITIL industry. No authors from Asia. No authors from government, health, engineering, non-profits, or small business. Well done!

The P T Barnum Gold Cigar for the Most Hyped ITIL Concept of the Year goes to a consortium of vendors for their brochure-ware proposed standards for CMDB repositories.

The Skeptic's Banner of Best Individual Contribution to itskeptic.org goes to the anonymous "Claire" of Practical Service Management for proposing "We could look to some sort of Continuous Hype Improvement Process (CHIP) - sustaining ITIL through a never ending series of refreshes and book reissues....."

Finally, the one you have been waiting for ...Envelope please... **The Grand Sagan Candle for IT Skepticism** goes to Robert Glass (in the Communications of the ACM 49:8, August 2006) for reportedly applying scientific method to one of IT's many assertions, the Standish CHAOS Report.

This is the one that gave us those oft-quoted numbers (known on this blog as "crap factoids") "a staggering 31.1% of projects will be cancelled before they ever get completed ... only 16.2% [of] software projects that are completed on-time and on-budget. In the larger companies ... only 9% of their projects come in on-time and on-budget".

Glass points out the inconvenient fact that "Objective research study findings do not, in general, support the Standish conclusions" and makes some telling criticisms of the Standish methodology, which appears to be much the same as those of most industry analysts: anecdotal, unscientific (no random selection, no controls, no full disclosure of data, no double blinds) and unreviewed. Whether Glass is right or wrong, he is the one following best research practice, not Standish. [1]

2007[2]

The Terminological Debasement Cup goes to Sharon Taylor, ITIL3 Chief Architect, for vague and varying usage of the word "process" in ITIL Version 3, and for describing several processes for the Service Strategy book where the original authors declined to recognise any.

The Marie Antoinette Memorial Cake for Most Patronising Attitude goes to Pippa Bass of the Office of Government Commerce (OGC) for keeping the community "involved" by sending them newsletters; and releasing the ITIL3 books in secrecy to a hand-picked list of reviewers as a "public review".

The Gartner Ribbon for Most Preposterous Statistic goes to McKinsey for saying that "only 34 percent say that they are more effective at introducing new technologies than their competitors are" (like saying "only 34% are tall"). The runner up is Dennis Drogseth of EMA for comparing different populations between surveys.

The Andrés Escobar Memorial Shield for Best Own Goal goes to IT Service Management Forum (itSMF) International for signing a contract to publish the ITSM Library in direct competition with their contract with TSO, causing publication of ITSM Library books to be suspended until the mess could be sorted out. They also receive the Trump Medal for Most Inappropriate Empire Building for the same contract.

The Snake-Oil Championship is won by Ken Turbitt of BMC for promising "ITIL out of the box".

The Joseph Stalin Award for the Revision of History goes to OGC for quietly deleting the 1.1.1 section of ITIL2 books that referred to ITIL as "public domain" and "publicly available" that "any organisation can use".

---

[1] [This was brought to our attention in that excellent blog erp4it.com – thank-you Charlie]
[2] http://www.itskeptic.org/node/430

The News of the World Trophy for Services to Journalism goes to Matt Stansberry, Site Editor, SearchDataCenter.com for saying that Alasdair Meldrum "literally wrote the book on the IT Infrastructure Library (ITIL)" and thereby perpetuating the myth that IBM wrote ITIL1.

The Deng Xiao Peng Memorial Spittoon for Services to Democracy goes to itSMF International for whispering the call for nominations for its new Executive Board, eliminating five of twelve candidates on a technicality, releasing the results ahead of time, and then electing the Chairperson in a process contrary to that agreed with the full Board.

The Mata Hari Mask for Nefarious Activity goes to whoever was behind the pseudonym Dr Julie Linden.

The Tony Soprano Memorial Best Friends Steak-knife is awarded jointly to The Stationery Office (TSO) for undercutting itSMF by selling V3 books to major buyers direct around the same time that itSMF was funding and organising the worldwide promotion of those same books for TSO, and to itSMF International for taking a cut on the discount they pass to local chapters of itSMF. Both parties also receive the Angus and Malcolm Young Dirtiest Deeds Ribbon for the same achievements.

The P T Barnum Gold Cigar for the Most Hyped Concept of the Year goes to the UK Communication Workers Union for describing acoustic shock as "a devastating 21st Century industrial injury problem ruining call centre workers' lives and costing industry millions" then extracting over two million pounds from BT and other employers, narrowly edging out last year's winners the CMDB Federation of vendors for allowing another year to go by without any standard for CMDB federation emerging (they lost first place this year by finally getting a first draft out in August this year).

The Dumbdown Cup goes to APMG for two stupendous contributions: designing an ITIL3 training program designed to maximize revenue instead of learning, and reducing supposedly masters-level ITIL exams to multiple choice format.

Finally, the one you have been waiting for ...Envelope please... **The Grand Sagan Candle for IT Skepticism** goes to Steve Andriole of Datamation for 10 "New Rules" for IT

2008[1]

The Three Silver Thimbles for the Grossest Statistical Trickery goes jointly to BMC and Forrester for obfuscation on a scale never before seen by the IT Skeptic even by the ethically challenged standards of the software industry. They triggered Chokey the Chimp's most severe Crap Factoid warning of the year by claiming the pure crystalline essence-of-bullshit figure of $1M savings per year from CMDB, achieved only by ignoring obvious and essential activities, under-pricing others, and totally ignoring the license costs to buy the product (you read that right: license costs zero). An extraordinary effort. Do not let anyone look you in the eye and quote this figure. The IT Skeptic re-analysed Forrester's data and deduced that rather than save a million a year, BMC Atrium CMDB just about maybe pays for itself after two or three years in a favourable case, if you can get them to give it to you for $100k. May we never see a report like this one again. The industry is way overdue for some code of practice around this sort of thing.

The Service Management Entrepreneurial Championship for 2008 was won by Ron Muns who cashed in his HelpDesk Institute, also known as ThinkHDI, also known as Think Service Inc, for a cool $30 million, give or take small change. An inspiration to us all.

Runners up were it-processmaps.com for charging twenty thousand dollars for a set of ITIL process maps. No services, just a download.

The Trump Medal for Most Inappropriate Empire Building goes to TSO for charging 5,750 big fat British pounds (real money) for a corporate annual subscription and £2,500.00 for an individual one (yes, you read that right and yes, per year!) to an ITIL Live (TM) portal that originally was going to be "available to the ITSM community at no cost".

The Ironic Twist is awarded to APMG, OGC's accreditation agency, whose own accreditation was suspended by the United Kingdom Accreditation Service. A supplementary Ribbon for Valour is awarded for getting the accreditation back. Even the most strident of APMG critics must be sympathetic about having to wend such byzantine pathways of bureaucracy.

The Terminological Debasement Cup is not awarded this year because far too many people use "governance" when they mean "management" to be able to single out a recipient.

The Andrés Escobar Memorial Shield for Best Own Goal goes to EMA for declaring there is a CMDB tidal wave when the IT Skeptic's

---

assessment of their own numbers reckons 2%-5% of IT shops have something like an ITIL-defined CMDB.

The Acapulco Gold Medal for Most THC-Induced Marketing goes to Managed Objects for thinking social collaboration (which just happens to be a current fad) might be of some relevance to the tightly controlled backroom CMDB, which led to their product MyCMDB and a "What are they smoking?" response from the IT Skeptic.

The Alf Garnett Cultural Sensitivity Totem-pole goes to David Wheeldon for eating fish and chips in Singapore.

No, just kidding about that one :-) Happy retirement David.

The Marie Antoinette Memorial Cake for Most Patronising Attitude goes to the ITIL Qualification Board for referring to the "itSMF UK Q&C committee", one Aussie and possibly a few others as the "itSMF community".

The Shoe-in-the-Door Most Intrusive Product of the Year undoubtedly goes to Plaxo (which was not a new system in 2008 - it just annoyed me and apparently others again)

The Little Blue Pill for services to fiscal sanity goes to Google book search for providing a way to access the ITIL Version 3 books (and many others) online that is legitimate and free.

The Robert Soloway Big-House Award for the Worst Commercial Comment Spammer (on the IT Skeptic blog) goes to manny from stratavia for fine fiction. Runners up were:

- the un-named Indian SEO bumbler from or on behalf of NewStar (yeah let's name names) for ineptness beyond the call of duty (comments now deleted)

- Scott from Interfacing Technologies for sheer chutzpah

The Coronation Street Pint For Longest Running Saga goes to the ITIL Qualifications Board for the ITIL V3 Foundation syllabus.

The Transparency Cup goes to itSMF USA for clearly making the first of "the specific objectives of the Corporation" be about "commercial organizations and vendors of products and services". itSMF members get a mention in the eighth objective.

The Pink Slip for Most Career-Limiting Move goes to the unnamed executive at EDS who announced "EDS Asia Pacific Standardises on BMC Software Atrium CMDB to Improve Service Delivery" one month after HP acquired EDS. (Thanks to William Vambenepe for pointing out this one)

The Deng Xiao Peng Memorial Spittoon for Services to Democracy is won for the second year in a row by itSMF International, this year for deciding that if you aren't one of the itSMF establishment you can't speak to the organisation's leadership.

Runner up was APMG for running a public survey for "your valuable feedback" on the ITIL V3 Foundation Syllabus with a whole five days to hear about it and respond. No mention of a sign saying "Beware of the leopard" but one wonders.

The Onan Award goes to FHD, a London advertising firm, for their daring new logo for OGC.

We present **The Cobbler's Children's Shoes** to OGC, the gurus of release management who put out the second edition of ITIL V3 by stealth.

The Dumbdown Cup is presented to OGC for the long-promised Lifecycle Process Model for ITIL V3. It is pretty much useless in its published state.

The Bell-less Prize for Mathematics goes jointly to Dimension Data and Datamonitor for revolutionising statistical science by declaring that deliberately selecting a skewed sample population is merely a "methodological nuance" and then drawing conclusions based on a 10% swing whose "statistical significance ...could be the subject of further scrutiny".

Finally, the one you have been waiting for ...Envelope please... The **Grand Sagan Candle for IT Skepticism** goes collectively to the people of the Netherlands. After a few days in the Netherlands, the IT Skeptic can say it is an unusual country. It is unusually flat, with an unusually large number of canals and ditches, but that is not what is meant. It is unusually friendly and orderly and honest but that isn't what is meant either. It must be the only country in the world that is widely skeptical about ITIL. The Dutch seem to be naturally open to options. They want to see the possibilities before committing to a course of action. They respect dissent and are curious about debate. And they are hard working and diligent, systematically working though the considerations and covering all the angles. No wonder they take to bodies of knowledge - process and frameworks and methodologies - like the proverbial ducks to water (of which they have plenty: ducks and water and BOKs).

A special mention goes to Jan van Bon and Herman van Bolhuis for the Best Practices in IT Management conference in the Netherlands in April 2008, and for assembling Ian Clayton, Brian Johnson, Paul Wilkinson, and the IT Skeptic, aptly described as "The most unbalanced team you can currently find."

Defending the blog

In September 2007 the blog, and my own integrity, came under attack[1]. I responded...

I stand accused of hypocrisy and dishonesty. I have been open about why I blog and why I was anonymous. For the benefit of those who came in late, I blog the IT Skeptic because I want to learn how to build a site up. My personal stretch goal is a page rank 7. First I need to get to 6.

I was anonymous because I have professional responsibilities within itSMF. I still feel exposed in that regard: there are some ugly political animals in itSMF (only a few, happily) who may yet make life hard for the NZ editor.

You need to recover some objectivity, Stone-caster. ITIL is just business. It is about people operating computers in business. It is about people making money helping companies work out how to do that. I'm not interested in personalities or personal agendas, except where they negatively impact on my own interests, one of which is to see ITSM advance and grow in a healthy manner. Some of the people who comment here are probably not people I would go camping with. So what? Some of the people who blog here do so because they want to increase their income. So what? I'm interested in what they have to say, not why, nor who is saying it.

Nobody is into ITIL or itSMF because it is their spiritual quest in life. If you want to do charitable volunteer work, go help UNICEF. Some have so much of their life invested in ITIL or ITSM that they care at an emotional level, which I think is not healthy but that's OK if that's what they want. Some just like to see things DONE RIGHT. Likewise, I think it is healthier to be able to let go of that when necessary but whatever. For many more, their interest is entirely commercial and I don't have a problem with that. ITIL isn't sacred, to be kept pure and unsullied by venal motives, it's business.

Everyone has a personal agenda and that's fine; they almost always result in positive energy for the ITIL movement. For a person to lift themselves out of the torpor of their daily existence enough to comment here means they have some personal motivation driving them to do that.

So I don't give a toss who people are or why they contribute to this blog, so long as their comments contain some interesting ideas to be debated.

---

[1] See www.itskeptic.org/node/360

Some great ideas will come out, people will change their opinions, I might even change my mind (it happens). People want to read stimulating ideas and test them with debate. They are not interested in venting of spleen except as a passing freak show.

As for the silent majority, you don't get a blog to page rank 5 [back to 4 as of Feb 2009] unless people are interested in what you have to say. And I allow anyone to have their say. The only time I have edited posts was when Julie Linden made libellous statements.

Finally I am not anti-ITIL, nor are any of the people who post here that I can think of. You need to look at your own personal issues if you think that everybody who challenges the content or establishment of ITIL is anti-ITIL: that is too binary. Even those who promote competitive IP. An intelligent business person realises that competitors build and educate the market. And they realise they will only displace powerful incumbent competitors by creating something better. We'll either get a better alternative or ITIL will be prevented from becoming complacent, either way is for the good of us all. You can't throw your toys out of the cot every time someone criticises something you are affiliated with.

ITIL is not going away any time soon. As you say, it is what people want right now. I for one don't want anything to happen to ITIL: I still depend on it for a living. ITIL is big and strong enough to withstand a bit of robust critique and debate: it will be the better for it. That is the point of this blog: the openness and honesty created by public forum helps things grow; secretive dishonesty and meddling poisons them from within.

This website is about debating ideas not personalities. If you have some useful ideas to contribute, I look forward to seeing one, whether I agree with it or not.

...We have had only one really good troll on the blog (and a few lesser trolls). I never did work out who it is. The following conversation goes on a bit but it is interesting and I'll be accused of all sorts of things if I edit it. I have to make an exception and include the troll's comments too...

Pots and Kettles

Submitted by Spam Watcher (not verified) on Sat, 2007-09-22 23:09.

I strongly dislike spammers of all types. It is not nice is it?

The pity is that YOU are as bad as anyone for it. Yes, YOU.

I have been around the blocks reading plenty of websites in this market over a very long period. And I have seen plenty of it from you. Crude link placing at its worst.

Yet when someone does it on your turf, you come with the clean guy act?

Excuse me for laughing.

If you are going to poke at people for playing a dirty grubby game like that, stop playing it yourself.

unsubstantiated accusations

Submitted by skeptic on Sat, 2007-09-22 23:32.

I haven't had time to be around the forums and blogs for quite a while, but I believe I have always had something useful to say when commenting. If you have some examples of "crude" spamming why don't you offer links to them here and let readers make their own evaluation instead of slinging unsubstantiated accusations.

Sigh: I was going to take this thread down soon and let Matrix off the hook. I can't now until this little issue is resolved...

Mind Games

Submitted by Spam Watcher (not verified) on Tue, 2007-09-25 22:14.

Come off it. Are you trying to fool yourself, or just us?

I have seen PLENTY of this type of spam from you. It is very easy to find.

It ranges from trivial worthless comment posted as a paper thin excuse to spam your link, to crudeness like "get the latest on .... at www.itskeptic.org".

This isn't in the mind, it is real. Maybe you have blanked it out of your mind, but it is still around for everyone else to see.

If you are going to sink to that level, that is your choice. But posting as though you are an innocent when someone does it to you insults the intelligence of anyone reading this.

Contribution to public discourse: zero

Submitted by skeptic on Tue, 2007-09-25 22:31.

Personally I think there is a qualitative difference between on the one hand saying something meaningful on the topic, then telling people you have something more to say over at your blog when you really do, for which I don't apologise, and on the other hand saying "hey folks" and signing with a link to a commercial website that offers no value to the topic, which is what happened.

If it was some overeager person pumping another commentary site by dropping a meaningless comment I probably would have ignored it - I've had one or two of those - but it wasn't. It was a commercial consulting firm trying to drive traffic to their brochure site. Contribution to public discourse: zero.

Maybe you haven't noticed but the web is a web: people actually appreciate links that direct them to more related information because they are interested. That isn't spam. If you are incapable of telling the difference then how about you go study how the web works and what the etiquette is before you accuse me of being "crude".

Facing The Truth

Submitted by Span Watcher (not verified) on Wed, 2007-09-26 09:39.

You seem to be having a problem facing up to your own actions. It is a matter of record that you drop links to your own commercial website just like Matrix have done. The quote I posted last time was pretty much taken directly from one of your comment spams I came upon. It says nothing apart from "come to my website".

You now even seem to be in denial about the nature of your website too, as though it is somehow pure and clean. It isn't. It is commercial. I see adverts all over the place. Adsense, books, grockle, you name it.

So what makes you different to them? Not a lot really. Although you add insult to injury by the ridiculous denials.

And I really don't need lessons on net etiquette from a comment spammer.

That would be spamming.

Submitted by skeptic on Wed, 2007-09-26 18:39.

Regular readers will be aware that this blog is a learning tool for me to experiment with different web revenue generators. So far the blog has paid me somewhere approaching $200. Total. Ever. I estimate that I have spent well in excess of $100,000 worth of my time on it. So when I say this blog is not a commercial blog I feel fairly comfortable in that assertion. It is here to learn and enjoy.

This blog is not a static brochure website advertising my business. That is here[1]. And that isn't comment spam. It is a link to a site for those who might be interested. It is also a link in the hope that you might actually grasp the difference.

You seem unable to point us to a single example to support your continual pestering, but let's accept for the moment that I once commented by saying there was more to say on the topic on my site. I don't recall it but you seem determined that I did, so whatever. I'm not ashamed of that. I have never placed an unrelated link or out of context link: the link has always been there because it was something that would be of interest to the readers of the comment, not because I would derive commercial benefit from deceiving a reader into following an out-of-context link. That would be spamming.

You Need To Wear Objective Spectacles For Self Assessment

Submitted by SpamWatcher (not verified) on Wed, 2007-09-26 22:35.

Yes, it would be spamming, which is what you have done repeatedly in many places.

I have just checked on that last example I found and it is still there in all its glory for the whole world to see. It seems that you have comment spammed so often that you have forgotten where you have done it.

Adding "get the latest on .... at www.itskeptic.org" as the sole contribution to an article is not what a genuine person would consider adding value. It is exactly what Matrix did above, and what you have been crying about. It is spamming.

So now that we have established that you are a spammer, a spammer who can dish it out but not take it, let us look at commercialism. There are adverts all over this website. Everyone can see that. The more visitors you get the more money you make. Everyone knows that too. So the more you comment spam the more you make. Yes, the world knows.

The amount of money you make from this is not relevant, even though we only have the word of a comment spammer for that. It is the intent that matters.

So when you complain about others placing links to their commercial websites and accuse them of doing exactly what you do to your commercial

---

[1] www.twohills.co.nz

website, maybe you can see how you look. Or maybe not. You seem to have a problem looking at yourself through objective spectacles don't you?

I don't. I see you clearly. Unfortunately for you a lot of others on here do to.

I don't think I'm the one with the problem.

Submitted by skeptic on Thu, 2007-09-27 08:07.

I don't think I'm the one with the problem. You and all readers have the option to read elsewhere. I've made my case. You seem incapable of understanding it. I don't intend to respond to you any further.

QED

Submitted by Spam-Watcher (not verified) on Thu, 2007-09-27 21:16.

Yes, the case is indeed proven.

You behave exactly as Matrix did. In fact much worse and over a much longer period. You then wring your hands in denial when you are caught out.

You can justify your spamming to yourself all you wish, but do not expect us to buy it.

I and others I have spoken to have long found your comment spamming habits to be distasteful. You just add insult to injury by wriggling on here, a commercial website, trying to play the innocent. It doesn't wash.

Ok this is dead

Submitted by Leave the Skeptic Aloe! (not verified) on Sat, 2007-09-29 14:49.

Leave the Skeptic alone and lets move on to the next topic.

What Goes Around Comes Around: 2

Submitted by Spam Watcher (not verified) on Tue, 2007-10-09 12:03.

Let's hope that he leaves others alone then, rather than infest them with his unwanted spam. It works both ways, unfortunately for him.

...and there were days when I had to clean up my own mess...

I got my facts wrong. Without prior feedback or pressure from anyone, I would like to apologise to OGC, the itSMF and others involved in the ITIL Version 3 Refresh for the imputation that there was no public consultation prior to the authoring of the ITIL Version 3 books.

There was in fact considerable effort:

> "OGC and itSMFI are working together to consult UK and overseas public sector users, corporate and business users and suppliers globally. itSMFI will additionally seek feedback and coordinate responses from their members in over 27 countries. The two ITIL Examination Institutes, EXIN and ISEB, will organise responses from the training community." (OGC Information Bulletin - 21 January 2005)

Just as importantly, there was a web-based survey as well.

These resulted in reportedly "530 written responses and over 6,000 comments, representing 80% of the countries with an itSMF chapter"

The conclusions were published in a public report. This was a major piece of work that I should not have overlooked.

Having said that, this was a one-off exercise that was commendable but only goes part of the way towards community involvement.

I maintain my position that there has been and still is no official community mechanism for ITIL. This apology does not affect the statements I made in ITIL Must Embrace the Collective.

I also maintain my position that the process of preparing Version 3 has been perceived by many in the community as lacking transparency (and in communications, perception is reality).

And I continue to believe that the basic approach and philosophy is patronising rather than participatory. The ideal is somewhere in between: see *ITIL reform needed*[1].

However I regret that in comments made I have overlooked these efforts and have suggested there was no participation at all: for that I unreservedly apologise.

When I wrote about speaker eligibility for the upcoming itSMF International Chapter Leadership Conference (CLC), I got mad and I allowed that to cloud my judgement and affect my language. I was rude. I apologise for the tone of the posting, to Ken Wendle whose name was on the document in question, and to itSMF in general. I'll understand if you speak to me like that when next we meet, but I hope I can keep things on a more professional level here on in. Sorry.

I have edited the posting to moderate the tone.

...Enough self-congratulation. On with some of the ideas from the blog. Some parts of this book are direct extracts. Other sections are edited and compiled into fresh material for this book ...

People Process Technology

The IT industry does not have a good track record for introducing new things. Projects fail, products don't fit, results are unexpected, users are unhappy. "People Process Technology" is a useful model to help us do better, but it gets ignored more often than it gets applied. The IT Skeptic suggests redefining it to new terms will improve its acceptance. If we apply it more, we should have less IT failures.

The model "People Process Technology" has been a popular one for years. It gives a fine insight into where to set our priorities in any IT innovations such as new applications, new ways of working, or new technologies. I am unsure of its origins (I would love to hear from any reader who knows). It goes back over a decade in the software engineering world. It says that when we are planning or designing or doing anything, we should consider the people, the process and the technology. And – I like to add – in that order! This means roughly equal attention and effort, not passing lip-service.

It is quite extraordinary how often this rule is honoured in the breach rather than the observance – how it is ignored. Attune yourself to the model, and then apply it to everything you read: proposals, emails, memos, articles, websites, forums. You will be amazed how often IT people leap straight to the technology:

• If we buy this it will fix that

• The problem is that there is no monitoring tool

• I'll code a fix

• We need a form / database / spreadsheet to track it

• We could build a system to do it

• The errors are creeping in because the screen is designed wrong

That should be no surprise I suppose, for a number of reasons. We are attracted to this industry because we like technology. It is easier to blame objects than people. We know more about how to fix technology than how to fix process. Technology is more tractable than culture.

If only we stuck a People Process Technology poster up in every office the problem would be solved. Having it on the wall would remind people to apply it, and if they see it every day eventually they will come to believe it. Maybe not (unless of course the poster has an animal on it – apparently that makes posters work).

People Process Technology. How many times do we hear that? (Or ITIL sources add a fourth dimension: Partners[1]. An even more complex model includes vision and strategy, steering, processes, people, technology, and culture. [2]

The key is to start them in that order (People then Process then Technology) and keep them in balance. IT people too often start with the technology, occasionally start with the process, and seldom start with the people (culture, team, approval, support, enthusiasm...).

Technology works where it is a tool to assist people and support process, where it has been selected or designed to suit those processes and people, and where the people and process work with or without it. Technology makes people more efficient and processes more reliable (or is that vice versa?). It seldom makes something possible that was impossible without it.

The artefacts produced by an ITIL project are documents, tools, communications, events and sometimes organisational structures and roles.

These products are created in order to describe and manage new ways of doing the processes to get the IT operations job done. So a more important visible output of an ITIL project should be new processes in action.

But the primary objective of any ITIL project must be cultural change: change the mindset, attitudes and behaviour of the IT operations staff (and to a lesser extent their users). Culture, in a business context, is just a fancy name for "how we approach things round here".

If there is no – or insufficient - cultural change, there can be no long-term project success.

In some projects, the processes never see the light of day. There is a small mountain of documentation produced after a flurry of assessment, benchmarking, consultation, work-shopping and design – activities that

---

[1] An Introductory Overview of ITIL, Colin Rudd, itSMF 2004.
[2] Planning to Implement Service Management, Vernon Lloyd, The Stationery Office, 2002)

the consultants feast upon. Training is delivered, forms are posted, expensive new software installed, manuals printed and distributed, new portals appear on the intranet. Then life goes on as before. The tool is never adopted beyond some pilot group, the processes are ignored or circumvented, and the manuals gather dust.

Other projects count themselves as a success because the process goes into operation. But after a year or two the actual process has drifted away from the documented one, many controls have been relaxed or subverted, uptake has not expanded to all forecast departments or processes, subsequent phases have been forgotten, the project has been disbanded and ownership lost, and the organisation is slipping back to where it was before the project. It didn't stick.

Failure to implement anything, or failure to maintain momentum, is almost invariably due to neglecting People, the first of our three key factors: People Process and Technology (and yet it is the last of the three that is often blamed).

We often talk about "implementing" ITIL or "doing" ITIL. These are the wrong words but we all use them, including this author. ITIL is a transformation not an implementation. The processes are there already - we just change them to a standardised (supposedly best) way of doing them. We transform them through process re-engineering, and we keep them that way through cultural change.

If the process works, technology can make it more efficient and better measured and managed. If the process doesn't work or the people don't accept it, the technology just wastes your money. "People Process Technology, in that order" – make it a mantra.

We are drawn to IT by a fascination with complex technology. This is unfortunate because it blinds many of us to the importance of the People Process Technology (or Things) trilogy.

Change and Configuration Management are processes. If the process is working, they collect and maintain good configuration data (in a repository that you can call a CMDB if you insist). If the process is broken technology is not going to fix it. Bang your head hard against the desk while repeating five times "technology is not going to fix it".

If your people do not have a service management culture; if your service management processes are not well designed, bedded in to the organisation, and measured and monitored; if you do not have this situation then all the cool tools in the world are not going to fix it dammit!

Once you have the right people doing the right things in the right way, only then can you indulge yourself and spend what is left of the project budget on the shiny geegaws peddled by the vendors.

OK, that is an exaggeration: there is a place, well into the process design, when we identify opportunities for tools to help manage the process and in rare cases even help automate the process. Once we understand our people's capabilities and desires, once we understand exactly what we want the process to do, then yes we may be able to build a solid business case to buy a tool, most likely a service desk but also other operational software or even document management systems etc...

That does not in any way undermine my basic premise though: if you have a process problem there is not a technology solution.

So, folks, please let's grow up as an industry. If you are paunchy and aging, buying a red sports-car does not fix the problem. If all the kids shun you at school, a HotWheels set is not going to change that. If you can't get your people to write down what they changed, a shiny "Automated Application Dependency Mapping" (or any of the other gadgets being peddled around the ITIL world right now) is not going to make any difference.

People Process Technology. The order is important: People come first. IT folk too often start with the technology, occasionally start with the process, and seldom start with the people. Once we understand what will and won't work culturally and what we need to do to get there, only then are we in a position to design and implement processes (unless of course you like doing it several times, or failing). There is no best practice, only generally agreed practice. So no definition of process is sacred; they all need to adapt to the receiving organization. The link between People and Practice is education: inform, train, coach.

So Practice/Process comes after People. It follows naturally. It must be said that not everyone sees it this way: "data design comes before coding"; "buy a tool and let it dictate the process"; "a good repository is the starting point"; "you can't do anything until you have acquired some data".

There is an interesting debate in IT between action-oriented thinking and object-oriented (we are talking more generally than the programming-related meanings here). Here is a crude linguistic test for process orientation or technology orientation: do they talk about verbs/actions or nouns/things? The data/process, technology/process, objects/activities, nouns/verbs arguments are like the nature/nurture one: The reality is somewhere in the middle as both are important. The culture of IT as the first decade of the millennium heads to a close is off-balance, object-centric. IT gets more complex and unstable every day. If you listen to the vendors, apparently the solution is not to look at how we do things and the quality and culture of the people doing them. No, it is to introduce yet more technology.

There is a point, well into the process design, when we identify opportunities for tools to help manage the process and in some cases even help automate the process. Once we understand our people's capabilities and desires, once we understand exactly what we want the process to do, then yes, we may build a solid business case to buy a tool. In order to select the tool, we need to understand what we have to achieve with each transaction, and how we plan to perform the transaction. So you need to be well advanced down the process design path before you start selecting tools. Personally I would wait until the processes have been tested in walkthroughs, but you can only hold the geeks off for so long. The main thing is not to let them start the project by looking at tools.

Most business issues that IT addresses are process problems. If you have a process problem, there is not a technology solution. If you are paunchy and aging, buying a red sports car does not fix the problem (though you may feel better about it). Technology works where it is a tool to assist people and support process, where it has been selected or designed to suit those processes and people, and where the people and process work with or without it. Technology makes people more efficient and processes more reliable. It seldom makes something possible that was impossible without it. The term "Things" is better than "Technology" because the fixation is more general: with products, documentation, forms..., all kinds of objects. You even find people treating process as a thing (stay with me here). To implement new practices you need to look at the people doing the implementation, and the process for implementing the process (the "meta-process"?), before you capture the process as a document. Yet some projects start by designing the forms, then work out how the forms will function. Sometimes organizations do nothing but post a form and declare a new process is in place. It is the same old Things-first thinking. And they fail. The forms sit unused.

Likewise we see projects where the process was written up as a document and distributed, and that was the implementation. Once again, they fail. The documents gather dust. Look around: how many process flowcharts hang on walls or sit on shared drives or in binders on shelves without having any instantiation in reality?

People Process Technology. People Practices Things. Whatever the model, please consider the culture first and the things last, and you will find implementations of new services, systems, practices and software go so much better.

People

"You can't manage what you can't measure". Who on earth came up with that one? One of my big concerns about the application of ITIL is it's emphasis on KPIs. Useful but dangerous.

Management is about the operation of a function or process. Even though I bet somewhere we have sanitary disposal managers these days, back in the real world "manager" means someone who manages people. They build processes around people and they make them follow those processes but at the end of the day managers manage people.

And you can't measure people. Oh, we try. But you can't. Einstein got unimpressive grades. So many modern corporate ills stem from managers trying to manage people by numbers.

First, I have seen brilliant people (read: valuable corporate resources) laid off because the numbers fingered them. Bad managers applying bad numbers.

Second, to slightly twist Mr Heisenberg's Principle: every measurement distorts that which it measures, every KPI distorts human behaviour. No KPI perfectly reflects the desired outcome - it always leads the measured subjects off the desired path. Management by measurement leads to some weird results (every civil service is awash with them).

Third, the KPI hasn't been invented that measures "good". I used to have to rank my staff, 1 to 12, no equals. What a nonsense. The ranking would shift from day to day depending on the challenges the team faced. It would change from hour to hour depending on who had pissed me off last.

Management by measurement is only a substitute for inept management. Put another way, it is an organisation's compensation for its inability to attract, create and retain good managers. Any decent manager can make correct assessment of staff based on instinct and subjective observation. Numbers help, and they particularly help fire someone, but you can manage what you can't measure. Good managers do it every day.

Now, governance - that's another matter. Perhaps you can't govern what you can't measure...?

1.2   Principles of Real ITSM [see www.realitsm.com]

Anyone who has experienced the contented tranquillity of a mature and stable IT organisation will long for such a work environment.

Such a pleasant place to work is achievable with some commitment and the rigorous application of Real ITSM principles, known as Realitsm and pronounced ree-uh-litz-m, near enough to "realism".

The main threats to IT stability are change, accountability and reduced spending. Realitsm is about eliminating these threats from the IT environment, in the best interests of all in IT. A harmonious IT environment requires adherence to the following Realitsm principles:

- Ensure a stable operating environment

- Maximise adaptability to change

- Promote involvement through collectivist decision-making

- Maintain morale through reduced group accountability

- Maximise revenue and funding for the IT department

- Maximise benefit and value for the IT staff

1.3   Real ITSM vs. ITIL

ITIL presents "best practice" , an idealised model for us all to aspire to. ITIL is all very well for theorists, academics, consultants and IT managers, and all others similarly detached from reality.

Down here in the real world, at the coalface, an entirely different model prevails: Real ITSM, which represents Real Practice.

Real ITSM involves its own lifecycle, activities, roles and metrics, analogous to those of ITIL but entirely different. They differ because, unlike ITIL, they must engage with the real, physical world, populated by "wetware" - those cussed, unpredictable and generally useless devices known as People.

When any idealised model meets People, the laws of logic are suspended, and rationality flies out the window.

When ITSM frameworks go through this realitsm transformation, the output is Real ITSM. Most BOKs are process-centric. Real ITSM is people-centric: it understands that what really happens is dependent on the people – their motivations, culture, personal agendas, fears and desires.

...from *Introduction to Real ITSM*, R. England, Custom Books 2008.

For a whole book on the topic of people in IT, *see He Tangata: IT is the People*, R. England, to be published in 2009

Process

ITIL V2 was process-centric. ITIL V3 works hard not to be. It wants to be service-centric but...

Wholeheartedly agree that process can be overdone and there isn't a fixed link with service capability. Nevertheless this is funky modern thinking. ITIL V2 was all about process. Letting go of process as the foundation is a big step for many organisations. I would also put it to you that "funky" = "immature", and abandoning process as a discipline is akin to many other post-modernist rejections of fundamentals (and common sense) that have ended in tears (or will).

I'm the first to say process needs to be done with restraint, and I point to my CoPr and SM4SME[1] work to support that.

But I don't intend to throw the baby out with the bathwater. I'm old-fashioned enough to believe that good service requires good process at appropriate maturity levels and investment levels.

And that process maturity can be measured. I'm more interested in what is pragmatically useful in the trenches than what is ideologically correct or compliant with the theory du jour.

My concern what the post-modernists will do with these ideas. "process doesn't matter", "any approach has to be seen as valid", "it's not what you do, it is what the service feels like", "the service has to WANT to change" ...

Past discussions on this blog have suggested that a process fixation such as ITIL's engenders an inflexibility and ponderousness in an organisation. Whilst I am a process fan, there is an important point to be addressed here about how ITIL relates to nimbleness and adaptability.

From the *Introduction to Real ITSM*:

> "Repeated procedures ingrain habit, which stifles staff creativity and flexibility. The more different ways a procedure is performed, the higher the probability that one of those ways will still work after cataclysmic change. This is simple Darwinism. Repeatable processes are like the agricultural monoculture of a cloned crop: highly productive in good times but highly vulnerable to disease, pests, climatic extremes or other stresses."

---

[1] http://www.itskeptic.org/node/1114

This is of course tongue-in-cheek but there is a grain of truth here. Does repeatable, managed process reduce flexibility and adaptability in the face of changing conditions? Does evolutionary theory have a warning for us not to be too rigid?

A more specific question from the original premise: for a species to survive in the face of abrupt change it relies on the diversity born of mutation in order to rapidly adapt. Monocultures of cloned identical crops fare very badly in the face of new diseases or changing environments. Do approaches such as ITIL stamp out diversity and thereby limit our options in the face of challenging change? If we only have one way of doing things and "punish" those who don't follow it, are we creating a Monsanto monoculture of process?

The more we standardise process and punish those who have their own variants (which may be less efficient in the current conditions), the more we remove adaptability from the system.

Real ITSM consists of

- a Deathcycle which follows a service from misconception to abandonment

- a set of Activities performed

- related Roles to be put on wetware's business cards and otherwise ignored

- Metrics used to distort behaviours

- Complimentary Guidance

Unlike ITIL, which uses the word "process" with a cavalier disregard for any generally accepted definition of the word, Real ITSM prefers to refer to "activities". We do this partly because it is a better-suited word and partly to keep the OGC lawyers at bay. This does mean that the "four Ps" doesn't work any more (People Processes Products Partners), so Real ITSM uses the alternate model of Wetware Activities Stuff and Parasites which is just as mnemonic: WASP.

Real ITSM activities are carried on in all Deathcycle phases independent of services. The Deathcycle is, like, just a model, you know. Real activities carry on regardless.

Technology

An article[1] raises the interesting question why there are far more Service Support tools than Service Delivery tools. The article concludes "the lack of powerful and highly touted tools for Service Delivery is a natural consequence of the process definitions and the current marketplace." I don't think so. I believe the germ of the answer is in the article: "Service Support processes are more tactical in nature while Service Delivery processes are more strategic." Service Delivery processes are strategic: they can be run on a Word document. As the article also says, there is a need for Knowledge Management to help with that. But not ITIL Knowledge Management: there is no specialist need beyond standard Knowledge Management tools, and everyone seems to sell one of those these days.

There is a place for point solution tools within each of the Service Delivery processes: service level measurement and reporting, asset register, backup and recovery automation, network and systems performance database... These are well served already by available technology. The article says "few are directly tied to IT Service Catalogues and fewer still to a CMDB ... there are none that cross all the technology domains and also none that roll up their information to assist in developing the ITIL-required Availability Plan". Perhaps the authors are more demanding of software than the IT Skeptic, unlikely :-), or perhaps they haven't looked at the Big Four lately (BMC, CA, HP, IBM), but I would have said those guys covered most things pretty well and roll up to a service view pretty well (as much as can be done by a tool).

But the article looks for a tool for the whole process: "they do not cover any of the other many attributes and requirements of the overall ... process (communication, coordination, documentation, strategic planning, etc.)" The bits of any Service Delivery process that need automating have tools available already. The rest of it is process. It is not a technical problem so there is no need for a technical solution. Tools can't do strategic thinking (perhaps more modelling tools would be good to support that thinking process, but this is point solutions again).

As I have said before: People Process Things, in that order. Technology exists to make process better, where it can. If the process does not need technology, or if the process cannot be done by technology, then don't assume there is a one-to-one mapping from every process or function within a process to some piece of technology. Vendors can't sell strategic process tools because strategic processes don't need technology solutions.

---

[1] http://www.itsmsolutions.com/newsletters/DITYvol3iss7.htm

Tools don't work. Not for what people ask them to do, which is to fix a problem. Put your tools in, maybe even design a process around them, but it will fail. It might take 12 or 24 months to fail but it will fail.

Start with the people, change the culture/mindset/habits/attitude, then help those people look at process. Once process requirements IN THAT ORGANISATION are understood, find a tool to fit. Any other sequence is imposing a change on a culture that has not accepted it and is therefore doomed. SO in my usual exaggerating fashion, I'd say "tools don't matter".

The Real ITSM monitoring device is the Telephone. This device is extremely sensitive to any interruption to service and will ring within a time inversely proportional to the importance of the service to users.

Not only that, but it will tell the Service Desk precisely what the impact is, and the required restoration time.

Therefore the Telephone renders redundant all the complex systems management tools, event monitors, alerts, service catalogues and other encumbrances employed by other ITSM frameworks.

It is cheap to implement, uses redundant systems, has very high availability, requires little administration, and its implementation and maintenance are outsourced.

It is an exemplary piece of state-of-the-art IT equipment.

Governance

Governance is hot. "Governance" is the "in" word right now in IT. It is also a word that is suffering badly from terminological debasement, something the IT Skeptic has railed against on this blog before.

Governance is not management, not doing. It is steering the organisation. Command and Control. Or as the new standard has it: Direct, Evaluate, Measure. As the term becomes more debased, governance is most often confused with two management activities: measurement and policy compliance. Governance is done by governors. If they are not a governor (within the domain of consideration) then what they are doing is almost certainly not governance. What they are doing is serving governors: implementing mechanisms to enable governance, providing information for feedback to governance, acting to meet directives of governance; making corrections to stay within policy bounds.

The IT Skeptic adheres to a purist usage of the word "governance" which aligns closely with the new ISO38500 standard. The word is often used to mean management: running a business unit or function. This is just plain wrong. But somewhere in between is a set of activities in a grey area.

Governors don't set up security policy and they don't detect exceptions and they don't administer or oversee project portfolios (let alone individual projects) and they don't run reports: to me this is clear misuse of the word governance. Governors don't measure. They consider measurements when monitoring the business, but they don't do the measuring. Governors don't audit. They consider audit results when monitoring the business but they don't perform the audit.

Where it gets grey for me is the activity of collecting, collating and analysing information for the governors; and the activity of implementing, communicating and policing the policies and strategies set by the governors. Even though it probably isn't done by the governors, is it governance? Perhaps. Or maybe we need a better word, like policing. Personally I'd like to see governance restricted to a strict interpretation as ISO38500 is trying to do, but I suspect the bird has flown.

The word "governance" is in danger of total debasement. ISO38500 may be only half-cooked but that is because it arrived just in time... or perhaps too late.

But there is plenty of evidence around that 38500 is desperately needed, and possibly too late to save the total erosion of meaning of "governance".

Take this article[1] as just one example:

> Every organization, large or small, must make decisions about how to use their resources in the best interests of the enterprise. The demand for data, projects, people and money always exceeds the supply of those resources. This is the core of governance: how to make those decisions in the best interests of the enterprise – not what is in the best interests of a particular function, but in the best interests of the organization. Of course, we all have different opinions about what that means. A governance process that ensures that the correct projects are completed and the correct people are involved in prioritizing them is essential to success.

They are talking about management. Governors might check that managers are making these decisions well.

> choosing projects that create value is inherently a strategic activity and should involve corporate leadership...Much of the written work on governance focuses on the structural features or methods for managing a collection of projects. Topics such as policies, procedures, standards, data definition, roles, responsibilities, accountabilities, business rules, data redundancy, master data, structured and unstructured data, privacy, security, data usage, data quality, auditability, authorities and decision making are all valid and important to address. However, research and experience indicates that effective governance processes are characterized by both methodological comprehensiveness and social interventions where key stakeholders build collaborative relationships and shared understanding.

Putting aside the consultant-babble of "effective governance processes are characterized by both methodological comprehensiveness and social interventions where key stakeholders build collaborative relationships and shared understanding" that would win me Bullshit Bingo in one sentence, the bits I can understand are talking about management. If this is governance, what does the Board do? If this is not management, what is?

There is no governance in ITSM (though it creates some data for governors to use). There is no governance in IT (though it also creates data for its masters). Governance is performed by governors, who don't work in IT (heck governors don't work)...

---

1 http://www.b-eye-network.com/view/7597

Governance and Assurance

Interest in IT Governance is rising rapidly, but a new ISO standard will make clear that the term is often misused. What we are really seeing is a rise in interest in IT Governance and Assurance. Along with Service Management these will provide the three supports for business-IT alignment.

IT Service Management started something. It broke IT free of the shackled thinking that IT was about doing things with technology and writing programs. It said that there is a higher level of thinking about how we do that stuff.

It introduced a second idea too: that "how" is about process, and process doesn't need technology, it needs Bodies of Knowledge (BOKs, my term not ITIL's: ITIL talks about "framework"). In the case of ITSM, the focus of that how is around understanding how well we do IT and defining "how well" in terms of what the organisation needs us to do. Of course this "how well" was framed as a process issue and it spawned ITIL as its BOK. ITIL is often seen as the "answer" to IT's Service requirement, but it isn't. The change required to meet the requirement is not a process one, it is a people one, and the answers are cultural not procedural (let alone technological). The tools to support changing the people include ITIL.

Now there is a new area of "higher level thinking" emerging in IT, and it is all in a muddle. It is a mix of the concepts of Governance, Risk, Assurance and Compliance. Governance shouldn't be mixed up in there. Governance is something distinct. The passive part of Governance is tracking the business against strategy objectives and policy: taking a navigational fix not weighing the cargo. The active part of Governance is setting policy not issuing commands: setting a course not steering. So IT Governance is understanding how right we do IT, and defining "how right" in terms of policy and strategy of the organisation. Note that Governance is not reporting, or security, or dashboards or risk management, or – as I've seen lately – project management. Management is not Governance. All these things that are recently being mislabelled as Governance are about executing the commands of the governors, or providing them with information, or ensuring the organisation complies with their policies. Steering the ship is not governance. Even more so, rowing the ship is not governance.

The bulk of Risk Management is not Governance. Most of Risk Management is operational. The closely intertwined concepts of IT Risk, Assurance and Compliance are about how safely we do IT, and defining "how safely" in terms of safe for the organisation (not in the sense of human safety, though that is one subset). The governors are concerned with setting policy and bounds. They aren't concerned with fixing things that go out of bounds. Or if they are then they are no longer governing. This is not wrong; it just needs to be clearly understood when the governors are taking an operational role.

Help is at hand to rescue the much-abused term "Governance". The international Standards organisation, ISO, has released a new standard defining that very word, *ISO/IEC 38500: Corporate governance of information technology*. The standard defines Governance as three activities: Direct, Evaluate and Monitor. Now the new standard makes it clear to the IT community that Governance pertains to command and control - not measurement, policing or adjustment - we can hope to see the emergence of a term that nicely wraps up the operational (i.e. non-Governance) aspects of Risk, Assurance and Compliance. Assurance is a good catch-all word. I quite like Policing but I doubt it will catch on – too threatening for these PC times [for our British readers that is PC as in Politically Correct not Police Constable].

With that new concept gaining centre stage alongside Service and Governance as the third leg of the IT tripod supporting business-IT alignment, we can control how well, how right and how safely we do IT. Just as the change required to meet the IT Service requirement is not a process one, it is a people one, so too with IT Governance and Assurance. Nevertheless, the BOKs and the tools are required to support that change.. People will look for BOKs aligning as neatly with IT Governance and Assurance as ITIL does with IT Service. COBIT and related publications are nearest to the IT Assurance BOK, and the ValIT publications are on the way to being the BOK for IT Governance.

The growth of IT Service Management as a discipline within IT has been a good thing, and long overdue. But it has been a lopsided process: Service Management is not everything (not to hear some pundits tell it). Now we are seeing rising interest in "IT Governance", which if you look into it is actually interest in both IT Governance and IT Assurance/Policing (and the underlying technology and processes to provide the data for both Governance and Assurance/Policing, and to enact their directions).

The ITIL industry is worth several billion dollars a year. Now there are two new markets opening up, the vendors are salivating. The reaction of some CIOs will be horror at whole new vistas of IT spending, but just as ITSM is becoming a normal expectation of IT so too will Governance and Assurance. In twenty years we will wonder what the fuss was about (remember how exciting it was to actually monitor and manage your computers?). In the meantime, look forward to some excitement as IT Service's star fades and two new ones burst into the sky.

What governance isn't

One of the less endearing behaviours of the IT industry is to take terms that once had a meaning; and then misuse and overuse the word until the original meaning is all but lost. Vendors are the main culprits, eager to redefine a term to fit their offering, but the analysts are at it too, trying to find creative new meanings for formerly well-understood terms. Some authors, commentators and journalists contribute simply by not understanding the proper meaning of the term and so taking it places it was never meant to go.

"Management", "consultant", "solution", "knowledge"... there is a long list of victims. One of the latest is "governance". In an attempt to stop the rot before this word loses all usefulness, we should define what governance is not.

What Governance is

Often the easiest way to understand something is to first define what it is not. However in the case of "governance", it is not difficult to define what it is, or rather what it was back when the word had a clear agreed meaning. So let us begin by defining the term.

The Concise Oxford Dictionary (Sixth Edition 1976) defines to govern as "...regulate proceedings of (corporation etc.)". Despite all that has been done to the word since 1976, this is still the essence of governance: regulation. And "regulate" is defined by the same source as "Control by rule, subject to restrictions; moderate, adapt to requirements..." Governance is the practice of controlling behaviour/activity/process/practice by

- Creating a controlling mechanism by defining roles, responsibilities, decision rights, and accountability

- Setting the rules (the trendy word is "policy")

- Defining the bounds to restrict behaviour

- Reacting to excess to bring it back within bounds

- Moving the bounds in response to changing requirements

So there are two main functions to governance:

- Directing. Setting and adjusting policy and bounds in response to external stimulus: the behaviour the business requires to survive, compete and comply.

- Controlling. Enforcing the bounds in response to internal stimulus: demanding metric reports and comparing against the thresholds defined by the bounds; requiring correction where metrics go over thresholds.

Governance is actually very simple in definition and execution. Governors are not highly paid because what they do is clever or complex. They are highly paid because they carry the risk through their accountability for non-compliance.

They say you can't manage what you can't measure. In the same way you can't govern what you can't measure. This is often interpreted to say that if we cannot measure something we should not manage or govern it. This is incorrect. If business requirements dictate a certain policy and we cannot currently measure compliance with that policy, then we have two options: (a) implement process and tools to measure it or (b) accept the risk of an unregulated policy. Better to make the risk transparent than to leave the policy off.

In particular, changing technology means that the capability to measure is a lot more volatile than organisational policy. If new metrics become available, it is easier to enforce an existing policy than to introduce a new one.

One of the most powerful and widely applicable models in IT is "people process things". (Often this is said as "people process technology" but that is far too narrow. People and process are underpinned by many artefacts such as forms, books, files, even whiteboards and sticky notes). Governance is first and foremost a state of mind, then an activity, then the tools to enable and assist that activity. A measurement tool on its own is not governance, despite what the vendors claim, without the organisational attitude and the repeatable processes to make it useful.

What Governance isn't

Which brings us to our topic: what governance isn't. The philosophers among us will remind that "what something is not" is an infinite topic. We will restrict ourselves to "what governance isn't but people sometimes try to make it". Here are seven interrelated areas often confused with governance:

- Measurement, reporting and audit

- Management

- Optimisation

- Financial control

- Policy enforcement

- Vision and strategy

- Rule

Measurement, reporting and audit

Governance is not measurement or reporting or audit, though it may employ these tools. As is the way of most tools, these can be used for multiple purposes, one of which is to report back to governors. Real governors seldom use tools themselves: they require governance feedback information from employees.

Doing the reporting or audit is not governance: it is executing the requirements of the governor. Don't let tool vendors tell you otherwise. And "people process things": if the activity of reporting is not governance then even more so the tools are not governance. Nor do they enable or improve governance. If you improve your culture and process you might identify how tools could assist that improvement, but implementing tools in a vacuum will not make a difference.

Management

Governance is not management, at least not the operational activity that is the core meaning of management (or was before the word lost all meaning). Just because someone is making a decision does not make it governance. Most decisions are not governance, they are management. Only policy decisions are governance.

The government and the Governor do not operate a country: the civil service does that. The governors set policy, rules, guidelines; they delegate the power to enforce them; and they demand information and tribute.

Governance is one function of senior management, but only as it is delegated. The ultimate responsibility for governance rests with the owner, board of directors, or government, depending on the type of organisation. The execution of governance can be delegated to executive management: the accountability can not. In recent times, the Sarbanes Oxley Act has made that quite clear in the USA; so too have various OECD, EC and national Acts and regulations.

Optimisation

Governance is not optimisation.

Governance asks "are we doing...?" but not "how are we doing it?" Profitability, ROI and other such operational metrics are of interest to governors only in so much as they have set policy to say "We must be profitable" How we achieve this or why we are failing to achieve it are management functions not governance ones. Executive management is responsible of optimising the performance of the organisation; governance is responsible only for ensuring it remains within bounds.

Financial control

Financial processes are not governance, not even controlling processes. All financial management is part of the operations of the organisation. Some financial metrics will be required by governors to ensure operations remains within financial policy bounds, but this is a small part of what finance does and even then getting the data is not of itself governance.

This includes many activities often tagged as governance: Project Portfolio Management (PPM), Asset management, budgeting, annual reporting... Even fraud detection is not governance: it is an operational security process.

Governance sets financial policy: financial management executes it.

Policy enforcement

Governance is not enforcement of policy.

This is perhaps the most common misuse of the word "governance". Governors mandate that policy shall be complied with. They measure to ensure the organisation remains within the bounds of policy. But the day-to-day operational activity of keeping the organisation within the bounds is management not governance. Governors are watching not doing.

So bounds functions like risk management, change management, financial management, security and audit are not governance. They are the means by which the organisation satisfies governance requirements by keeping the organisation within the bounds of policy.

Vision and strategy

Governance is not setting vision or strategy.

Another area that is often confused with governance is creating the vision, setting the direction of the organisation, and devising strategy. Governors appoint an executive to do this, and give them a framework and policy within which to do it. In some organisations, the governors get actively involved in the process and don't fully delegate it. But this means that the governors are involved in high-level operations, not that the activity is part of governance.

Rule

Governance is not always rule.

A king may rule but in the modern model he/she does not govern. Equally in many large organisations the nominal figure-head has little to do with governance. A government minister or secretary has only nominal control over his civil servants (watch "Yes Minister" on TV). The Chairman of the Board may do no more than occupy the chair. Note that this is not a consequence of simple delegation. The British people constitutionally removed their monarchy's right to govern at sword-point. In theory the US president is answerable to the Senate (though in practice some would say the republic has an emperor). The civil service in every nation evades control. The Chairman may simply be ineffective.

IT Governance

So far we have talked about governance in general. This article is about IT in particular, so what of IT governance. If we focus on IT, does it change this discussion any?

The principles of IT governance remain exactly the same: direct and control. The practices of IT governance are of course more specific. IT governance is very well defined by Val IT [1], that excellent product of the IT Governance Institute. Val IT starts slowly and looks deceptively light after you have read it, but it is a nice comprehensive framework for governing and managing value from IT.

Val IT defines the IT governance as

- Ensure informed and committed leadership
- Define and implement processes.
- Define roles and responsibilities.
- Ensure appropriate and accepted accountability.
- Define information requirements.
- Establish reporting requirements.
- Establish organisational structures.
- Establish strategic direction.

- Define investment categories.

- Determine a target portfolio mix.

- Define evaluation criteria by category.

Val IT also helps define what IT governance is not. It describes Project and Portfolio management

- Maintain a human resource inventory.

- ...

- Establish an investment threshold.

- Evaluate the initial programme concept business case.

- ...

- Make and communicate the investment decision.

- Stage-gate (and fund) selected programmes.

- ...

- Monitor and report on portfolio performance.

...and Investment Management:

- Develop a high-level definition of investment opportunity.

- Develop an initial programme concept business case.

- Develop a clear understanding of candidate programmes.

- Perform alternatives analysis.

- ...

- Assign clear accountability and ownership.

- Initiate, plan and launch the programme.

- ...

- Monitor and report on programme performance.

- Retire the programme.

As we discussed already, governance is not operational management, even where that management is the implementation of governance policy. Val IT agrees.

If we revisit our list of seven examples of areas that get shoehorned into the definition of governance, we can see how they have a different context within IT but they are not changed.

Measurement, reporting and audit

In IT, we are blessed with the COBIT framework as a useful definition of practices and metrics for measuring, reporting and auditing IT. In addition there are of course ITIL and CMMI and other frameworks that extend and complement COBIT too. IT is something of a thought leader in this area: try to find good KPIs for HR or marketing. We in turn take our lead from manufacturing where TQM and Six Sigma have pioneered many of IT's concepts.

Management

In the last decade or so we have moved from IT people managing to managers managing IT: the understanding that management is a skill that many IT people do not grow into, and effective management can be brought in from outside IT. The rise of ITIL is a sign of that maturing as non-IT managers look for effective frameworks to impose. But IT managers do not govern. They serve their governor masters like all managers do.

Most importantly, there is no such thing as IT governance in the sense that nobody within IT governs, except as delegated from the governors. When we narrow our focus to IT Governance, one thing does not change: the governors of the organisation own it. Accountability for IT Governance rests with the Board, or owner, or minister/secretary, just like any other governance. IT is governed just as Manufacturing, Distribution, Finance, HR and so on are governed: from the top.

Optimisation

Again nothing changes. CSI is not governance. Doing things better within IT is part of the operational management of IT. We do it to stay within governance's policy bounds, but we do it outside of governance.

Financial control

IT does a lot to facilitate financial management and financial governance by providing the software to make the processes effective, but the tools are not governance any more than a hammer is carpentry.

Policy enforcement

IT plays a pivotal role in modern organisational policy enforcement in areas like audit and security, but we merely deliver to the operational processes that respond to policy: this is along way removed from calling what we do governance.

Vision and strategy

It has been well argued of late that there should be no IT strategy: IT is one aspect of the organisational strategy. Certainly IT's emergence as a function more aligned with the business with outward facing management means we push for a seat at the top table, but that does not mean CIOs take a governance role. It means they take an executive management role.

Rule

There is no distinct IT governance role so there is no distinct ruler of IT, but try telling that to some CIOs.

In theory the practice of governance is simple, though in practice not so. The definition of governance is simple: policy making and monitoring. But the vendors will make governance mean what they sell; the analysts will make it mean something new and oh so clever; and many writers will make it whatever they think it means. This article's quest is probably futile: the word "governance" is doomed just like "partner" and "paradigm" and "legacy" and "virtual" before it. Maybe there is still a chance. You will make this writer happy if just once you say "that's not governance".

Wandering topics

The IT Skeptic is nosey. He pokes into topics that don't concern him. He is unafraid to comment on topics he knows little about (some say that includes ITIL). He always has an opinion.

VOIP

These are ugly times for telcos, a topic I look forward to exploring a little more on this blog. Today's topic is VOIP and the anti-competitive behaviours that would logically induce in a telco. Let me share with you a recent email from my broadband ISP.

First some background. My ISP is a telco, the big dominant telco. They also provide me phone lines. Actually they try to pretend they don't, by branding the ISP arm as an excitingly named subsidiary, but it is a pointless sham really when it all comes on one convenient monthly bill.

Why would I get my broadband from a big ugly telco? Well I didn't have much choice really. I live in a village of 700 houses, mostly blue-collar (and yes, it's idyllic, when the wind stops). The cable goes straight through here to more lucrative suburbs without a tap: we get our pay TV by satellite. The nearest broadband wireless base station is miles away. I can get satellite broadband, but I run all these websites. I need to upload the fruits of my development as much as I need to download backups and scantily clad women, and satellite broadband is VERY asymmetric (like some of those women). So that leaves me with ADSL, which comes through the copper, which is provided by the telco.

Since I signed up, the government has forced the aforementioned telco to unbundle the local loop letting competitors get at me, but too late for me. (And the telco had the gall to claim they would have done it anyway. LMAO. Couldn't sit for a week.)

Another recent development is that my power company claims they can pipe me broadband down the power lines, thus locking me in with a different ugly corporate giant.

Besides I prefer to deal with one pack of support morons not two. So for good or ill I'm in a contract for broadband with the phone company. Which brings me to the very exciting email from the very excitingly-named ISP subsidiary:

> We're eager to keep you informed of what new developments you can expect in broadband services in the near future.
>
> Right around the world broadband services are constantly developing, and [this country] is no exception.
>
> Back in April, new [exciting name] plans were introduced delivering maximum download speeds of up to 3.5 megabits per second on supported lines. We also announced that we will be introducing new technology in the future that will enable even faster broadband speeds for customers, depending on their location.

Hot off the press is the news that [we] will be providing new unconstrained speed options later this year.

These new plans will include options which will deliver unconstrained speeds for both downloading and uploading. So instead of being provided with individual maximum line speeds, these options will deliver the maximum the network is capable of delivering at any particular location and time. [I live in a technologically primitive country. YES this is considered an exciting development. I know. I know.]

With these plans customers may find it easier to do things online that are "bandwidth-intensive" - e.g. downloading / uploading music and files, watching video, sending and receiving large email attachments such as photos, and playing online games.

Now, for a starter for ten, what bandwidth-intensive activity is very pointedly NOT included in that list? Yes, very good. VOIP. As in Skype, Google Talk... Lynch-pins of several of my businesses, the greatest invention since the internet itself. Why not? Well the telco doesn't want you to do it do they? In fact they are not going to even mention it because a lot of the people in this country - who still think unconstrained broadband is an exciting development - haven't actually heard of it, and the telco for one are not going to tell them.

Switch now to a meeting I went to where there was much discussion of this same telco who have been hotly denying rumours that they have been using QoS[1] in routers to recognise and degrade VOIP traffic. This would probably be viewed in most circles and even in a court of law as anti-competitive practice. In fact it is monopolistic, in that I believe the telco in question provides pretty much all the fat-pipe backbone in and out of the country.

One lady in the meeting asked "Why do they do that? Why can't they accept the world has changed and embrace the new technology as something exciting?" Well, the left-wing, hairy naivety of the question had me gobsmacked (fuzzy thinking always brings out the P J O'Rourke in me).

"Because they are a giant corporate conglomerate in one of the most fiercely competitive industries, you pixie-dust idiot" (...I felt like shouting but didn't, being a nice chap off-blog).

---

[1] It seems remarkable to me that there are people who know less about this stuff than me but there are, so here goes:
Internet (TCP/IP) network devices these days have a Quality of Service (QoS) function that allows them to recognise different kinds of traffic and allocate proportions of their bandwidth to each. So if your network is drowning in email, they can throttle it back to only use say 20% of the bandwidth. If downloads are swamping it they can throttle those. And so on, including VOIP traffic.

Because they still have billions of sunk investment in copper and exchanges and vans and phones to wring an ROI from. Because they swaggered into the mobile phone market thinking they could bully and gouge there too and had their lunch eaten by real capitalists in a truly competitive market for a change. Because they pissed further billions up against the wall on the 3G nonsense like most other telcos (a topic for another day). Because, hallelujah, they are finally answerable to shareholders (yes I live in one of THOSE counties where that too is an exciting new development). Because they are mad as hell over some long-haired bunch of hippy upstarts giving phone calls away for freekin' free, across THEIR pipes!! Right under their freekin' noses!!!!. Whaddya think they say about that in the telco boardroom? "Isn't new technology exciting"? "We must take a hands-off approach and allow the market to find its own level"? I DON'T THINK SO. They are saying "Screw those muthas down so low in the QoS all they can see is their own toes, and if you tell anyone we'll sink your pension and come after your children". That's what they are saying. Outside of some over-conscienced techo blowing the whistle on them who would ever know what the QoS settings are? We have a saying here when they cry innocent: "Yeah, right!".

So all this exciting new unconstrained bandwidth that they are so eager to tell me about isn't worth a pinch of drek to me for one of my bandwidth-intensive activities of choice, because this little black skeptic doesn't believe for one moment that they are going to let me get away with it. What about YOUR country?

VOIP is a disruptive technology. As always, those being disrupted complain loudly. But there is nothing dishonest about using VOIP. You buy the bandwidth - you use it as you see fit. The telcos better adapt to VOIP or die. But those using VOIP are just doing what capitalists are supposed to do; exercising their prerogative in an open market. The difference between a phone system and an internet bandwidth system is that the IP access can have massive bandwidth through simple off-the-shelf commodity components. A copper-based phone system is sourced expensively from proprietary (and hence non-competitive) over-engineered components, and uses outmoded expensive wires to deliver its service.

The confusion and debate over VOIP arises because many consumers are still stuck with accessing IP via an expensive custom-built voice network.

Bandwidth is cheap. I buy it in bulk. I should be free to browse the web, talk to friends or do whatever I want with that bandwidth. VOIP is as valid a traffic as any for me to put down that pipe and there should be no differentiation.

The voice network (the "local copper") is dead. It will take half a century to die, since the return has to be realised on the current investment. But it is stone dead. My grandchildren will access the world via radio, cable and satellite. In the interim, I'm afraid the telcos have been caught in the nasty bind that faces any industry that requires massive capital investment: they grow fat in the good times; they suffer horribly when an alternative competitor arises because they do not have the liquidity to get out.

It happened to railroads. It is happening to telcos. The reason telcos are piling so enthusiastically into mobiles and cable and content is that they have to replace the copper as a source of income and very quickly. Well, sorry for the telcos, and their shareholders. They were blue-chip investments in their day. They may be again if they can avoid going the way of the railroad. The analogy is those (very few) railroads that reinvented themselves as transportation networks: trucking, warehousing, air... [or became bulk long-distance carriers over existing infrastructure and abandoned the last few miles.]

VOIP is a perfectly valid technology sold by business people responding to an opportunity and a demand. They are doing nothing wrong and nobody is being cheated. To continue the railroad analogy: the railroad can have basic safety rules around what you put in your containers, but they don't prevent you from shipping what used to be carried in their boxcars. They just adapted to carrying containers instead. They also had to adapt to a smaller slice of the transport market as shipping became more attractive and passengers went to airlines instead.

Right now I get bandwidth via ADSL down the copper only because an effective competitor is not yet available out here. ADSL represents an interim salvation for telcos much as containerisation did for railroads, and they may get enough benefit from it to save themselves and realise their ROI from the copper after all. But they need to stop whining about what traffic I choose to put down that pipe.

Just as soon as I can get a better and/or cheaper service through another pipe I'll switch. The current telco better be providing that alternate pipe else they'll lose my business.

Guess what: they won't be providing it. Nimble intelligent competitors are laying cable and hiring satellites and putting up wireless base stations. They will get to my village first. The only place the telco is competing is in mobile, and badly. They are fat and lazy and they will go down to better competitors.

It's called capitalism and it is in the best interests of the public, except those members of the public silly enough to leave their money in copper-based telcos.

Privacy

People demand online privacy as if it were some god-given right. Privacy is an aberration of recent history, a transitory phenomenon that is evaporating quickly in the hot light of technology. Privacy is dead - get over it.

Today's musing is prompted by this quote seen in The Pointless Privacy Debate[1]

> In response to criticism from a british [sic] privacy group and European Union data overseers, Google recently announced it would anonymize data it retains on user searches after 18 months... The EU applauded the move as it had lauded Google's agreement to comply with its 2005 directive requiring service providers to retain all identifiable records up to two years. Huh?
>
> When it comes to consumer privacy, lawmakers can't seem to contain their frustration and even outrage with businesses that retain detailed, personally identifiable data. Yet when it comes to investigating crime—terrorism and child pornography being the favorites—they just as passionately take the opposite position. Consumers are equally ambivalent: We're creeped out to find photos of ourselves showing up in Google maps, but infuriated when the movements of alleged terrorists and other criminals through public spaces aren't captured or stored.
>
> ...You give away far more "private" information in exchange for small discounts at the grocery store or pet store every time you use your loyalty card. And that's not necessarily bad. The data is valuable to retailers and manufacturers, and you're willing to sell it.
>
> ...Maybe it isn't a debate at all, but a negotiation.

What is "normal" privacy anyway? Scott McNealy of Sun Microsystems said that consumer privacy issues are a "red herring... You have zero privacy anyway... Get over it". Expectations of total privacy are a Twentieth Century phenomenon, that emerged as we moved away from communal housing and village living. There is no reason why they can not be rolled back again. Privacy is a transitory modern phenomenon amongst the wealthy developed nations – it is the exception not the norm across cultures and history. The issue is that it takes time to change something so conservative and personal. [The 20th Century will be seen as a time when privacy peaked.]

1

http://www.cioinsight.com/article2/0,1540,2159182,00.asp?kc=CIOMINEP NL072707

Privacy is gone. If your alter ego in some online community is a diaper-wearing goat-fondler, people are gonna know, just as in the village of old your predilections would soon be revealed.

The difference now is that you exist and interact in the online world as streams of information. Nobody has to record it, nobody has to disseminate it. You do all that by the very act of existing online. To think that this flow of data can somehow remain confidential is patently absurd.

Equally absurd is the idea that people have a right to online privacy. The only people who have anything to fear from such loss of privacy are those who have something to hide. If your political beliefs are not to your employer's tastes; or you are tupping the wrong person; or you have a penchant for bukkake; or you are running a tax-free business on the sly; then don't do it online. Do it in the privacy of your own home's four solid walls, like we did before the internet. Don't do it by broadcasting a stream of personal data across an open network to the other side of the planet on servers managed by people you don't know, then act surprised when word gets out.

As the amount of data grows and as it becomes more integrated, a natural trend is to use data mining for more advanced security. The world has barely started down this path. There is much more that can be done to apply existing data technologies and techniques for

• Statistical analysis: deviance reporting ("take the ratio of funds transferred to declared income and investigate the top 2%")

• Pattern analysis: exception reporting ("no-one has signed on from there before" or "this individual has never come in at night before" or "there are an unusual number of deductions happening from this country")

• Profiling: ("this individual will probably react this way")

There are some fundamental technical criticisms of this kind of data mining (leaving aside the social issues for now). As Scientific American put it in an editorial "Every data set has patterns. At issue is whether they mean anything ... Terrorism is very rare – which is good for us but bad for data miners. Even with a low error rate, the vast majority of red flags will be red herrings ... In short, the data miners commit the fallacy of determinism: they falsely assume that if you just amass enough data, you will know what is going to happen".

In one year post-9/11, more than 30,000 travellers were mistakenly linked to names on terror watch lists when they crossed the border, boarded commercial airliners or were stopped for traffic violations, according to a report by the Government Accountability Office.

Nevertheless, the application of advanced technologies like neural networks gives us hope of finding the evil needle in the haystack. And the stakes are too high not to try.

As our security capabilities become more advanced, the world is changing to make it all the more urgent that we deploy these capabilities. As we face escalating terrorism, hacking and identity theft, it is clear society must respond to protect itself. But to do so raises challenges. How do we protect without destroying what we seek to protect: freedom and democracy? How can we use the collected data for the benefit of its subjects? How will we respect the right to privacy?

The changing world creates pressures to employ technology advances for our protection. As these advances compromise our privacy, they also drive social change in our attitudes to privacy. Business and government are working to set standards and policies to ensure these security advances deliver us benevolent security: Big Uncle, not Big Brother.

Either is possible with the technology: benevolent security is dependent on the legal, social and business policies that govern the technology.

Immense amounts of data are assembled about us, gradually eroding privacy. The application of advanced technologies gives us hope of finding the evil terrorist needle in that haystack. Modern concepts of privacy are just that: modern. In most places and times, people live with far less privacy than the Western world has become accustomed to.

Now things are returning to normal: get over it. We can be quite apathetic about much of this change, but the community will speak up whenever it goes too far – defining the limits through outcry.

More security systems that intrude into our privacy are inevitable given the rise of terrorism. Society will get used to conceding privacy over time. But the initial reaction of many to these more integrated security systems will be that they represent "Big Brother". Originally Big Brother was the supreme ruler in George Orwell's novel 1984:

> At the apex of the pyramid comes Big Brother. Big Brother is infallible and all-powerful... Nobody has ever seen Big Brother... BIG BROTHER IS WATCHING YOU... There was of course no way of knowing whether you were being watched at any given moment. How often, or on what system, the Thought Police plugged in on any individual wire was guesswork. It was even conceivable that they watched everybody all the time... You had to live ... in the assumption that every sound you made was overheard, and ... every movement scrutinised

In contemporary usage Big Brother is a mythical entity who is all knowing, all powerful, secretive and despotic. The image is often invoked in privacy discussions, always pejoratively.

If we accept that increased security is essential in response to modern threats, we must all ensure that the resulting erosion of privacy does not result in an erosion of freedom and democracy. It especially falls on IT workers to ensure technology is put to work benevolently.

The result of increased security does not have to be Big Brother. It can be "Big Uncle": a powerful force working in the interests of the community to preserve and protect. Smokey the Bear with wiretaps.

BIG BROTHER	BIG UNCLE
All knowing	Appropriately knowing
All powerful	Answerable
Secretive	Transparent
Despotic	Benevolent

Most of us willingly surrender privacy every day and will do so increasingly online (except for the most paranoid among us: you know who you are and so do we).

Even in modern times we concede privacy to others who watch over us. Doormen are allowed to watch our coming and going in return for their protection. Neighbours are given permission to spy on our homes through friendships or within the framework of Neighbourhood Watch. Local police patrol our streets, allowed to pry with more freedom than other citizens.

We agree as a condition of employment to clock in and out of the job, to pass through access control systems, to let our employer watch and police our web surfing and email at work, to be answerable for our whereabouts and activities during work hours.

High levels of privacy are only a phenomenon of large wealthy cities. In poorer urban communities and small towns and villages, people draw together and expose their lives to family and neighbours in return for the security and protection it brings.

We concede privacy by delegating trust in return for protection. It is a permission-based process which we have some control over, at least as a group if not always as individuals. There is no reason why electronic security cannot operate the same way.

We will allow access control systems to know more about us (e.g. biometrics) so that they can recognise when our identity has been stolen. Any human gatekeeper knows that a wealthy senior woman is unlikely to look like a 14-year-old school-boy, but currently anybody on the Web can pass themselves off as someone else with a minimum of credentials. If two things are known about us already, it should be OK to put them together in order to spot the unexpected, just as a human might do.

We will allow authorities to find us via our mobile phone when we have crashed the car or had a heart attack or wandered with dementia, but trust them not to tell our spouse we are philandering or to map our political activities.

For another vision of this kind of paternalism (and the origin of the title for this paper), see Big *Uncle says chill out*, New Scientist 20 October 2001: "Combining expert systems containing the knowledge and experience of scores of behavioural psychologists with the CCTV cameras could predict the consequences of the human interactions being surveyed. Is that man getting angry? Is that child too trusting?"

We will delegate trust to peers (family, colleagues, and friends) to allow them to access our email when we are sick, to vouch for us when we forget our passwords, to ask the building access system where we are.

Most of all, we will recognize that rights to privacy that we conceded and the trust we delegated in the physical domain can logically have an equivalent in the electronic world, so long as it is on the same terms.

It is up to all of us to ensure that the result is Big Uncle not Big Brother.

Communities get the government they deserve. Despotism arises with the tacit consent of the majority, and is overthrown through rejection by the majority (or a powerful minority). IT professionals are at the centre of the implementation of all modern security measures. We owe it to ourselves, our professionalism and our community to ensure that these measures are imposed with benevolent intent: and to blow whistles when they are not.

The world has changed for the worse. Security will increase and privacy decrease. Advanced technologies will deploy to make it so. The IT industry - as a group and as individuals - has a central role in ensuring that technology delivers the benevolent security of Big Uncle, not the despotism of Big Brother.

Information engineering

When we speak of a new profession(alism), could it be that by focusing on IT we are focusing on the wrong thing?

My other interest besides being a nuisance is railroads. I just read the line "railroads nurtured the new profession of civil engineering in the 19th Century" (...in America. It's one of those "the world ends at the shining seas" books[1].) This resonated with me. Can we paraphrase to "Information Technology nurtured the new profession of"... WHAT?

We - or at least I am always on about the profession of IT, or I prefer "Information Engineering". But maybe the real profession isn't about information any more than civil engineering is about railroads. Maybe the profession is about building complex people systems, about - dare I say it - process, and of course the cultural change to introduce/refine/grow that process.

I put it to the audience that the information age, digital technology, and the internet, (and probably some more factors like the rise of the corporation), have all combined to lift people-process to a new level of complexity, just like railroads forced civil engineering to new levels by the railroad's demand for gentle curves and gradients.

The real profession that we see emerging or maturing is.... what?

> Systems engineer? (And not as we meant it when that was a trendy IT title)
>
> Process engineer?
>
> Or is Information Engineer a good description anyway?
>
> Or something else...

Historically bridges were always the big driving force for civil engineering, but up until the 19th Century most of them were made by people who had little idea what they were doing. They had no scientific basis for it. They just used gut feel, guesswork and copying to build their bridges. The most experienced built the best bridges, but some still fell down and nobody exactly knew why. Sound familiar?

The industrial revolution changed that. Suddenly canal aqueducts and later railroad bridges were required that had to carry enormously higher loads while staying nice and level and steady. And they were much much longer and higher: with a road you can dip down into the valley as far as

---

[1] *Landmarks on the Iron Road*, W. Middleton, Indiana University Press 1999, ISBN-13: 978-0253335593

possible, have a nice short bridge, and then crawl back up the other side. Not so with canals or trains. Lastly, when double-heading steam locos thunder onto a bridge at 60 mph, believe me you need a whole new order of engineering. Along with that came tunnels and cuttings and fills on a scale never conceived of before.

And it wasn't just the design that changed. It was the logistics of building on such a larger scale. When my Dad ran a data centre, there was 64k of memory. It basically added up the day's cheques and deposits for the banks, and spewed out a bunch of totals. These days ERP and CRM and the Windows desktop is a whole different ballgame.

Also in *Landmarks on the Iron Road* on page 4

> In the decade between 1870 and 1880 railroad and highway bridges collapsed at a rate of about forty a year [in the USA]... Frequently, designers had an imperfect understanding of the forces... or of the potential dangers... Steadily increasing loads often subjected bridges to stresses for which they had never been designed... All too commonly bridges were hastily built by the cheapest means... Quite generally, too, bridges were designed and built for the railroads by independent bridge companies on a competitive bid basis.

Woooooo spooky.

Open source is not the answer. I don't think open source has anything much to do with IT. IT is about the application of software tools to business requirements. Whether those tools are built by open source or a mega-corp makes little difference. The in-house systems of each discrete organisation have to be assembled/enabled/instantiated somehow and therein lies the engineering problem.

IT exists to manage the flow of data, in the same way that railroads exist to manage the flow of freight and passengers.

My point is that the professionals who built railroads weren't railroaders. They also built for canals and, later, for freeways and pipelines and airports and ...

At a layer of abstraction removed from IT there is a profession emerging that builds complex people systems, of which IT is currently the major enabler just as railroads were the only engineering game in town in 1880.

Business cases

Too many business cases contain arguments that are simply not compelling. They seem compelling to the business case author because the author is too self-absorbed to see things from the perspective of their target audience. Usually this boils down to whining.

The following arguments seldom work:

"Because we ought to". "Because it is the right thing to do". So are a thousand other things you aren't doing right now. Why this one?

"Because it is better". You got by last year, why can't you get by next year? "Better" actually works but only once you link it to one of the other arguments listed elsewhere: you look better to the clients you want to attract; you have to get better to meet the quality standards of the new contract.

"Because I think we should": "it is my recommendation", "I strongly urge", "it is evident to those at the coal-face that"... If your opinion mattered so much it would be your decision. Put another way, your 5000 colleagues are doing it this way and you want to do it that way. On the balance of probabilities...

"Because I need it to do my job". Either you are not doing your job now or you are managing with what you have now.

"Because it will improve staff morale". This will get lots of affirmative lip-service but unless poor morale is actually costing or risking something forget it. If there is an underlying cost or risk, address that instead of whingeing. My favourite poster: "sackings will continue until morale improves". Or a great slogan for ITIL projects: "if you can't change the people, change the people". So don't go banging on about morale - they just might do something about it.

"Because everyone else is". This can actually work, especially if the decision-makers have been reading about it in McKinsey Quarterly or CIO or ComputerWorld or the Economist or Time. (Once it is in USA Today or Readers Digest it is probably time to move on). But it works as part of the persuasive language (to be discussed in a future blog). You include lots of the usual drek from Gartner to make them feel good about the decision - but it is not an argument. It is not part of the case itself. On its own it will not do - it is just supporting evidence.

These arguments do not work because they have no value to the organisation or the decision-maker. Maybe you haven't noticed yet, but in business what matters to you matters only to you. Put another way: if the multi-{million/billion}   dollar   corporation   with {hundreds|thousands|tens-of-thousands} of employees thinks differently to you, which is more likely to have to change: the corporation or you?

This self-absorbed, self-important, prima donna view of the world is especially prevalent among technology geeks, who think the world is too stupid to understand what they are arguing. On technical issues this is often true. On business issues it seldom is. Deciding where to spend money is a business issue.

So argue from the organisations perspective, not your own.

Find The Money. What if you can't FTM? Relax. It does not have to be real money. It just has to look like money.

Returns on investment can be above-the-line or below-the-line or both. "Below-the-line" means cost savings, efficiencies, lay-offs. "Above-the-line" means more customers, new products, more sales, higher prices. Below-the-line money is easier to make tangible, to put a solid figure on it. It is also harder to prove because people understand the current process and have some measures of it. Above-the-line numbers tend to be more speculative (read: "made up") because we are talking about new fields, the unknown.

Here is how to find the money for your business case:

Look for below-the-line savings. There are some analyst BS-papers that give you Crap Factoid percentages to wave around: 25% less calls to the helpdesk, 15% less downtime, whatever. Find some existing cost metrics within your business (dollars per call, dollars per hour down). Failing that use yet more analyst wet-finger-numbers. Do some impressive spreadsheets (colours are good) to show the expected savings.

If the resulting numbers still look a bit light:

If you really need serious money for a project, claim that you will save ten minutes per person per day, and thereby increase everyone's efficiency by 2%. Then calculate the entire staff costs and claim 2% of it. If you are scoffing: I have seen it done for a web portal product. This is of course nonsense. If I gave you an extra ten minutes per nine-hour day (who works eight any more?), how much more would you get done? None, you would spend ten minutes more at the coffee machine.

When the below-the-line numbers don't stack up, look to above-the-line: also claim an increased productivity in the company of 2% so add that to annual gross return and calculate the increase in profits. Claim that.

Find strategic issues that are hot in your organisation right now; growth, flexibility, quality, customer. Show how the project contributes to those.

You can also appeal to the argument that there is no return - ITIL is just part of the cost of doing business. This is obviously weak, with one exception: risk. Reducing risk can be a compelling argument if (a) there is focus on that risk right now due to scrutiny or a recent embarrassment and (b) the person who owns the money owns the risk.

Finally if all else fails to come up with the money: nick it.

The new SAP rollout has a five-hundred-million-dollar budget, so pipe some your way by showing how the ITIL implementation is essential infrastructure for the new system.

You know the Department is under-spent for the year: offer to help mop up some of the surplus.

Your peer manager is out of favour with your boss, so go after his budget.

...you get the idea.

You can get the content right but fail at the communication of it. The pitch is as important as the story.

Make sure the way the case is explained does these things:

1) Take away pain or fear. Humans are basic creatures. All the rational intellectual arguments in the world are but dust in the wind if the person is in physical or emotional pain or genuinely afraid of something. Convince them you can remove the cause and you will get anything you need.

2) Deliver on key people's personal agendas. Never mind what the organisation wants: what does the decision maker want to hear? Steady consolidation with no major change because he is headed for retirement. Radical transformation because she is new to the job and wants to be seen to have made a difference. The same basic content can be presented either way. Guess what happens when you get it the wrong way round.

3) Align with key business initiatives. Another way of saying this is to align with the decision-maker's KPIs (key performance indicators: what they are measured - and paid - on). So it is a variant of (1) above (every criterion for a successful business case is). The company has a drive for SOX compliance. The Minister has decreed cost cutting measures. The Board has announced to shareholders an exciting new program, Transformation 2010. Shape the whole business case around the language and ideas of the initiative you are aligning with. Measure the business case in terms of the initiative's deliverables.

4) Use the right buzz-speak. Read the Annual Report. Read what the decision-maker has been writing lately, and what they have been reading lately. Pick up on the language.

So the strength of a business case is money (real, imagined or ... ah ... diverted). The strategy of a business case is how it is aligned with the target organisation. With strength and strategy, and a little luck, and no whining, you can succeed.

IT terminology

The persistent erosion of meaning in IT terminology is a damaging practice endemic across vendors and analysts. When a concept gains some currency and everyone wants it, suddenly all the vendors have got it - often by re-labelling a feature of their existing product. And the analysts keep confusing the definition so no-one can call the vendors out for this obfuscation. I used to really struggle with this. I thought I kept getting the wrong end of the stick with new terminology, until I realised that is was other people moving the stick.

Most of us have been around the industry long enough to remember when "knowledge management" actually meant something. You added value to data to make information, and added value to information to make knowledge. Knowledge management was about gathering information into a knowledgebase, where it could be organised and accessed at a conceptual level, where the IP of the organisation would be captured and shared, and where new concepts and strategic insights would emerge. Now anyone whose tool stores files or lets you type text in has a knowledgebase. By some current vendor definitions, Windows Explorer is a knowledgebase.

Before that it was Executive Information Systems. EIS was about providing the information to support corporate strategic decisions, by distilling out KPIs, preferably in real-time. After a while, any end-user reporting tool apparently supported EIS.

In recent years, it has been ITIL. Suddenly every vendor has ITIL. ITIL is technology-agnostic. Strewth, you can do ITIL with Post-It Notes, and the way things are going it won't be long before 3M are advertising Post-it Notes as "ITIL compliant". But it seems to me that there are some clear criteria for a reasonable person's definition of "ITIL compliant".

It is far too easy to slap the word "ITIL" on any operations tool (or pay some firm to do it for you). This only serves to debase what ITIL means and to confuse the community.

More recently, the victim has been Service Oriented Architecture or SOA.

> our own research shows, that organisations are increasingly confused by the seemingly endemic and varied use of the term SOA in vendor propositions. [Macehiter Ward-Dutton Advisors , May 04, 2005]

And now this, the last straw: from EMA, analysts who should know better.

> "The point is the CMDB is not a 'thing', it's a landscape, it's a system," said Dennis Drogseth, VP of EMA. "So, the CMDB is exactly that political-cultural process of getting organizations to define a trusted source of information for a given environment and to share that info in a consistent way with parts of the organization." [ITSM-Watch August 3, 2006]

No it isn't. Leave it alone. It's a thing.

> Configuration Management requires the use of support tools, which includes a Configuration Management Database (CMDB)... The CMDB is likely to be based upon database technology that provides flexible and powerful interrogation facilities. [Service Support, p124].

CMDB is NOT "a landscape ... a system" or a "political-cultural process". Bullshit. I'm not sure whether this reflects the author's ignorance of ITIL or blatant lack of respect for the meaning of terms, but either way: stop it! Invent your own bloody terms and leave CMDB alone.

Project management

One of the things ITIL3 improves is the whole development/production interface, introducing radical concepts like production readiness, acceptance, evaluation... oh and testing. Heady stuff. But something that was omitted from ITIL V3 was documentation of Dead Cat Syndrome.

Service Transition alludes to it in a few places, but it is such a chronic condition in the industry it needs to be described explicitly. In many organisations, putting a new project into production is akin to lobbing a dead cat over a wall. IT Operations needs to put controls in place to prevent this. Projects benefit from these controls by having a better definition of the end goal and a better end product.

When is a project ready for production hand-over? In some organisations this is when it has passed testing. Testing addresses what ITIL v3 calls Utility and Warranty: it does what it should, and it does so reliably/dependably (see *Service Strategy* (the "leaf book"), p 33). But there is more to consider. Without these further considerations, many projects are as welcome in production as a dead cat, and those in IT feel they have as much say in receiving the system as a neighbour does in receiving the cat over the wall.

Some organisations accept a project after it has been in production for a warranty period (not the same meaning of "warranty" as ITIL Version 3). That is, the project team operates and supports the system and resolves all incidents and problems for a defined period after go-live. This is an excellent idea, but on its own it only means we are deferring the cat-toss for a month.

ITIL v3 talks about operational readiness: testing that the system can be deployed and deployment can be verified, the service can be monitored and measured, it can be operated, users and service providers can access it, and it meets service levels (see *Service Transition* (the "peas book")g p 101).

This is a most important concept, and operational readiness should be formal test criteria, as it is in ITIL v3. One way to think of this is that the IT operations group perform their own acceptance testing, as well as the users doing so. There is an element of locking the stable door in operational readiness testing. We need to work back to the start of the lifecycle and influence operational robustness (not an ITIL v3 term), i.e., how the system was designed and built.

Does the system include functions and processes defined and tested for start-up and shutdown, availability checking (end-to-end test transaction), user provisioning, releasing locks, processing logs, data archiving, reversing a transaction, recovering a deleted object, data cross-check, reporting cross-check, ands data quality audit?

Is it a self-correcting system: transactional integrity, referential integrity, automated error recovery, automated rollback and restart?

Is it an integrated design? I see too much "Tarzan software". When Tarzan sets out swinging from vine to vine, it needs just one vine to be in the wrong place for him to end up on the jungle floor. Applications that pass data into a database file for a batch process to pick up; broadcast messages hopefully without confirmation; rely on external spoolers ... these are a recipe for error if they do not have control and visibility over the entire transaction from end-to-end; if they cannot check that a transaction is viable before starting it; if they do not confirm the transaction was successful; and if they can't roll it all back if it wasn't.

Okay, now the cat is at least alive. But it will still be a mangy cat unless we look at the last consideration for an acceptable project deliverable: The organisational infrastructure. In terms of my favourite mantra, we have addressed process and technology but what about people? No system should be accepted into production until it has:

- A mechanism for the transfer of IP from the project into production support (level 1 and 2). Normally, this is done by seconding production people onto the project, then returning them to their production teams at the end of the warranty period.

- Underpinning contracts negotiated with third party suppliers (usually software and hardware vendors) that match up with...

- SLAs agreed with the business.

- Administration roles agreed and demarcated between IT application support and the business's own systems administrators, defined all the way down to discrete functions such as user provisioning, password resets, adding values to reference data, help with using the system, fixing user data errors, backups, scheduling jobs, regular maintenance.

- Functional and hierarchal escalation paths agreed between all IT, business and service provider groups. Functional escalation means Level 1, 2 and 3 support arrangements decided and implemented, with OLAs (i.e., internal SLAs between support groups) on how incidents and problems get passed around.

Now we have a healthy cat.

How to get to know the cat and have some say in whether it gets chucked over the wall or not?

There is a tribal effect in any group of humans. Once the group reaches somewhere between 20-and-100 people it will start to fracture into two groups. (Personally I reckon 80 is the magic number, at least with Kiwis). The separation between development/solutions and production/operations is a natural plane to break along. So, in any reasonably-sized IT shop there is usually an us-and-them mentality between these two groups. Once they are on separate floors or in separate buildings it is pretty much a given that there is some gap in communication.

In order to have any control over what is chucked over the wall, it is essential to bridge this divide. IT should establish liaison relationships with architects and with project teams. I have never yet found a relationship between production's infrastructure architects and development's solutions architects that rose above the dysfunctional. It always seems to degenerate into butting antlers. Liaison people are communicators and negotiators, not pontificators.

The main objectives of liaison are to:

- Educate architects, designers and developers on operational requirements;

- Influence design standards; and

- Review projects at an early stage to gain agreement on operational design.

Most ITIL processes seem to have their proactive and reactive aspects. Think of this as proactive IT operations: influencing the design of systems during their genesis to ensure a satisfactory outcome for everyone. A good place for it to reside is with the Availability Manager.

Conversely, projects cannot follow a strategy of ignoring operational requirements because it won't make the problem go away. Project teams should reach out in return and encourage corresponding communications with production, to ensure these requirements are addressed early in the project, when changes are cheaper and easier.

So, operational acceptance should depend on proper testing, warranty period, operational readiness, operational robustness, organisational infrastructure, and liaison relationships

More requirements to worry about and a higher bar to clear might seem like the last things a project manager wants to hear. But, by meeting these criteria, a PM knows exactly what he or she is shooting for. Moreover, there will be minimum fuss at the end of the project and a quality product will be delivered. Hand a happy purring cat to willing owners instead of tossing a feline corpse over the wall and running away.

I don't feel that ITIL has this problem clearly nailed yet. In fact I accuse *Service Design* of actually fostering it. The diagram on p31 is just wrong. It shows the project team's job is done at the start of the pilot or warranty period. A project team should retain ownership through the warranty period until acceptance has been signed off.

When a project is being designed, production readiness should be designed in. Along the way the project should be coached to prepare for Go Live. If they don't listen or don't want to play or don't play nicely, then there should be production-readiness criteria and if they don't meet them they don't go into production (Real ITSM calls it the Service Porthole they have to squeeze through to get aboard).

1. Define a "production readiness" standard (does ITIL offer any help at all here?)

2. Get it included in the architecture: in design specs, in requirements gathering, in deliverables, in required infrastructure. The Architects usually go along with this readily - they are mostly non-partisan on the Dev/Prod divide.

3. Get CIO mandate for: "no Operations signoff on production readiness, no production change". This is the hard bit but it is easy to make a business case for this: cost of failures and degraded service, cost of manual support processes, cost of re-working apps to make them supportable

4. Push in to dev project-start-up meetings and make it known this is how things are from now on - nicely. Then help.

5. Try to get as much as possible retrofitted into in-flight projects - lots of coaching and sleeves-up help required here. Be seen to be helping.

6. Get a "head on a pike": make a project late by refusing signoff. The more fuss and debate the better. Whether you win or lose this fight in the end does not matter. Project managers like a smooth ride. They'll take note and get readiness engineered in to their other projects.

It is all about communication. This is a People issue not a Process one. (Nor a technology one: "we need better lifecycle tools"). Go along to project meetings, especially in the early days and especially those projects that make you nervous.

1. Explain why we need this stuff to make a project into a successful service.

2. Explain how much of it is design thought and documented information and only a little of it is actual engineering in the system.

3. Explain how Operations wants to work with the project team to help design it and document it (then deliver on that promise).

4. Explain what will happen if it isn't there. Tell the story of the project that didn't play nicely.

If this gets steamrolled then there should be waivers signed: "Operations will make best endeavours... but accept no responsibility if..."

Nobody deserves a Dead Cat.

It is essential to define a suitably narrow criterion for permissible services.

The Service Diameter (SD) defines the number of degrees of freedom allowed to customers when requesting services. Real ITSM is about minimising this number.

The resulting specification through which a service must pass in order to be accepted into production is known as the Service Porthole.

The following mechanisms are used in minimising the diameter of the Service Porthole:

- Service Valuation: this figure can readily be inflated beyond any CFO's pain threshold.

- Service Improvement Plan: used to divert resources that otherwise would be available for new services

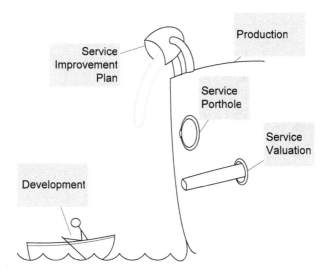

Intellectual property

It occurred to me today that defending your digital IP is like having a puppy [warning: yet another puppy analogy].

At home at the moment we mount regular Puddles and Poos Patrol (thank heavens for polished wood floors). Likewise the price of digital respect is constant vigilance. Keep an eye out, run scans, check eBay, ask around. Be aware of what people are up to. Devote a little time each month to policing your own material. Even dear old Google is effective: spot an unusual turn of phrase in your work, quotate it and google it. There are free tools on the web, or if you can afford it then look to firms that provide a commercial solution [no I'm not promoting any].

And whack thieves. There are no cops on the internet (except the private cops of the big corporations, like the railroad detectives of old). It is the Wild West. We have to look out for ourselves (and each other) and carry a gun.

And you can hit them. I had a piracy site taken down by the simple expedient of complaining to their web host. I got pirated content of mine taken down. I failed to get eBay pirates removed but I like to think I worried them with my complaints to eBay... maybe (eBay don't give a {what my puppy leaves}).

I hate digital piracy. You should too. It is the laziest form of theft. Like any theft or corruption, it introduces economic drag, and it acts as a disincentive to creativity, business and entrepreneurism. Please don't confuse what I am saying with the DRM issue and drag us into that argument. How pop culture gets shovelled out to the masses is of little interest to me.

Sharing content is good. It is how we do it that matters. We can quote, or link, or use attributed extracts within fair use. That is what the internet is for. But theft is theft and I think we all know it when we smell it, which brings me back to my starting analogy.

So let's all stand up for decency on the internet and take action when we see it defiled, please.

DespoITSM

Like similar closed non-public-domain BOKs, Real ITSM is copyrighted and trademarked. RITSI protects its intellectual property rigorously, policed by the DespoITSM program.

The Program (as it is known, as in "Oh no! Not The Program!" [dramatic chord]) enforces:

- Misuse of copyright material

- Violation of trademark

- Parody and satirical mockery of Real ITSM

- Unpaid bills

- Overdue subscriptions

- Overdue books from the RITSI Library

Enforcement is outsourced to Lou and Stan's Debt Collections and Intellectual Property Enforcement Inc. Lou and Stan have an uncanny ability to avoid drawn-out legal arguments and a remarkable number of affiliates in other countries.

Web 2.0

The hype wave of Web 2.0 approaches a crescendo. Apparently it is going to transform IT and reengineer the business. The IT Skeptic thinks not. Actually I think "not again".

I have been holding off on the Web 2.0 topic until I could do something learned, erudite, pontificating. But the whole thing is as slippery as a soapy baby so I waited as I tried to pin it all down [WARNING this is a mixed metaphor: do not try to pin babies]. As usual an article has set me off and I wait no longer. The catalyst is Web 2.0, Sea Changes and the Enterprise[1].

The author, Steve Andriole, freely admits

> I was in the very heart of the dot.com bubble... We took lots of companies public in those days. Only a few survived. Many ... crashed and burned and lots of good people suffered. Is anything that different now? I find myself muttering phrases like "sea change," "game over," and "killer apps" way too often. I really thought I was cured.

I think he isn't.

> 1) Wikis could revolutionize the way that companies document policies, processes and procedures.

No they won't. Wikis are a useful tool for a large group of people to collaborate on writing stuff down, but good useful documentation is authorative, structured, consistent, complete and meticulously accurate, none of which are attributes of wikis in general.

Impact on the business on a Richter scale of ten: 1

> 2) Blogs can be used to vet ideas, strategies, projects and programs. They can – along with wikis – be used for knowledge management... They can also be used as living suggestion boxes and chat rooms...

Well, yes... in as much as a blog is a webpage that folk can write on, much like a piece of paper only more complex and expensive (actually I think he's including forums when he refers to "living suggestion boxes and chat rooms"). Knowledge management? No. KM is one of those much-abused labels that people slap on anything handy. Chucking facts in a bucket is not KM.

Impact on the business: 0.1

---

[1] http://itmanagement.earthweb.com/entdev/article.php/11070_3663881

3) Podcasts can be used for pre-meetings, in-meetings and post-meetings documentation. Repositories of podcasts can contribute to institutional memory and together comprise a rich audit trail of corporate initiatives and decision-making.

Oh my, he's really winding up now. We have been able to record audio for a century. The reason it hasn't displaced paper is that it is inconvenient, impossible to index or search or copy, and bulky. A "rich audit trail" I think not, unless "rich" means "impenetrable". Voice mail was an advance in communications?

Impact on the business: 0

4) RSS filters can be used to fine tune information flows of all kinds to employees, customers, suppliers and partners

Phew, back to earth. Agree on this one: RSS feeds and filters would be a much more useful mechanism than the barrage of emails I used to get (and not read) within the corporation. But filtered crap is still crap. This addresses the symptom not the problem of corporate communications - nothing fundamental here.

Impact on the business: 1

5) Mash-up technology makes it easier to develop applications that solve specific problems – if only temporarily. Put some end-users in a room full of APIs and watch what happens.

Lost me on this one. "end-users in a room full of APIs" will result in precisely nothing, as anyone who has struggled with JAD and similar methodologies will tell you. Mash-ups are as dodgy as the name implies. Just like prototypes, ad-hoc queries, user programming and spreadsheets: they should be allowed nowhere near a real production IT environment; and their use by the business will result in as many errors as successes.

Impact on the business: 0

6) Crowdsourcing can be used to extend the enterprise via the Web and leverage the expertise of lots of professionals on to corporate problems

Back to earth again with a bump. The potential of crowdsourcing is real ["outsourcing to the wisdom of the crowd", or posting your problems on the internet and asking for solutions]. But not infinite: crowdsourcing fatigue will set in, the crowd is not always right [a future blog], it will fall victim to spam and nutters, and it can only be used where commercial confidentiality is not important (don't want to telegraph a new development to competitors before it has even been designed). R&D has not been transformed - it just has one more useful tool.

Impact on the business: 1

> 7) Service-oriented architecture ...is actually a decentralizing force that will enable companies to solve computational and display problems much faster than they ever did in the past. What will it be like when we can point to glue and functionality and have them assemble themselves into solutions?

I can hear the wild arm-waving. I grew up a bit earlier than Steve, and I remember all the magic solutions that were going to transform IT or business. Every one was accompanied by similar arm-waving pundits shouting "follow the gourd" [Life of Brian, Monty Python]. SOA will allow us to do things better and smarter by adding yet another layer of complexity to be integrated and managed and kept stable: three steps forward and two back.

Impact on the business: 2 if it works.

Any one of a dozen similar articles could have been the basis for this one. Sorry to pick on Steve. He's not alone of course. There are armies of them, just as there were behind all the previous waves of irrational exuberance. How about this one[1] from a blog called EarlyStageVC

> Mash-ups represent a potentially powerful way to create new ad hoc Web applications out of existing enterprise data and web services... Ultimately, they will emerge as complete business processes that mash (integrate) enterprise applications with applications in the cloud. And SOA and Web 2.0 will fully converge.

...and black and white will live in peace and harmony. Shockingly he is talking about Web 2.0 as passé ("on the verge of going from Wired to Tired"), and Web 3.0 as the next big thing. But there was one great point in that same article

> Collaboration in a business context has a goal other than the act of collaborating itself. We used to call these goals business processes. Collaboration is one important component of a business process, but it is not the whole process.

...or even a large part of it. The real world runs on a lot more than a few wikis and tag clouds. Returning to a common mantra of mine: technology does not fix process. Most business problems are people and process problems. We have technology up the wazzoo: more is not going to help. In as much as Web 2.0 concepts and technology expedite people and

---

[1]
http://earlystagevc.typepad.com/earlystagevc/2006/04/web_20_now_what.html

process, they are a good thing and they will play their small part in making a difference. But they aren't going to change the world, and Web 2.0 and/or SOA are not going to transform business.

Blogging is developing into this incestuous industry of bloggers writing about blogging and each other. The resulting spiral has the industry rapidly disappearing up its own fundamental orifice.

Fuelled by the vanity of everyone having their own soapbox, a money engine is emerging where blogging is seldom about anything useful or relevant outside of its own onanistic world. Bloggers are all busy selling advertising and affiliate programs to each other. Their content is on how to blog, or how to make money from the internet which usually involves ... wait for it ... blogging.

The only model offered by 90% of the good advice is to provide content sufficiently interesting to attract readers and thereby generate advertising and affiliate sales revenue. But so often that content is about the act of blogging and the readers attracted are themselves bloggers. Other times the content covers Web 2.0, the internet, and other topics that are really only of interest to those generating the industry. The quintessential example for me is ProBlogger but look at Technorati's top 100 blogs to see the trend.

The model blog for how it is supposed to work is, for me, Manolo's shoe blog[1]. The writer had the genius (or good luck) to combine humour, celebrities and fashion shoes, and as a result reportedly makes a good living from it. But the results reported for such blogs are unaudited claims made by those with a vested interest in maintaining the blog frenzy. More importantly there are only a handful of Manolos at the top of a vast pyramid of 15 to 70 million bloggers scrabbling for another hundred readers of their self-absorbed posturing, all chasing the lure of easy money – write a blog and get the cheques.

Clearly this is a self fuelling bubble no different to the Dutch tulip frenzy or the dot-com scam. Perhaps the human race will never tire of exposing their thoughts online to a disinterested world. More likely the fad will eventually die away (Who reads this stuff? And where do they find the time? Who actually clicks on the ads?) and with it the revenues, and a much smaller number of sites will remain who actually have a topic to talk about and something to say.

---

[1] http://shoeblogs.com/

Webpreneurs

...or "Internet, I Gave You The Best Years Of My Life"...

The world is full of those chasing fame and fortune on the Internet. The glittering lures of e-commerce, Adsense and cult hero-dom draw them from far and wide, looking for easy money, good hours and groupies. It is not like that.

Just as the rock-and-roll industry has its Rolling Stones, Madonna and Led Zeppelin, the Internet examples of hitting it big are all there for us. Tim Ferriss achieves widespread fame with his (excellent) book and website The Four-Hour Work Week. Manolo's Shoe Blog is reputed to pull six figures a year. And of course Mark Zuckerberg at the ripe old age of 22 turns down a billion dollars for Facebook.

Many of the reports of untold Internet wealth come from those who profit from the frenzy in the industry – their objectivity is often questionable. And just like the music biz, for every shooting star there are thousands of Internet wanna-bes banging away in seedy bars while holding down a day job.

Internet entrepreneurship is very like pop music. If Sony knew for sure how to engineer a hit they would only publish a few CDs a year. The model is that you keep throwing them at the wall and see what sticks. Same with websites. So many aspiring webpreneurs seek that one great idea that will go platinum, like Craigslist or Skype or Facebook or Digg or YouTube or Wikipedia or MegaUpload or GameFAQs or so many others.

I have my favourite examples, where I think "dang, I should have thought of that!" These include Neopets, tinyURL, Wikia, MissBimbo and the New York Times.

(Just kidding about that last one, but let us consider it for a moment. It illustrates the point that along with the Internet poster-children of pure e-commerce, there is another large group of sites that succeeds on the Internet because they are just another channel to a successful bricks-and-mortar business. And contrary to common assumption, Amazon is more part of this latter group. Even though it was born from the Internet, it needs serious real-world infrastructure investment and management, so I do not consider it a pure Internet play. Other examples are CafePress and Lulu.)

But for every success there are thousands of failures. Right now my most successful site has a traffic rank on Alexa of 1,341,140. That's right -– it is on its way to being the millionth-most-popular site on the Web.

Blogging is the latest big thing: we'll all grow rich by exposing our brilliance and wit to the world, who will come in droves to click on Adsense links and product referrals. ProBlogger tells us about the six-figure sites, but Technorati tells me they are "currently tracking 112.8 million blogs".

The odds are against us.

The ones who really get rich in the music industry are the venue owners, publishers and promoters. In the same way the big winners on the Internet are the advertising middlemen like Google, and the myriad hosting companies. Thousands of aspirants risk their time and money each month chasing success and almost all of them lose.

The IT Skeptic has a Google page rank of five [back to four in early 2009], and it draws tens of thousands of page views a month. It pays me over a hundred dollars a month, heading toward two hundred. If I charged the time I spent on it at my usual IT consulting rate it would owe me over a hundred thousand dollars. That isn't good ROI.

Many hopeful rock bands spend tens of thousands on instruments and amps and lighting, then can't get a gig. On www.websitebroker.com a site was offered for sale:

> "...This website cost a little over $20,000 to develop. It is a complete Flash 8 video streaming website with a content management system and registration system ... Price: $8,000"

This is even worse ROI – real money gone.

And then there are the dreamers. Successful entrepreneurship requires good business sense and gritty pragmatism. How about this ad on www.buysellwebsite.com:

> "...currently developing a video game trading site which will allow users to trade video games with each other...Are there sites like this already? Yes, I have seen a couple and they all make money and you can too if you market it properly... Price: $60,000"

This for an unfinished site entering a market with established competitors.

Most sites for sale go for a few hundred or at most a few thousand dollars, so don't go spending tens of thousands on developers and designers. Launch the site as rough and ugly as you can and just test the waters to see if anyone actually cares -– the equivalent of banging out a few numbers at the local pub on a Saturday night to see whether the crowd produces cheers or bottles. AdWords is a superb medium for testing ideas and marketing for a very low cost – you only pay if they click so lousy ideas cost you nothing!

If the crowd loves it and you take off, then you can use the revenue to pay for the fancy stuff in a self-fuelling process that will grow readership. Dump the sleazy manager you started with and find some classy gigs to play at. That is, move on from Adsense and DirtCheapHosting.com to targeted advertising services and robust hosting platforms.

Until then don't give up your day job.

The Folly of the Crowd

There is much excitement about the potential for Web 2.0, in particular what is known as the Wisdom of the Crowd. Wikipedia becomes the repository of all knowledge, Google search statistics are the zeitgeist of the times and MySpace is the face of the world. Page rank is a measure of authority. Corporations appeal to the public for solutions to problems. The ivory tower is replaced by the democracy of the commons; the proclamations of the cathedral displaced by the hubbub of the bazaar. Not so fast.

The Crowd listens to the wisdom of Oprah and reads USA Today. The Crowd doesn't understand how their status-defining mobile phone works. The Crowd believes in Roswell and psychics and crystals. The Crowd litters the Web with blogs nobody reads; inane twitterings bereft of insight, the daily drivel that was once mercifully hidden away in a diary. The Crowd looks to rock stars and movie stars for leadership.

Majority does not equal truth. Voting is good for social decision making but not for advancing knowledge. The majority once wanted to burn witches. The majority seems to think alternative medicines are superior to pharmaceuticals. The majority thinks the outcome of Survivor is important. The majority mocked Darwin and were stumped by Einstein.

It isn't even a majority anyway that fills the forums and blogs and wikis. It is the voice of a fanatical few. Either they hold views so strongly they are motivated to work on the content, or they have no life and spend all their time on a computer. Either way they do not represent the views of the majority. They represent the views of extremists and social outsiders. This explains why some of the most successful blogs are blogs about blogging.

The Wisdom of the Crowd is the final triumph of post-modernism: the belief that any position is as valid as another; that it is all relative to the people involved; that there is no absolute truth; that shamanism has as much to tell us as science.

As a result, the Crowd equates fame with wisdom. The views of someone who has spent a decade absorbing the accumulated wisdom of all civilisation (and passed stringent tests to prove they have succeeded) are no more important than the views of a high-school dropout who can play an electric guitar, or a drug-crazed tart who can act.

The Crowd also fails to discriminate between sources of information. Google pulls up webpages from learned institutions intermingled with the ravings of the lunatic fringes. Creationists, conspiracy theorists, new agers, nutters and racists thrive on the web, and the Crowd laps it up.

Wikipedia may be more extensive than Encyclopaedia Britannica but it will never be as authorative. Google gives us access to information but not to knowledge, let alone wisdom. MySpace and Facebook and Wordpress do precisely nothing to advance the human race. Hailing the Wisdom of the Crowd only cheapens the Wisdom of Civilisation. Wisdom belongs among the guardians who have preserved and built it from generation to generation, the academics; not spattered across a billion websites like textbook pages thrown to the wind.

The internet has shredded knowledge. It has torn it up into digestible little pages and blended an amorphous mass that Google dips into almost at random. We don't need to learn or remember or think because we can pull up an answer on demand. Nobody studies textbooks any more, or even reads journals. Information rains down in the patter of RSS feeds or flicks past in email headlines or babbles in sound-bite videos or scrolls by as news-pages and blog headings: so much information from so many people who know so little.

Just like me and this article.

This is not to say that Web 2.0 is a Bad Thing, nor does it argue that community involvement is counter-productive. The message here is to avoid putting the Crowd on a pedestal as some font of wisdom. It is an unreliable unpredictable superstitious mosh-pit of ideas and data: potentially fruitful if managed; potentially dangerous if idealised and idolised.

Scale

The key is to manage the Crowd, and the main thing to watch is scale. On a large scale like Wikipedia, the Crowd does average out to something approaching a stable depiction of accurate information. An excellent example is the entry on homeopathy which had a wild ride before settling down to an objective rational entry, though debate remains brisk and may never end, because the Crowd is an incubator for ideas good and bad, scientific and superstitious.

The idea of community knowledge becomes more problematic as the Crowd gets smaller. If we look at a niche community such as ITIL practitioners - closer to home for readers of this article - then even the Wikipedia entry becomes the work of a handful of people, and specialist wikis are either the work of their original founders or die from apathy.

Bring the community down to the even smaller population of the staff of an organisation and the whole idea of the Wisdom of the Crowd starts to fall apart.

Wiki-style help or documentation systems work only with the energy of a responsible owner and/or an enthusiastic few. They tend to be patchy, difficult to navigate, rapidly outdated and eventually fall into dusty disuse (like just about every knowledge repository within organisations).

Discussion mechanisms are mildly useful in a geographically-dispersed company, but email serves just as well. More importantly, email doesn't get displaced by the forums, so discussion tends to get fragmented between the mechanisms. In theory a forum is an open discussion and email a closed one, but in all but the largest and most dispersed organisations the practical difference is moot. The forum mechanism seems to provide a useful long-term record of what was discussed, but who will find it? Only those who remember what was said, or a lucky few who have the time and tools (e.g. Google Desktop) to be searching it. Open archiving of the emails would serve just as well.

Moving back up in scale to the internet, forums do provide value, and the most extraordinarily useful titbits turn up on Google. Unfortunately once again these need to be treated with extreme caution and treated only as suggestions because they are subject to even less review and debate than wiki entries.

The forum equivalent of Wikipedia is probably Yahoo! Answers, and even with the largest possible Crowd this provides information of mixed quality. The factor at work is again scale, and more so with forums. The forum world is highly fragmented and each Crowd is small. Taking ITIL as an example again, most ITIL-oriented forums are moribund. Of the few active ones, most are full of newbies asking inane questions and self-appointed experts providing questionable answers. Only the forum owned by the itSMF has middling activity level and attracts authorative participants, precisely because it is not owned or moderated by the Crowd.

Filtering

Even in the best of cases, the useful information is still polluted by misinformation. So the second consideration after scale is filtering. On the internet there is sometimes filtering in the form of moderation. There is occasionally filtering in the form of an expert review panel. The vast majority of websites have no filtering other than the discriminating ability of the reader, and sadly in the post-modernist world critical faculties are being destroyed not developed.

Within an organisation, there can be much better filtering. Staff are accountable for what they say, and anonymity may not be permitted. Resources can be assigned to review and quality-assure the information. In some cases an open forum is desired – to stimulate debate and creativity – but mostly the accuracy and reliability of the information is paramount. The wisdom of the organisational Crowd is only as good as the people who own and manage it.

In summary, the Crowd does gather data. That data gets turned into information if it can be searched adequately. That information tends towards useful reliable knowledge if it comes from a large enough community and is subject to sufficiently robust filtering. In rare cases the Crowd may accidentally produce wisdom, but only if the reader has the capacity to separate it from the dross.

Open source

Many of you will be familiar with that seminal work The Cathedral and the Bazaar, a manifesto of the open source movement. If not, I recommend you read it. Today I want to talk about a different perspective: the Craftsman and the Bazaar.

The craftsman is an expert in his trade who builds to last. He creates quality heirlooms that people will be treasuring and restoring in centuries to come, long after it is forgotten who made or originally commissioned them. The bazaar sells trashy geegaws that don't last. They suit our society driven by commodity, novelty and innovation.

Mainframe systems are recently retired or still around after thirty years of service. As our industry matures (and IT technology matures) eventually the enormous rate of change will slow and systems will be expected to stay around for even longer. Change in the aircraft industry has slowed: look at how long the 737, A320 and 747 have been around and still undisplaced as the workhorses of the international skies. Automobile manufacturers try desperately to find novelty in a field that has pretty much exhausted it. New bridge technologies don't come out every year or two, so bridges are expected to stand for the lifetime of their materials or their usefulness. Software doesn't wear out per se, though its quality will degrade over time with constant maintenance, especially if architecture and/or documentation are poor. Ah, documentation. Hated by most, done (properly) by few. In the brave new IT world we apparently need it less - which brings me back to open source. My experience of open source code is that in-code comments are rare, and accompanying documentation minimal. If you look beyond usage notes, documentation is usually non-existent.

Why were certain design decisions taken and what were the options and considerations? What are the critical aspects of the architecture that must be preserved in future? What is the architecture, the standards to which it is built? What mistakes have been made and fixed, so as not to repeat them? A code craftsman, building for the future, would consider this documentation as essential as an install script.

Open source developers, on the other hand, are writing for the bazaar: their targets are to get something working, to get immediate uptake (and recognition), to have fun coding. Their products are cool, shiny, eye-catching, reflecting the latest fashions (Ajax, XHTML, video, Google Maps, RSS...).

They are like the toys my son buys from the $1 shop: made cheap, made to be picked up, not made to last more than a day in the front yard. They are so cheap they are effectively free, and he won't be handing them down to his children. Contrast them with his Märklin trains, his wooden Thomas trains, or his Lego. These are designed by professional engineers. They are robust, useful, compellingly fun, and compatible throughout their range. The play value lasts for years, long after the novelty is gone. And in twenty or thirty years he will be pulling them out of the attic for the next generation. These are craftsman toys. Am I saying he will be dusting off the old Adobe Photoshop (insert your favourite well-engineered software here) disks in thirty years too? Well, no, I doubt that somehow. Unlike the other engineering disciplines, IT is still caught up in a pell-mell rush of evolving technology that means the same considerations don't apply as they do to bridges or toys. Even craftsman software (if there is such a thing) becomes obsolete quickly. For that reason, what the open source people are doing is OK right now, I guess. This entire website rests on the LAMP stack (Linux, Apache, MySQL, PHP .... and Drupal) so I must think open source is useful. There is little justification for craftsmanship in anything that is going to be obsolete so quickly.

What concerns me though, is the habits we are forming and the direction open source is taking. Many in that movement will be completely mystified by these comments. "Surely open source code is better, of higher quality, than most other code? Developed by a large pool of enthusiastic and committed programmers, designed free of commercial imperatives, tested by thousands of others..."

Software is different to bridges or toys or furniture. It is different to most other artefacts produced by Man, in that it changes, constantly. It evolves to meet new requirements; it shifts to adopt new technologies. Documenting why and how a bridge was built is mildly important. Documenting code is essential. And as we start to move into a new phase of the Information Age, a maturing phase, we will expect our software to stick around. The obsolescence cycle will get longer. The code itself will become one tiny facet of the artefact that is a piece of software. On its own it will be worthless. It will be one cell in a matrix of requirements and designs, frameworks and architectures, minutes and discussions, decisions and compromises.

If the human race is to have any hope at the end of the 21st Century, we will have rediscovered Quality by then. The trashy disposable pap that characterises Western civilisation at the start of this century will be seen as an embarrassing diversion, like the Naughty Nineties at the turn of the last one. Along with that broader trend, IT will grow up. IT is engineering and finally starting to admit it (ITIL is a good positive example of the new professionalism that I may discuss one day). Engineering does not set out to be fun, creative, spontaneous. Engineering is sober, disciplined, frugal and conservative. In the next few decades, software engineering will adopt the attitudes, practices and professionalism of the other branches of engineering.

Somewhere between now and then, software is going to have to start being built to last just like every other constructed system. Like any business infrastructure, we will demand we get maximum return on our investment before we decommission it. I like open source software. It is human, personal, sharing, communal, fun ... and cheap. Much of it is also, by engineering standards, trashy junk. I don't think Linux is junk, nor other of the big foundation systems that get enormous input from many people. But I worry about the code where each module is written by one or two amateurs in their spare time, which describes huge quantities of the open source stuff out there. I work in that kind of code a lot, and much of it is pretty rough. But more importantly, most of even the well-crafted code is just that: code. Little or nothing else exists to assist when the current volunteer has babies and a promotion and suddenly isn't interested in unpaid code development and someone else steps into the breach. When the individuals move on, much of this code will fall apart like a twenty-dollar remote-controlled car or a no-name DVD player or an Ikea bookcase. You get this stuff on trestle tables in the Bazaar and it isn't going to last long. It does not represent the future of software (I hope). The future is going to need the work of Craftsmen.

In all but the largest of online communities the supposed consensus community content is actually created by a fanatical few. This is made worse by the online world's distaste of people making a living. To take one example close to home for this blog, recently a link to *ITIL's dead elephant: CMDB can't be done*[1] was removed from Wikipedia on the grounds that it is on a blog. Let me stress that I didn't put it there and I don't know who did. But someone thought it illuminated the debate and added balance to the otherwise rosy depiction of CMDB, until Wikipedia's intellectually elitist policy overruled. A blog is only opinion and yet an online magazine (govtech.net) or CIO Magazine columnist Dean Meyer (who knows little about ITIL) are OK.

This followed an earlier debate over whether a site with Adsense ads on it could have anything worthwhile to say (generally held in contempt by the high priests of Wikipedia). And recently I copped criticism on this blog from a member of the "open" community for my Ops4less site asking for content contributions in order to get access to the goodies. I'm not taking this personally; I'm just citing examples from personal experience. Many other examples abound. While the Drupal community is receptive to folk

---

[1] http://www.itskeptic.org/node/25

selling consulting services, anyone attempting to charge for a contributed module would get nowhere, and there is no mechanism to do so. Some users get quite abusive if none of the (free) support volunteers answer their questions straight away or to their satisfaction.

This distaste for commerce amongst the open community strikes me as the height of silliness. The number of contributors is restricted enough already. If they can only contribute when they have zero benefit from doing so beyond either ego-stroking and posturing or the genuine satisfaction of contributing to the community or for some intangible future profit, then the pool will be further limited to the truly fanatical and will become even less representative of the community. The open movement might spring from socialist ideals but it ignores capitalist reality at its peril. Every socialist state has discovered most people don't contribute without reward.

The foundation stuff, Linux, MySQL etc is robust and good. (But where are the admin and query tools for MySQL on Linux? PHPMyAdmin is beautifully functional - though a decade behind the MySQL Windows tools, but I find it hilarious that the same people who wrote and use it are probably slinging mud at Windows and IE security, because PHPMyAdmin security is a joke. And as a user of Apache, without having seen the source, I must say some of it looks a bit klunky, dare I say kludgy, usability-wise. I like to assume that is because all the design is focused on the internal engine, which appears to be rock solid).

No, I'm more concerned at the stuff that fizzes around on top of these: CMSs and application packages and tools and such, user-contrib stuff rather than committee-managed core stuff.

Modern minds

I found a fascinating article[1] from the ever-interesting Nicholas Carr (remember "IT Doesn't Matter"?) on how Google is making us stupid.

I reproduce an extract here as you won't have time to read it:

> Over the past few years I've had an uncomfortable sense that someone, or something, has been tinkering with my brain, remapping the neural circuitry, reprogramming the memory. My mind isn't going—so far as I can tell—but it's changing. I'm not thinking the way I used to think. I can feel it most strongly when I'm reading. Immersing myself in a book or a lengthy article used to be easy. My mind would get caught up in the narrative or the turns of the argument, and I'd spend hours strolling through long stretches of prose. That's rarely the case anymore. Now my concentration often starts to drift after two or three pages. I get fidgety, lose the thread, begin looking for something else to do. I feel as if I'm always dragging my wayward brain back to the text. The deep reading that used to come naturally has become a struggle... My mind now expects to take in information the way the Net distributes it: in a swiftly moving stream of particles. Once I was a scuba diver in the sea of words. Now I zip along the surface like a guy on a Jet Ski.

I'm reminded of a phrase from the delightful *Doctor in the House* books by Richard Gordon, about last-minute cramming for medical exams, which went something like "dashing pell-mell down the corridors of knowledge, snatching handfuls along the way". Google is all about snatching handfuls.

As I quickly scanned this article it occurred to me to give you three more factors besides Google:

Magazines had already superseded books because they were the only way to stay current before the advent of the internet. I still read books for stimulation, but I long ago stopped reading books to stay up with the latest developments. As a result people were already becoming accustomed to two-or-three page summations, to having their knowledge pre-digested by journalists and delivered in little chunks like pet-food.

Television had of course already destroyed most traces of critical analysis or systematic thought in large tracts of the population, especially what passes as news and current affairs today as compared to even twenty years ago. Most TV news makes the USA Today newspaper look in-depth. If it can't be delivered in a thirty-second sound-bite it isn't covered.

---

[1] http://www.theatlantic.com/doc/200807/google

The third contributor to speed reading is software user guides and manuals which are so packed with useless repetitive puerile crap and contain so few nubs of useful information that nobody actually reads them any more. Most IT people are adept at extracting the juice from a hundred-page manual in a few minutes. Nowadays most manuals are only provided in pdf on a CD which only hastens the process.

My mother is 84 now. She marvels at how I can read a newspaper article in less than a minute while simultaneously talking to her. None of my friends would notice.

On another topic [that one went on much too long], Carr's most telling point is "The Net's intellectual ethic remains obscure". I don't think it has one and I shudder to think how many generations will have to pass and how many horrors emerge before it develops one.

Gullibility

Telesales advertisers and other hustling snake-oilers no longer use images of "thousands of dedicated" white-coated scientists and bubbling test tubes. Science is out of favour with the general public due to the rise of post-modernism, new age, alternative this and that, and other bilge thinking. The only positive to this gradual erosion of the Western world's intelligence is the demise of science as an image of credibility with marketers.

The same has not happened with computers. Deliver anything on a glowing panel and the public thinks it must be true or possible. PowerPoint adds authority to drivel. Software won't sell if it isn't sexy. Graphs, preferably three-D surface graphs, depict problems dissolving and ROI soaring. And every quack and nutter finds a willing audience on the Internet.

Part of the problem is Arthur C. Clarke's dictum that "any sufficiently advanced technology is indistinguishable from magic." What Clarke didn't say is that people only think it is magic if suddenly exposed to it. If accustomed to it in everyday life they know it isn't magic, but they subconsciously give it mystical properties. Most people don't have a clue how tiny chunks of sand can make the Internet appears on a flat piece of plastic. Most of the public doesn't grok electricity. Even some IT people don't understand this stuff below the abstract level of what they see on GUIs and HTML pages. So when an e-mail promises that Bill Gates wants to give you $100 or that a little girl in Kansas won't die of dyslexia if you forward the e-mail to 10 others, people buy this drek. When a website persuasively argues that antiperspirants give you Alzheimer's, the truth is only a Google away, but people are not taught to think critically. They don't know to seek the contrary view and balance the arguments to make their own judgment.

People are credulous. They always have been: by burning your neighbour alive you can test whether she is a witch; the world is flat; mice form spontaneously in old rags; perfume keeps away disease; the king is a deity; women can't run a country; crop circles are made by aliens; Bono's opinion matters; Iraq is about democracy...You would think it wouldn't take an Einstein to see through these.

I went to a friend's house one evening and the microwave was gone, replaced by one of those little grillers. I asked why and they proudly showed me the Web pages their 12-year-old son had printed out, about how microwave ovens fry your brains with leaked radiation. They sold a near-new microwave to go back to a technology from our parent's generation. Next time I was there I slipped their son a few pages printed from Snopes.com on how this is a load of bunk. He went pale and scuttled away. I bet he never told them but maybe he learned a lesson...or not.

Ah, Snopes.com. Along with Urbanlegend.com, Snopes has done more to preserve my Internet sanity than any other Web site. Every now and then a rumour comes along that is so good I'm not sure, and I turn to these sites for a touchstone of rational information. Without them I think I would have given up on the Internet long ago.

The problem is not restricted to the Internet. Software product demonstrations play on the same weakness. This stuff must work – I saw it. Nobody would buy a car based on driving it ten yards across the dealer's lot, but a vendor can demo one icon turning red and convince buyers they have a CMDB. Say after me: if it is running on a lone laptop in the meeting room, it isn't reality.

Worse still is the screenshot in PowerPoint. Seemingly nobody has heard of graphics editors when vendors talk about their upcoming product as if it actually existed.

Then there is the spreadsheet. This humble tool has brought down mighty companies and misdirected governments. If I work something out on the back of a napkin everyone wants to query how I got the result, but have the number pop out of a spreadsheet and it's gospel. The first rule of business cases is to deliver them in spreadsheet format with the dodgy assumptions buried in a cell formula on page five. The COBOL code that calculates a single customer's discount is subject to rigorous testing by experts. The code that calculates the company's profitability for the year is written in Excel by a tired accountant one evening and tested by the same person the next morning...sometimes. I know of a company that spent two billion dollars on another company based on the fact that they could conduct business with better profit margins than anyone else in the industry. After two years, an auditor (investigating on behalf of the Board to work out why it didn't seem to be working after acquisition) discovered that the spreadsheet that reported the profit divided by the same factor in two different cell formulae. Margins weren't 5%: they were 2.5%. Due diligence at purchase missed it.

In fact it is not just computers: it seems to be any screen. Don't get me started on what documentaries and news media get away with that wouldn't wash in a book or newspaper. Moving animations of medications hit the spot on curiously neutered see-through bodies. Movies tell of kids using a laptop hacking the Pentagon to remotely control missiles. News reports show smiling soldiers. Something about illuminated information paralyses the mental faculties. Whether it is television, demo, movie, spreadsheet, Web site or presentation, be doubly on your guard for what Clive James once called "the ancient Japanese art of bullshido."

The iPhone

The IT Skeptic's little brother is so excited by the iPhone he wrote an article about it:

im so xcited by the iPhone really they are just everywhere! the other day my friend's uncle saw somebody with one.

aparently it's a whole new paradime of user interface. ive always wanted a new paradime. every time i zoom something on my computer i think how much easier and more fun it would be to do it on a small screen with thumb and finger. im sure it will be accurate and easy to control too, and i like zoom all the time. really

and that way cool way it knows which way up it is. hey! what happens if im lying on my side using it? cant wait to find that one out!

im gunna get rid of my crappy pocketpc that i bougt on ebay for next to nothing. its years old, still going strong, theire pretty hard to brake but so uncool specially next to the sleke iPhone. i bought it, the pocketpc that is, so i could do writing and spredsheets and email and stuff but its just a bit too small for editting papers even with the excelent handwriting recognision on windowsCE.

i kno the iPhone doesn't have recognision but im sure the on-screen keybord will be just excelent, kind of like texting with thumbs only cooler you know?

and they've made all the iPhone controls nice and big and fat so you can use your finger to touch them. no more using a stilus with all those fiddly little lists on the pocketpc. fingers are much better. pocketpc sure could get a lot of stuff on one screen tho... im sure the cool scroling on the iPhone will make up for that!

i never did use the windowsCE diary so much either: its handy for knoing where i have to be next becos i get so confused so easily, like really! but for working out what day next week to go like blinkdating its too hard to see. u have to remember what all the little colored marks on the days mean and if I could remember that i woodnt need the calender silly! so i wait until i get back to my pc where i can see the diary on the big screen then i use my pocketpc to call people back to make apointments, if i remember to call them that is which is where the pocketpc is kinda cool cos i can make a recording to myself or write a note or set a reminder in the calender.

achually i text more than i call, cos the pocketpc handwriting recognision is so good for short messages – like so totally easier than thumb typing you know? im gonna miss that but at least i can use the same Bluetooth earpiece with my new iPhone i hope the iPhone takes as good a photo as my pocketpcs 2 megapixel camera – i bet it has way more than that. sure the pics r no good for printing real big but they r great for emailing – i used to use the pocketpc for emailing pics – and video, the pocketpc does video - but it used something called "3G" and it got so expensive you know? now i just use it as an ordinery phone and save heaps!

i bet the iPhone will use something cheaper to send pictures cos everyone does it in the ads, and anyway i bet iPhone does it in some way that is just way cooler than the way the pocketpc does it, for sure. and i bet it organises pictures better than windowsCE too.

i have all these pictures on a 2Gig memory card my brother gave me cos he got it for free at some seminare, (man ive never even come close to filling that thing up) but i keep forgetting how to find the pics. my brother gets real rude about me forgetting stuff like that: he says if i set up one of the buttons on the front of the pocketpc to be the photo album i could get there in one click, and play my music tracks from the same place. but i dont need to work out how any more becos im sure the iPhone will be way cooler and smarter and everything.

becos everyone says the iPhone will change the way everyone does everything ive been trying to pursuede my brother to get one but he says his Palm still does everything he needs. i said he should use an iPhone to do his office work on but he just gave me one of those looks and asked if i'd ever seen a spredsheet on a screen that small.

i said the iPhone screen is really big. he thinks it is the same 3.5 inch as the pocketpc but anyway it looked bigger on youtube so i bet hes wrong as usual

anyway at least ill be able to use the iPhone to brows the internet and watch movies and stuff, so long as it doesnt use that 3G thing for those too because once ive saved up for the iPhone there wont be much money left for phone bills. and so long as its 3.5 inch screen is bigger than my 3.5 inch screen like im sure it is, because websites all look so crappy on mine.

not as bad as that WAP phone my dad had but crappy for sure. ooh i just cant wait, u know? tecnological progress is so exciting! u can just feel the world shifting and changing. things will never be the same, well except my pocketpc of corse which was kinda the same but in a dufus way. no way im gunna be seen with that thing anymore. i think ill sell it on ebay. i wont get much for it but at least it still works good.

Acoustic shock

The IT Skeptic takes a break from ITIL and talks about call-centre absenteeism. Call-centres are generally high-stress, low-morale environments – a recognised issue that has seen much progress in addressing it in recent times but it remains real. This is no excuse for the abuse of reason through hyped syndromes to justify absenteeism, and especially the cynical support for this by some doctors, unions and of course lawyers. The latest work-related illness is "acoustic shock".

Perhaps attention to it will encourage call-centre employers to treat staff less like cattle, but it is also growing a predatory industry.

"Employees who work in call center operations can be four times more likely than the other employees to miss work for psychiatric conditions such as stress or depression," notes Dr. Ronald Leopold, vice president and national medical director, MetLife Disability in a recent study conducted by MetLife. And no wonder – I wouldn't do their job.

But it is hard to show that work causes "depression", whereas a label like "acoustic shock" attached to the condition by a recognised medical practitioner offers a causal link against which to claim compensation.

According to a UK union, acoustic shock is "a devastating 21st Century industrial injury problem ruining call centre workers' lives and costing industry millions".

For those of you who may be unaware of this syndrome, the following is from the Australian National Acoustic Laboratories

> The problem
>
> Occasionally, intense, unwanted signals accidentally occur within the telephone network... Although these high-pitched tones can affect anyone, people using a regular hand-held telephone can quickly move the phone away from their ear, thus limiting their sound exposure to a fraction of a second. Call-centre operators, however, usually use a head-set, which takes considerably longer to remove from the ear were an intense sound to occur. They thus receive a greater noise exposure than for people using hand-held phones. The problem may be exacerbated if call centres are so noisy that the operators need to have the volume controls on their telephones turned up higher than would be necessary in a quieter place.
>
> The effects
>
> Unexpected high-level sounds have been reported to cause a variety of symptoms. Symptoms that have been reported during the exposure include discomfort and pain. Symptoms that have been reported in the few minutes after the exposure include shock and

nausea. Symptoms that have been reported to continue for some time after the exposure include headaches, nausea, tenseness, and hypersensitivity (discomfort) to loud sounds that would previously have caused no problems. In some cases, these symptoms are reported to continue for many days or weeks after the incident, although more commonly the symptoms are short-lived. Some operators who experience an acoustic shock may feel apprehensive about using the phone or about loud sounds in general.

The damage mechanism

The mechanism causing the adverse symptoms is not known with certainty. It seems highly likely, however, that the sound exposure elicits an acoustic startle reflex. (The same startle reflex can also be elicited by an unexpected touch or puff of air to the eyes). When startle occurs, numerous muscles in the upper limbs, shoulders, neck, eye and ear (the stapedius muscle and the tensor tympani muscle) are activated. If the noise exposure is loud, or if the person is in an aroused state (e.g. anxious, fearful) prior to the startle, the magnitude of the muscular response is heightened.

Note the longer term symptoms are "headaches, nausea, tenseness, and hypersensitivity (discomfort) to loud sounds" – all chronic symptoms with no clear causal mechanism (although there is plenty of speculation around muscle tension) and no objective measure of their validity (they don't show up in blood tests, ECG etc).

Already the acoustic shock industry is gearing up: there are government inquiries, British unions have already handled more than 700 acoustic shock cases securing more than £2million in out of court settlements for workers, consultants are offering policy and process, and of course technology can be purchased to limit noise bursts.

According to the BBCBT has already paid out £90,000 to one worker. Solicitor Adrian Forden is representing another 83 BT employees who are complaining that they have suffered injury through "acoustic shock". "It could be the tip of the iceberg," he told the BBC's Today programme. "I've travelled nationwide interviewing people from all sorts of backgrounds who have experienced this problem."

I bet you have.

Dr John Welch says in the latest New Zealand Skeptic newsletter [sorry, members only] "It pays to have an employer with deep pockets... this is not an occupational disease but an attempt to attribute personal angst to the workplace".

How does the UK government's Health and Safety Executive view this new threat?

HSE's initial thoughts on acoustic shock syndrome were based largely on physiological evidence for hearing loss, with a strong link between an individual's exposure to noise and the level of risk to their hearing (how loud the noise was and how long it lasted).

An extensive HSE study incorporating evidence from 15 call centres in the UK indicated that call centre workers were not normally exposed to levels of noise that were considered likely to cause permanent hearing loss. Even on those occasions where operators were exposed to high-intensity noise, which might cause permanent damage to hearing (such as loud screeches and alarms being let off down the phone), such noises would be excluded by the protection built into the operators' headsets. The associated risk was therefore considered to be low.

Since HSE carried out its research, new medical evidence from Australia and Denmark has emerged. This was presented at the first ever international seminar on acoustic shock in Fremantle, Australia in September 2001.

This evidence was based on symptoms found in Australian and Danish call centre workers claiming to suffer from acoustic shock. The symptoms ranged from numbness and tenderness around the ear, to hypersensitivity to sound in extreme cases.

The research concludes that noise of high intensity and high frequency might cause symptoms at exposure levels which are lower than was previously thought to be the case. In addition to loudness and the duration of exposure, the research identifies a range of previously unconsidered variables, which may affect whether exposure to high intensity noise might cause symptoms. This includes factors such as: the sudden onset of the noise, stress, and an individual's personal susceptibility.

Initial clinical suggestions as to the physiological causes of the symptoms include muscular spasms of the middle ear region.

Over a hundred cases have been recognised in Australia, and a lesser (but still significant number) have been reported in Denmark. On the other hand there have been few reported cases in other countries. It is possible that the few reported cases in the UK could have experienced symptoms as described by the Australians.

Prior to the new evidence from Australia and Denmark, HSE had no cases of acoustic shock reported to it.

Note that factors include "... stress, and an individual's personal susceptibility".

Based on some light Googling, the wave does not seem to have reached the USA yet, but the IT Swami says watch this space!

Though out of scope for this blog, the Metlife report referenced above offered some excellent advice on improving the well-being of call-centre workers.

- Assess the work environment.

- Screen potential employees for skill sets. [...and for a nervous disposition]

- Allow for growth.

- Take advantage of technology.

- Involve everyone in health and wellness.

- Communicate the company's vision.

Check it out. There is no reason why call-centres should not install burst-limiting filters, and the current media activity may serve to make them universal – that is a good thing.

Likewise all the good people-management advice in that article would benefit call-centres that don't follow it now.

It is a shame however that prior experience with other occupational syndromes suggests that employers will have to payout because they made the mistake of offering jobs to anxious nervous people, and the valid claims for real harm will be swamped by hysterical claims from people who are tense and anxious before numbers eventually settle down to just the valid sufferers and the rorters.

The final word goes to John Welch of the NZ Skeptic: "I predict that the condition will remain unheard of in India... since there is no compensation available". Quite.

Ergonomics

Remember when a phone had a dial on the front with numbers, a TV had a volume knob and a dial with channels on it, and a record player had two controls: volume and speed?

Now:

- I have six remote controls on the TV room table, with more buttons than a 747.

- My deskphone has 25 buttons on it with four icons I don't even know and one called "R."

- My PocketPC PDA/phone keeps it secret that Bluetooth headset mode is disabled.

- There are five ways to connect a DVD player to a sound system but my sound system only has the four I don't need.

- I need to navigate a menu just to watch a movie.

- And my car needs a firmware upgrade.

I want to pick the phone up, dial a number and talk to someone. When I'm done I will hang up. I want to turn on one device (or turn on all the devices at once) to watch Sky, DVD or video.

I want to change channels, play/stop/rewind/forward/eject, adjust volume, and mute from one remote. (The mute button is the only valuable advance in user interface in fifty years of consumer technology.) The remote should park in a socket on the front of the box and recharge while it's there. I'm not going back into the TV room until the manufacturers get it together.

I want "dial tone" functionality for all the devices in my life, meaning they're always on, and they work by engaging them physically, e.g., pick up the hand-piece or open the door or stick a disc in. I don't want all this other stuff. Do you?

I'm not alone. A survey of 15,000 mobile phone users in 37 countries shows that "too many functions I did not use" is the number one device problem in all regions of the world. Of course manufacturers are not entirely to blame. As consumers we are naïve and childish, seduced by spec sheets and blinking lights. There are alternatives out there, if you can find them, such as Kyocera's A101k phone.

But mostly manufacturers are to blame. As a comparison to the Kyocera, consider what Vodafone Australia thinks is a simple phone: polyphonic ring-tone downloads, phonebook with PC synchronisation, SMS messaging, timer, calculator and alarm.

What is wrong with these people? Push the geeks out of the driver's seat and put someone normal in control of product design: someone who doesn't have a home LAN with a firewall server in the hall closet, or a Bluetooth earpiece and keyboard for their PDA/phone.

What we need is:

- Transparent technology: automation of customization. Let the device work out all the options. With every passing decade, Windows inches towards this goal, but the geeks run ahead sprinkling new obstacles in the path. The old voice phones are insanely complex devices, but the user sees none of it. I want a screen that is always on, has a touch screen, and allows me to browse the Web. No modems, no network properties, no passwords. Game machines will be the first to deliver.

- Design for the non-geek. Even we geeks get tired and have times where we don't want to wrestle with technology. Most people never want to. And they don't trust technology so don't ask them to. I heard a lovely story about the Toyota Auto-lock function that locks the door when you walk away: people would walk off, and then wonder if the door had really locked, so would walk back – which would unlock it...

- Design for humans. There has been recent discussion suggesting that the iPhone might be useful for business. It's not. It hasn't delivered anything that my Windows-CE PDA/phone doesn't already give me. They all suffer from one problem: the screen's too small. You can't pull a cow down a drainpipe and you can't use a phone to do work: you can't usefully read spreadsheets, or edit documents, or operate applications. Heck, you can't surf: a million WAP-enabled phones proved that. You can't even read. Why aren't the trains and buses full of people reading e-books? Because the geeks overlooked the simple fact that screens aren't good for reading (even big ones).

> "It is not pleasant to read things on the Internet with a backlit screen. It is hard on your eyes. Eventually maybe they will find a way to make it a lot easier to read.
>
> The other problem is that you have to scroll. It is primitive in the sense that the Internet is a scrolling medium. A printed book with pages was such an advance over scrolling. To go back to scrolls is to step into the past. That goes back to monks in the 13th century. A lot has happened since the 13th century to improve the technology of reading, and so far no

one has come up, for sheer reading ease, with anything better than hard copy pages." - Tom Wolfe

- Physical interfaces: the old devices had a wee button here and a switch there and a lever over there: car choke knob, camera shutter timer, phone receiver hook ... Now we have rows of identical buttons with cryptic icons or abbreviations, or multifunction joysticks where the down action has five different meanings depending on the context. This is not intuitive. Put physical buttons on it, give them each a single function, make them different shapes and sizes, and put them in handy places spread around the device. Consumer electronics should not look like 747 cockpits.

The sophistication of the modern world makes our lives easier, but it is apparently too much to ask that technology should make our lives simpler.

Quality

The world doesn't give a flying fox about Quality any more.

I don't mean the time-and-motion, lower-errors, slick and lean meaning of quality as we ITILers understand it from Deming and Baldridge and Shewhart et al. I mean Quality as in the pyramids, the cathedrals, steam trains, Rolls Royce as it was once, Tiffany... Real values of thoroughness, integrity, family, home cooked food... You older readers remember: QUALITY.

If I may be indulged by quoting from my personal blog[1]:

> The Twentieth Century abandoned quality as a concept. For a definition of what I mean by "quality" read Zen and the Art of Motorcycle Maintenance... twice.
>
> [In the 20th Century] "Good" was not defined by quality:
>
> pop art
>
> Bauhaus
>
> disposability and built-in obsolescence
>
> the rise of plastics
>
> punk rock
>
> universal "fairness" (equality of outcome instead of equality of opportunity)
>
> post-modernism
>
> cost cutting and shareholder value
>
> fast food and convenience food
>
> Disneyland
>
> B grade movies
>
> the sound-bite as politics
>
> blogging
>
> ...the list is endless.
>
> Quality was no longer a factor: people judged on price, novelty, fun, convenience, political correctness, deliberate rejection of traditional values. Along with quality we lost the related values of honesty and reality. Most Americans don't even know what is real any more, and the rest of the Western world is only one turn behind on the downward spiral.

---

[1] www.bothol.org

As I recall (though I cannot find it) Tom Wolfe predicted we would rediscover an appreciation of quality in this century. Let us hope so.

What passes for wisdom in IT is generally pap: superficial and trashy. I'm afraid this blog is a pretty good example, as are most IT websites. Even bodies of knowledge that aim at depth and introspection, such as the ITIL3 *Service Strategy* book (the "leaf book"), are cranked out in haste. Once upon a time a learned book took a decade to see the light of day.

If you are smashing your brain against a screen sixty hours a week you probably can't even see all this. It wasn't until I gave the corporate treadmill the big finger and pottered around idyllic Pukerua Bay for a year that I started to get a little perspective back.

I don't pretend to intellectual Quality, others do. But at least I know what it looks like.

Part 2:
ITIL and CMDB

Service Management

The Y2K spending overhang drove new attitudes to transparency and justification. This led to new techniques (or rather new adoption of established techniques) for business alignment, especially Service Management.

Post-Y2K, organisations are demanding greater maturity from their IT departments – they want to see them run like a business, and they want to see disciplines and formalisms as if it were engineering. The current thinking in response to this can broadly be labelled as Service Management, which represents a real paradigm shift (a much-abused term that is used correctly here).

This is part of a much larger philosophical shift in society that we cannot cover here: from a product-centric industrial age to a service-centric information age. See Peter Drucker[1] and Alvin Toffler[2] for the broader social implications, and John Zachman[3] for the implications for computing. This shift takes a generation or more and is in progress now (the end of the 20th Century and the start of the 21st).

The shift caused by Service Management is to base all IT planning and management on the business and the IT services it needs, i.e. delivering to the users of the services, instead of starting from underlying technology, from the stuff we have to build services with. This is a "customer centric" approach, which is very much in vogue in areas other than Service Management as well as being a fundamental of the rise of the Information Age.

---

[1] *The Post Capitalist Society*, P. Drucker, Harper Business 1994

[2] *The Third Wave*, Toffler, Morrow 1980

[3] *Enterprise Architecture: The Issue of the Century*, J. Zachman, Database Programming and Design, Miller Freeman, 1997

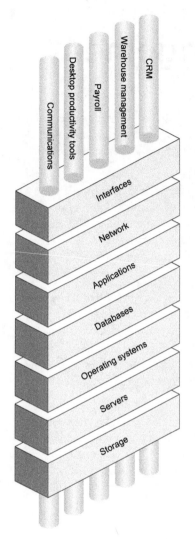

There is a matrix that can be drawn, of the technology silos that IT manages on one axis mapped against the services that technology delivers to the business on the perpendicular axis. Service Management is about turning the IT department around 90° so they look at the services they provide to the business instead of looking at the layers of their technology.

That is to say, service management is about getting IT people (or in fact any provider of a service) to think first about what matters to the user of the service and only then derive from that what is required of the technology and systems that provide the service. The users don't care what machinery is required to deliver the service so much as what comes out of the pipe.

The cultural shift from product to service has left IT behind in large organisations. They have been split off as a separate tribe with their own language and culture while the business has moved on and expectations have changed. Drawing on the advanced ideas of the Manufacturing sector, Service Management has grown up within IT (hence the common term ITSM) in an attempt to heal the rift and bring corporate computing into the new age. We are seeing a new development now where IT is taking Service Management to the business as an effective methodology for introducing customer-centric culture and processes across the organisation.

As a result of this shift in perspective, a second change results. Service management forces an IT organisation to think and structure itself around the services it delivers and hence the processes delivering those services, instead of around internal functional layers or technologies.

Finally, a third change results from starting with business strategy: it gets people thinking about strategy.

Once we understand what services we provide and what the users need from those services, we can plan, spend, operate, measure and improve on that basis. This is a very powerful concept that has widespread applications, and we will see much more of it in future.

Service Management applies the TQM concepts of customer-defined quality, continuous improvement, and measurement-based management. Services are defined in the terms of the people who use them. So are the levels at which the services are to be delivered. The starting points are the strategy and goals of the business, and how computing needs to support them. Services and service levels are agreed formally with the customers (ITIL distinguishes between the users who consume the service and the customers who pay for them).

Processes and roles are structured around these services, not around the technology. For example: problem, change, availability, service levels; not servers, networks, applications, desktop. Suppliers' contracts must support the service level agreements.

The technology comes last: what is required to fulfil the services now and in the forecasted future. If it doesn't make sense in terms of services and processes, we don't need it.

The focus is on maintaining and continuously improving quality of service. Service levels are measured. Processes are refined to improve them. This is an example of how ideas from the manufacturing industries have been showing up in the service industries.

Service Management has respectable antecedents, a good body of practical experience and good alignment with the macro-level trends in society. It is real. But that does not automatically mean we should all rush out and do ITIL.

Who left the IT in itSMF? Service Management can be about so much more than IT. What a shame we have kept our focus narrow. Perhaps one day Service Management will become a universal discipline.

A number of years ago - so the legend goes - there was a move to rename the itSMF to just plain SMF: the Service Management Forum. This was a recognition of the fact that much of the ITSM body of knowledge applies to services delivered in any context, whether staff services like payroll or HR, building services, or any of the service industries like travel or accounting or .... But some of the old crusties dug their heels in and the "IT" stayed. The compromise was to have the "IT" in lower case to de-emphasise it, and so it remains today.

I don't have the slightest shred of evidence for this story other than a reliable source, but it seems plausible. If it is true it was an opportunity lost.

I'd love to see ITIL generalised beyond IT one day. ITIL 4?

It could be called the Service Management Infrastructure Library, which one could surely not resist calling the Service Management Infrastructure Library Environment!

When we want to know how to, say, measure a service desk, we can find quite exact guidance everywhere. But it seems to me the depth and specificity (specifity? specificness?) and usefulness of advice is inversely proportional to the importance of the question. Consider the most important question we need answered in a service management initiative.

The standard consulting model, used in ITIL, is to determine the current "as-is" state through assessment, then decide the "to-be" state, and then work on the gap. ITIL V3 still fails to provide an assessment model, though COBIT does. So too do many consulting firms.

So we can find the as-is readily enough. But what about the other half? How do we pick the target "to-be" state? Very often the as-is and to-be are defined as some composite CMM maturity level from 1 to 5 (actually 0 to 5 - I've met zeroes: companies with one or more processes at a zero maturity level, no detectable trace). A consultant will give you the as-is to two decimal places, but how do we determine the to-be?

Seems to me the standard model is to extract a number from a suitable orifice. If you're a basket case you'll go for 2. If you are mainstream you'll shoot for 3. If you want to swagger you'll aim for 4. And if you want to use the result in marketing your company's services you'll find a consulting firm that will certify you as 5.

This is not exactly scientific or rigorous, and there is no process other than a brief gaze at the navel.

And yet is there a more important decision to be taken than the target maturity goal? The only one more important that I can think of is whether to even undertake the initiative or not. Why do we have whole books of guidance from multiple BOKs on lesser issues but when it comes to setting the broad scope, the ambition - and of course the cost - of the initiative, we allow someone to pick a number (or a number per process for the sophisticated ones)? On what basis? With what advice and guidance? Reached through what reasoning and methodology? None. Not in ITIL V3. Not in COBIT.

Services

The word "service" certainly gets some exercise. ITIL v3 says "A service is a means of delivering value to customers by facilitating outcomes customers want to achieve, but without the ownership of specific costs and risks."

This impenetrable bit of consultant-babble does not help those who are trying to grasp the fundamental concept.

The itSMF repeats the same waffle in their *Introduction*, but they then take pity on us by providing a practical example, where the outcome of sales people getting more customer face-time is delivered by a service which provides remote access to systems. (In reality, we all know that sales people spending less time in the office does not translate to more time with customers).

This is an advance from the ITIL v2 pocket book from itSMF which avoids the whole question of defining a service, though it does in passing say that a service is about "ICT infrastructure and management processes that deliver the information and solutions required by the business." ITIL v2 was centred on the process not the service, and in fact that other excellent itSMF pocket book for ITIL v2, *IT Service Management*, talks about "service" as a verb rather than noun in all parts of the book except the Serve Level Management section.

The ITIL V3 *Glossary* naturally repeats the party line quoted above, so we are no further ahead. Even the ever dependable Wikipedia omits a definition. This might be because defining a service is hard. It is one of those words where people know one when they see one but struggle to create a crisp, clear definition that covers all instances.

I prefer to follow the "Hitchhiker's Guide to the Galaxy" approach: it is okay if something is "relaxed" and "contains much that is apocryphal, or at least wildly inaccurate" so long as it is ultimately practical and useful.

Users regard IT as a utility delivering "stuff" in the same way as other utilities deliver water or power. IT is a pipe and what comes out the end are IT services. Users don't give a toss about the ponds, pumps, purifications and pipes needed to deliver out of the tap —they just care about the consumables delivered to the screen in front of them.

Customers and users care about all that infrastructure only so much as they care about the cost and standard of the delivered consumables. (Note: ITIL makes a good distinction between users and customers: the user uses; the customer pays.) So, services are what come out of the tap not what happens to get them there.

What do users consume from IT (or if you prefer, ICT)? They consume transactions running on technology. They add, update, find, view and report data. They execute a process. They communicate with someone. The value and quality of those services is measured by whether they are the transactions that the users need, whether they do what is required, and how well they do it. All those things are defined from the user/customer point of view, i.e. looking at what came out the end of the pipe.

Okay, so this, then, gives us a nice, crisp definition, right?: **IT Services are transactions on technology.**

Well yes, and no (of course). Now we will mess it up by exploring a grey area.

Not all customers want to trust IT as a total service provider (for good historical reasons). They are not willing to "black box" the services, to use the application service provider (ASP) model (now software as a service (SaaS) but still the same model). They are not willing to look only at what comes out of the pipe.

They either (a) want to know about the ponds, pumps, purifications and pipes and define the consumable in those terms or (b) they want to provide some of those themselves. In that case, they are treating IT as an infrastructure service provider (ISP) (and you thought it meant "Internet").

The customer wants to take some responsibility for their applications, and looks to IT for platform (servers, operating systems, desktops, databases, network, etc.), storage, bandwidth, and/or management (security, availability, backup and recovery, etc.). This is common in geeky departments like engineering but it can crop up anywhere.

Neither ASP nor ISP is "correct". Whether one or the other model is preferred (or prohibited) should be defined in the IT part of the business' strategic plan, and each service definition should make clear where it fits. What is important is for all parties to be clear on what the model is. Confusion and disagreement vanish the moment people realised they are talking on different levels.

If we can ignore that real-world intrusion into the idealised total service provider model we can come up with a slightly more precise definition that still does not become too waffly: **An IT service is the availability and/or consumption of a type of transaction running on technology.**

"Availability and/or consumption"? Every service provider sells the services they provide, even internal corporate service providers. There can be services that someone is already consuming, and there can be services that are there but nobody is taking them yet. There, we can't make it any easier than that.

...Here is something rare: the IT Skeptic pontificates about a technology...

Measuring a service as a black box is essential. Simply because it is impossible (in a practical sense) to discover and measure every link in a service chain, it is impossible to build a complete composite view of a service's performance bottom-up from the component CIs.

It is the boundary problem. Something is always outside your range of view: telco links, proprietary hardware, "magic glue" [EDI, EAI, SOAP, UDDI, LDAP, CORBA ...], the internet, service providers, outsourcers. Web Services, SOA and grid computing are not making it any easier.

The only way to accurately measure performance and availability SLAs is to monitor the user experience, i.e. black box the service. All the discovery, analysis and component-monitoring tools are there to alert us and to sometimes tell us why a service is not meeting SLAs, but they never(?) give us the 100% picture by building a service view bottom-up. (In the same way, the meta-view of the service can only be completely built top-down. The top layer links are all conceptual, perceived, existing only in wetware (people's heads). Further down the stack there are some links that exist physically but lie outside the boundary. Both these types of links in the service-view have to be manually built. This is why I say CMDB can not be fully automated.)

We are lucky that such black box service monitoring is not too hard. Measuring every single end user is impractical, but a good view can be achieved by selecting and measuring a representative subset of users by deploying an agent to their desktops. This gives us SLA reporting, and SLA monitoring and alerting. It also overcomes the old problem of users complaining and IT saying "well, we can't see any problem" using their bottom-up composite view.

Finally, lots of performance issues are user perception. Users never remember how it performed six or twelve months ago. Their frame of reference is always the last week or month. If IT says it has improved over the year, they will insist that IT is not measuring something. End-point monitoring at the desktop gives objective stats of the measured experience to show the trend over time.

You see, there are some technologies the IT Skeptic actually likes ☺

It has always seemed to me that most IT monitoring and measuring tools are very self-serving. They look at the world from the internal IT silo perspective. In ITSM terms they are mildly interesting diagnostic tools for incident and problem resolution, but in terms of service level measurement the only really useful tools are the ones that measure the end user experience.

I know these tools exist - there are plenty of them, the ones that measure response times from the desktop, that treat IT as a black box service provider.

They measure response time and availability. How do you define availability? I think the best definition is when response times are greater than some agreed value. This includes the case where response times are infinite which is too often the IT definition of a service not being available, but as far as a user is concerned very slow response is generally as useless as none at all. These are the only metrics that really map to what the user sees. All the network monitors and server probes and traffic agents and database monitors and snorage (sorry storage has never excited me) consoles... they are toys for the geeks but they don't tell us much about the service.

It is almost always impossible to consolidate their information up into a true depiction of the service. I've spoken before about the boundary problem: no matter how good your IT, there is usually something you can't measure adequately somewhere in the chain delivering the service. Even when it is possible, it's very hard.

True, the user experience tools aren't perfect either. It generally is not practical to put an agent on every desktop and measure every single user's experience. But I believe a representative sampling is enough.

Certainly users do. There is a sigh of relief when they finally see metrics that measure their world instead of the arcane insides of the IT beast. And yet when you listen to vendors, these experience monitors don't seem to be seen as the most important IT monitoring tool there is. They are ancillary. Accessories. Plug-ins. Add-ons.

They are not. They are your lead monitoring tool. All the others are the add-ons: the drill-down tools that let you work out why the user experience is outside the bounds of the SLA.

The very first monitoring to put in is the end-user experience (OK OK closely followed by the event console). Quick wins in service level reporting. And clear guidance in prioritising problems.

There's lots of them, including those that really DO sit on the desktop and measure the experienced behaviour, which to me is preferable, for perception as much as anything, or is that nonrepudiation? BMC has one, CA has one, and I bet plenty of others do...

SLAs work in large siloed formal organisations such as ...oh um... big British mainframe sites of the 1980s. This is a prize example of the cultural bias of ITIL and how it is non-representative of the broad user base it purports to appeal to. The Service Catalogue is a better central mechanism, and SLAs should be an optional addendum.

A recent comment was dead right about the limited appropriateness of SLAs. Abigail said

> "SLAs may work best ...in corporations, particularly those which have a cultural bent towards robust documentation, like maybe Big Pharma. However, in other types of firms (and specifically those in which you don't have a defined CEO type of role, such as in the case of Partnerships, e.g., legal or accounting services firms) I don't think it's either as feasible, or a particularly good idea. "

Absolutely. Some cultures do not readily accept formally negotiated contracts, and the "us and them" structure is actively counterproductive in some organisations.

But tell that to the authors of ITIL. This isn't just a case of adopt and adapt. SLAs are a fundamental part of the ITIL structure. They are used everywhere to define the responses of processes, to define and measure OLAs and UCs, and as the benchmarks for service performance.

There needs to be a more general mechanism in ITIL, and there is: the Service Catalogue. Instead of being a tiny throw-away mention on one page of the blue book, the Catalogue should be the centre of the ITIL world (not the Service Desk tool or - spare us - the CMDB).

If you must have SLAs, start from the Catalogue: Once the technical Catalogue has enough body to it, you can extract the SLAs from it and take them to the business.

The Catalogue is the singularly most important object in service management, and SLAs are a non-essential addendum to it. But ITIL doesn't see it that way and that is solely an artefact of the narrow culture and hence limited IP base from which it was (and still is??) drawn.

Here's one that a colleague wrestled with recently at a client site: how to treat hosted applications in the service catalogue. Here's my answer: that depends on the relationship between IT and the customer.

If the customer sees IT as an infrastructure service provider - if they are hands-on involved in how the service is provided (e.g. design, technology selection, standards, architecture) - then the service is "hosting" and each app is an instance.

If the customer sees IT as an application service provider - if they just want transactions to come out of the screen like water out a pipe - then each app is a service. Or more strictly speaking, each service is made up of an app or maybe a small cluster of what IT sees as apps but the customer sees as a single "pipe".

The world is unfortunately not this binary, ISP services vs. ASP services, so the model is seldom this crisp in real situations, but I think this forms a useful guiding principle. (There are two kinds of people: those who divide everything into two kinds and those who don't).

Some SLAs assign a key metric to how long IT is going to take to resolve incidents. Really. This is like firemen promising to put a fire out in ten minutes. Worse still if an SLA makes this mistake it almost always also has it the wrong way round.

The IT Skeptic's new book[1] is available now. One point it makes is that

> Some organisations give high importance to how long IT is going to take to resolve incidents, and they write this into SLAs as a key metric. Usually high priority incidents are to be resolved quickly while lower priority incidents can take progressively longer.
>
> This is akin to firemen promising to extinguish three-alarm fires within ten minutes but a backyard grassfire may take until tomorrow. It is absurd on three levels: extinguishing the fire takes as long as it takes, bigger fires take longer, and that little yard fire won't be so small tomorrow.

[Comments on the blog] imply that incident resolution is a single thread: "one fire squad", "get some low impact incidents out of the way quickly so that teams can focus on the high priority incident". It isn't. Even in the worst major incident, not everyone is involved, nor should they be. Some Service Desk and Level 1 people will still be quietly chugging away, working on lower priority incidents.

SLAs that say "priority 1 incidents: four hours to resolve" are crap. If we can we'll resolve it in ten seconds. If we can't it may take four days to get the vendors in and rebuild the system. Likewise SLAs that say "priority 3: three working days" are just an excuse for slacking off.

---

[1] Introduction to Real ITSM, www.realitsm.com

Every incident should be addressed as soon as possible and closed as soon as possible. It is how much we chuck at it that varies.

Using indirect KPIs is always a dangerous distorter of behaviour. if you want the SLAs to ensure the appropriate resources are applied and to drive the size and location of teams required and the spare part/hot swap stock size and locations, then write the SLAs so they define the appropriate resources to be applied by priority of incident for that service and define the size and location of teams required and the spare part/hot swap stock size and locations by priority of service. Don't make the behavioural causal chain any longer than it need be - you'll get all sorts of unintended consequences.

What I've seen happen is that everyone drops everything to work on a priority 1 incident and the smaller priority 2 gets worse and worse, especially as the priority 1's arbitrary resolution deadline approaches and a resolution is no closer.

In the satirical *Introduction to Real ITSM* I said

> "Real ITSM SLAs don't define response times. Based on priority, they define how many people will be assigned to an incident; how many hours a day it will be worked on; and what gets overruled to work on it. "

So a lowest priority incident gets .0025 hours per day of a Peon resource who gets pulled from reading the paper, while a higher priority incident gets 2 staff assigned for 8 hours a day managed by the Service Desk team leader and they can be pulled from staff meetings.

So if there is the agreed number of people working on that incident the rest of us can concentrate on everything else that is still going on. Of course as the User Priority rises (the spat dummies index), management will reassign more resource anyway but that is another driver to meet a different KPI.

We have this fixation that SLAs need to be written in terms of a small set of accepted metrics. They don't. Write them in terms of what matters.

SLAs are about setting expectations. Saying priority 1 incidents will be fixed within 4 hours is (a) impossible to know if you can do it (b) less likely than fixing priority 4 incidents within 4 hours (c) making a rod for your own back when you can't.

I'd rather say that

> Priority 4 will have one person assigned to it within four hours. They will work on it as they can. If they can't fix it within 3 days

we will ask you if we need to escalate it in which case it will become a higher priority.

Priority 3 will get one person assigned to fix within four hours. They will bring in additional resource as they need. If they can't fix it within two days they will contact....

...

Priority 1 will get a team of 5 assigned fulltime within one hour, including a Major Incident Manager, plus approximately 50% of the service desk manager's time. They will bring in additional resource as they need. They can pull resource from projects, training, meetings...

...or whatever. We can still measure time to resolve by priority as a KPI - just don't commit to it in an SLA. Users understand that it takes however long it takes. They are happy just to know the scale of the response they are going to get.

You don't place an SLA around who gets assigned (or you could I suppose) but we don't do that now. We assign people now and they know we do the best we can as IT professionals to find the right person.

As well as expectations, SLAs are about transparency. "This is what you are gonna get". SLAs aren't (in general) written to deceive or obscure what is going on - they are there to make it clear. Except in Real ITSM :-D

Different priorities get different levels of attention anyway, so make it clear. People are a bit less keen to demand priority 1 if they know what it will set in action.

As professionals we do try to close every incident as quickly as we can, i.e. right now we resolve it whenever it can be resolved. We're not saying we are going to extend the resolution time any more than it is now - we will always endeavour to keep those resolution times down. I just think it is silly to make promises. Setting a three-day expectation on a priority 4 just gives level 1 an excuse to not even start until tomorrow, especially if they are all bunched up over there trying to fix a priority 2.

Alternatives

Do we have to do ITIL to do Service Management? Of course not. To look and listen around the IT industry these days one would think so, but there is actually more than one game in town[1].

- **ITSM Library** published by itSMF. For interesting historical reasons, itSMF find themselves owning and approving an "alternate" set of books originating out of the Netherlands, mostly based around ITIL but often cheaper and often easier to follow.

- **MOF** from Microsoft is of course focused on their own Windows environment. It is a little different to ITIL but basically a variant (how unusual that Microsoft should create their own, slightly incompatible, version of a standard). Talk is that future versions will 'return to the fold'. In 2008 Microsoft released version 4.0 under a Creative Commons licence, effectively putting it into the public domain.

- **USMBOK** is an extensive body of knowledge that has had a rocky history but also has enthusiastic supporters, and the powerful mind of Ian Clayton

- "Implementing Service and Support Management Processes: A Practical Guide", Higday-Kalmanowitz and Simpson Ed., HDI, 2005 from the **Help Desk Institute** is, not surprisingly, a callcentre slant on ITIL. If you look around it can be downloaded for free by registering with some vendors ;-)

- **COBIT**: The IT Skeptic believes that COBIT has matured to the point where the supporting books constitute a body of knowledge (BOK) that is coming close to a credible alternative to ITIL [see p163]

If you just want to assess your capability, i.e. measure/benchmark your business, then there are several better alternatives. "Better" because there is no agreed standard for measuring ITIL: every consulting firm, including the OGC itself, use a different methodology to get different answers. ITIL is about defining "how" not "how well".

- **ISO20000** (and its ancestor BS15000). Despite some impressions given to the contrary, these are not 100% the same as ITIL. But it is the closest thing to an "ITIL assessment standard".

- **COBIT** is very comprehensive and widely embraced, especially for Sarbanes-Oxley compliance audit, and it is free for download along with an extraordinary amount of other material.

---

[1] For all the links in this article, see http://www.itskeptic.org/node/10

- The "owners" of CMM, Carnegie Mellon, have produced the **eSourcing Capability Model**. It provides incremental assessment for IT services whether they are internally or externally sourced: it includes both a service provider model and a client model. It also addresses the governance issues that arise in a multi-vendor environment. eSCM contains both a best practices model and an assessment methodology.

- The **IT Service Capability Maturity Model** uses the CMM maturity measurement model. It seems to be a very good model but has had little uptake since its release in January 2005.

- For Very Small Enterprise (VSE) look at **NOEMI**

...and other new approaches are emerging all the time. This is still a maturing area.

If you are looking for something simpler than ITIL, then there are several options:

- Check out the much anticipated "ITIL Lite": **ITIL Small-scale Implementation**, Office of Government Commerce, The Stationery Office Books, 2006. It looks useful but the proof is not in. The 1998 version (IT Infrastructure Library practices in Small IT Units, Office of Government Commerce, The Stationery Office 1998) seemed to me to be good but it got very little attention; it remains to be seen how this one goes or what the results will be. (BTW, what a great name the old book had: "ITIL in SITU" - how could they not reuse that?).

- **ISM**, the "out-of-the-box solution for IT Service Management". Always a bold claim but if anyone can pull it off Jan van Bon can.

- **FITS** does not get near the attention it deserves. Developed for UK schools, it is a nice simplification of ITIL

- The lighter **COBIT Quickstart**

- **Core Practice** (CoPr or "copper") is an interesting new development that bears watching. The premise is that we have a fixation with Best Practice. It should be limited to areas where there is a business case for it, and in other areas there should be no shame in just do the minimum necessary.

So don't get swept away on a tide of ITIL. Take a look at what best suits your business. ITIL is very good at what it does. It may be the right thing for you. Or not.

ITIL

ITIL is - depending on your perspective - either a set of books for sale, or a worldwide movement sweeping the IT community.

You don't need ITIL to run a static environment where nothing goes wrong and nothing changes and nothing grows. ITIL has nothing to do with technology, nor can it be implemented with technology. ITIL is about how an organisation and the people within it respond to planned and unexpected variations in the environment, from outages to changes to growth, in order to meet the needs of the business. ITIL defines human behaviour.

Every organisation needs the processes ITIL describes. Every organisation already has them. ITIL is just one way of defining a standard approach to performing them. You may not need ITIL but every IT shop needs to be doing what ITIL describes, one way or another.

ITIL is a creation of the Office of Government Commerce (OGC), a British Government body. Actually it was created by a more IT-centric predecessor of the OGC in the 1980s but this is not the place for an ITIL history lesson. According to the OGC[1]

> ITIL® (the IT Infrastructure Library) is the most widely accepted approach to IT service management in the world. ITIL® provides a cohesive set of best practice, drawn from the public and private sectors internationally. It is supported by a comprehensive qualifications scheme, accredited training organisations, and implementation and assessment tools. The best practice processes promoted in ITIL® support and are supported by, the British Standards Institution's standard for IT service Management (BS15000) [and now BS15000 is superseded by ISO/IEC 20000].

This is a modest description. ITIL is the most widely accepted approach to *IT management* in the world. Theoretically service management is only one way to approach the job of managing IT operations, but no-one has come up with a better one yet. Service management seeks to align IT with the business, a fancy way of saying they give the business what it needs not what IT wants to give it. This is just what everyone is trying to do these days, and ITIL is the best compilation of documentation, a "body of knowledge", on how to do that. It has been around for years but its time has come.

---

[1] www.ogc.gov.uk/guidance_itil.asp

The number one benefit of ITIL is undoubtedly standardization, a lingua franca. Auditors, consultants, service providers and new staff can quickly understand what is what and who is who if you use standard ITIL terms (and use them in the standard way). ITIL is the de facto standard for the industry.

The second benefit is the momentum of ITIL. By attaching the ITIL handle to a service culture initiative, it can help get approval and funding... or not, depending on the baggage carried by the approvers.

There are other benefits that are not unique to ITIL:

- a focus on a service-oriented culture/mindset

- a (fairly) comprehensive framework to check oneself against: what are we missing? What are we doing OK?

- a certification program for practitioners

- a catalyst for cultural change and process reengineering

- some raw material to get you started in designing improved processes and roles

On the other hand, ITIL has become something of a cult. That is, objectivity often goes out the window. "We follow the holy books, we do it because ITIL says so not because we have a business case, we do it the ITIL way not the best way, we will review all our processes not just the ones that are broken". ITIL for its own sake. There is nothing mystical about ITIL and much of it is debatable. As a result, ITIL projects can over-engineer and fix things that are not broken: i.e. they can be a poor use of funds.

Secondly, ITIL has become captive of commercial interests - something that was inevitable once it reached a certain size and momentum. This means decisions are not always taken in the best interests of the end user/consumers who are very poorly represented, nor of the overall advancement of the service management philosophy.

Finally, ITIL is aloof; it integrates badly with other important systems such as COBIT, ISO2700x, ISO900x, and CMMI; even the integration with ISO20000 is loose. The result is greater costs in bringing these systems together within an organization.

ITSM reference library

For those of you out there who are a bit cash strapped like me, you can find instructions for building a formidable body of low-cost knowledge at http://www.itskeptic.org/node/1182

Total cost $211 for an awesome BOK spanning ITIL, COBIT, ISO20000 and MOF - all that you need to work or consult in the ITSM industry.

This cool new tool from Google[1] makes clear the rising tide of interest in ITIL.

But what gives with Jakarta as a hotbed of ITIL interest? (Updated: oh dear! apparently an itil is bahasa slang for a certain portion of female anatomy)

---

[1] http://www.google.com/trends?q=ITIL

Best practice

I worked with a number of clients in a previous vendor life who were struggling to "do ITIL" because they felt (or had been told) they had to. There was little or no funding, often no project. And why? Because there was no business case. I'm a business case specialist. If there are good solid numbers with $$ before them, projects get up. They get attention and resources. They happen. We'll talk about the ROI of ITIL another day. For now let's focus on those poor people battling away to get something done.

And let's think of the company whose resources are being drawn off and distracted ... nay, wasted on misguided attempts to achieve Best Practice just because. As business commentator Mark Di Somma says[1]:

> Focused and achieved excellence is powerful, whereas striving for excellence everywhere (and not achieving it anywhere) is much less competitive. Better to be unbreakable everywhere and unbeatable in selected places than to attempt to be unbeatable everywhere, and not get there!

Di Somma has also said "World class best practice looks like everyone else". Gaining a competitive edge or differentiating yourself is not about doing what everyone else does.

It is not ITIL that is the issue here, so much as the uncritical acceptance of Best Practice as the only acceptable standard for everything. Take a look at Core Practice[2]:

> Not everyone can afford or wants best practice. We fully support best practices for those organisations that have the commitment and resources and reason to adopt best practice [within specific domains of the business]. For those who do not, something more pragmatic is required... For these organisations (e.g. small businesses, start-ups, and the cash-strapped) there is Core Practice. "If you do nothing else, do these things."
>
> We call it CoPr, pronounced "copper". Why copper? Well, because that is how the acronym sounds, obviously. But also because it isn't gold. You want the gold version? There are plenty of organisations who will sell you the gold version. This is the copper version. It is nearly as pretty and has all the same properties (near enough), but for a lot less cost.
>
> Best Practice has become something of a sacred cow in business. It is taken as a given that organisations want to achieve best practice in everything they do and an organisation that doesn't is somehow

---

[1] www.markdisomma.com/upheavals.asp
[2] www.corepractice.org/

less worthy than those that do. This should not be the case. Pursuing Best Practice is a strategic decision, which should be taken when there is an agreed ROI (tangible or intangible) for the resource investment required to get there...

We believe the world is ready for Core Practice: the strategic decision to minimise cost in a discipline of the enterprise by implementing practices sufficient to (a) meet obligations and (b) to make processes work to a standard sufficient that risk (to the organisation and to people in its care) is reduced to some acceptable level.

Do ITIL (or any "best practice") when there is a business case for it. When there isn't, don't flog yourself and don't weaken your organisation.

Is ITIL Best Practice? "Best" is a brave word. "Best" leads with the chin.

All the published ITIL documents define ITIL as Best Practice. (Do you recall how Winnie the Pooh said things in Title Case to show that they were Very Important?)

itSMF define Best Practice as "an industry accepted way of doing something, that works" and "the best identified approach to a situation based upon observation from effective organisations in similar business circumstances". Both of these are excellent and accurate definitions of how the term is used in the ITIL context. I have a concern with the word "Best". This is an emotive and judgemental term that to me implies several things:

- nothing else is better

- anything else is worse (so by subtle inference there is something wrong with you if you choose to do anything else)

- someone has evaluated it to determine it is best (so by inference it can be measured)

It is clear that is not what "Best" is supposed to mean. It is intended to mean "industry accepted" and "best identified". The fact remains that the word "Best" means something else.

ITIL is the product of a group of people who accepted contributions some time ago from a wide but not universal set of organisations and individuals. They then formed committees and came to a group consensus as to which of the submitted practices were "best". Then individuals wrote the books, using peer review and editing to remove personal bias from the result.

Now all those people are highly professional and expert and the result is an awesome body of knowledge. I imply no criticism of the people or the result – it is the most useful tool available for the execution of IT practices. It is just that word "Best".

Many believe that a consensus decision by committee is by definition sub-optimal.

Despite the rigorous professionalism of those involved, the result reflects opinion, derived from a subset of the community.

The ITIL domain is a difficult one to objectively measure and make relative comparisons on. There is no agreed standard for its measurement, with the possible exception of BS15000 or ISO20000. All measurement to date has been done by proprietary methods. How does a Pink Elephant "4" compare with a Lucid-IT "3"? The amount of rigorous academic research into the measurement of ITIL compares very poorly with say TQM or CMM.

ITIL is closely controlled by the governing bodies and changes only very slowly, in the form of major revisions. As a result it represents practice at a point in time. As advances are made, and as the world changes, these are only reflected in ITIL some years later. We need to make very clear to those not versed in the pedantic subtleties of the definition that what ITIL delivers is in fact Generally Accepted Good Practice. It may or may not represent the pinnacle of competitive excellence, as if anyone could measure that.

...Note: this blog entry was a quote from an editorial I wrote for *itSMFnz News*[1]. At the time the IT Skeptic was still anonymous. But I really wanted to use it on the blog. So Rob England, Editor, gave the IT Skeptic permission to reprint it. The itSMF was devoid of any code of practice, and to the best of my knowledge still is. The ownership (and reprint approval) of newsletter content is entirely undefined so I had no guidance, but this seemed a reasonable thing to do under my authority as Editor.

---

[1] Rob England, Editor, itSMFnz Newsletter Vol 2 Number 1
http://www.itsmf.org.nz/index.php?option=com_docman&task=doc_download&gid=11

ITIL Compliance

Many people argue that there is no such thing as ITIL compliance because there is no exact standard to audit against. Perhaps it is all semantics but I don't take such an absolute position - it seems to me that it ought to be measurable or at least assessable in some way.

I've heard this argument ad nauseum that a framework for ITIL assessment is either

- too hard

- imperfect

- a moving target

- not necessary because we have ISO20000 etc...

- available at a special price for you my friend from MegaBucks Consulting Inc or free with your MegaBucks CMDB

I'm not buying it for the simple reason that the user base is not buying it. People want ITIL and they want to know if they are doing ITIL and they want to know if their supplier is doing ITIL or if their megabucks consulting firm is giving them ITIL.

I think ducking the issue just shows that Castle ITIL is more focused on producing a product than meeting the needs of the users - the very attitude and behaviour that ITSM is supposed to fix. Funny that it wasn't too hard for COBIT.

On the other hand I think the opposite statement is clearly true: There is no such thing as ITIL NON-compliant software tools.

Pink Elephant will hasten to point out to you that they do not certify ITIL compliance (in fact I poked fun at them over it). Many people argue that there is no such thing. Certainly any software at all will support ITIL processes, the question is just how well, which is a question of degree. That is, there is no such thing as NON-compliant software - just some makes it more difficult than others. You can run ITIL on Post-It Notes if you want to, or Excel.

The danger when people start talking about ITIL tools is that some get the idea that they can "buy an ITIL" by installing the tool, but tools don't make ITIL. If you really want to test tools hard for ITIL "compliance" ask them these questions. To the vendor who proudly declared on this blog that your product is "ITIL aligned" you might like to measure that "alignment" against this list. ("Aligned" is the new slippery-speak now that "compliant" is on the nose)

The IT Skeptic's ITIL ~~Compliance~~ Alignment Criteria

OGC and itSMF let an opportunity slip and let down their constituencies when they ignored the whole area of product compliance. There are some obvious criteria for a reasonable person's definition of "ITIL compliant". Here are some searching questions to ask your prospective tools vendor, from the IT Skeptic. ITIL is technology-agnostic. You can do ITIL with Post-it® Notes, and the way things are going it won't be long before 3M are advertising Post-it® Notes as "ITIL compliant". The fact is that vendors are full of it when it comes to ITIL. It is far too easy to slap the word "ITIL" on an operations tool. This only serves to debase what ITIL means and to confuse the community. (The IT Skeptic has more to say about the debasement of terminology). You can sympathise with the vendors (as much as one can sympathise with software vendors... speaking as an ex-vendor myself). They can hardly ignore ITIL, yet OGC and itSMF both let an opportunity slip and let down their constituencies when they ignored the whole area of product compliance. No doubt they had good reasons for standing aloof from the whole sordid business but they have left unregulated an area that cries out for some control.

Today, there is no formal independent certification of ITIL compliance for tools. (Pink Elephant provides "PinkVerify™" commercial licensed certification. The IT Skeptic's experience is that this is not a good indicator of compliance to some of the following criteria). OGC set up individual professional certification early on, and now finally ISO/IEC has given us organisational certification (the 20000 standard). The product vendors have no choice but to make their own claims, and nowhere to go other than Pink to verify them in the event that their claims are in fact correct.

But it seems to the IT Skeptic that there are some obvious criteria for a reasonable person's definition of "ITIL compliant". So if you adopt ITIL, ask your prospective vendor these questions about their supposedly ITIL-compliant or ITIL-supporting tool (including some PinkVerified ones):

1. Who says it is compliant or that it supports ITIL? To what maturity and in what capabilities? Just because they think it supports Incident management at maturity level 2 is of little relevance if you need a Service Level Management tool to get you to maturity 4.

2. How many of their product designers are certified ITIL Masters/Managers? Is the chief product architect? If none, then who are the ITIL masters who consult on design? Ask for a conference call to discuss compliance.

3. Use of ITIL terminology. Part of the benefit of any standard framework is standard terms, so that new staff, service providers, auditors, trainers and contractors can all quickly understand your organisation and communicate clearly. So it is not OK if an incident is called something other than an incident, especially if an incident is called a problem and a problem is called a fault. Confusion will be endless.

4. Use of ITIL terminology. Just because it uses ITIL terminology does not mean it supports ITIL. The ITIL processes are clearly defined in the red and blue books. If it doesn't work to these processes (and a wide range of the variants that arise at implementation) it doesn't support ITIL. It is too easy to change the words on a few screens and declare compliance.

5. ITIL is all about Quality Management. How does the tool support this out-of-the-box (OOTB)? For instance, how does it support determining targets? How does it measure and report improvement over time? Does it explicitly implement a Deming Cycle (Plan, Do, Check, Act) in the tool?

6. Service Management is nothing without Service Level Management. Regardless of whether it is a tool for Availability, Capacity, Service Desk, Configuration, whatever.... ask them how it is SLA-aware and how it contributes to the monitoring and reporting of SLAs.

7. SLAs are multi-item written contracts. The contract defines who it is with, what period, who are the key people, what the vertical escalation path is. Each item can define support response times, time to repair, percentage availability, performance, resource usage etc. Setting a threshold time in which an Incident should be picked up or closed or whatever is not an SLA. It is one service level objective that might form part of an SLA if it could be defined on a per-customer basis. Do not allow vendors to redefine the term SLA to suit their own purposes.

8. SLAs relate to a service. This may seem obvious, but SLAs are not related to an asset or anything else: they define the levels for the service. One individual objective within an SLA might relate to a metric for an individual asset. SLAs don't.

   • From the top down: if an incident is raised against a service how to track how long the incident is open as a measure of the outage? How to know when an SLA is in danger of being violated?

   • From the bottom up: when a server or network device goes down, how to know what service(s) is impacted? How to roll up / consolidate device outages into a consequent service outage time?

9. Does the tool support workflow? (Pretty odd if a process-compliant tool doesn't). Does it come with the "standard" ITIL workflows (clearly flowcharted in the red book and blue book) pre-defined? (For example does it support diverging workflows for major or minor change? For requests and incidents?) How does the documentation explain implementing the tool in support of ITIL process? Pretty much every one of the larger players provides services to implement their tool in an ITIL environment, but check what comes OOTB and what is in the manuals. If there is hardly a mention of ITIL then you know their service guys have the tough job of putting lipstick on a pig.

10. Does the tool consolidate information to a service view? ("service" as defined by ITIL – there's a grossly-abused term) Tools that cannot measure and communicate in terms of a service are not ITIL tools (though they can provide a foundation of data for ITIL tools). For example: a monitoring tool should show current status of a service; a Service Desk should show current status of a service based on incidents, problems and changes; a Service Desk and/or SLA tool should provide historical reporting of consolidated availability information and cumulative statistics by service.

11. How many of their field implementation staff or partners have certification beyond ITIL Foundation? Foundation training is known in the IT Skeptic's part of the world as "sheep dipping". It is a basic process that everyone in IT operations should undergo. It provides just enough knowledge to be dangerous (the IT Skeptic should know, being a mere Foundation practitioner himself). If your organisation is of any size or complexity, you probably want more highly trained people, although of course you should look at the broader skills and experience of the individuals involved. Nevertheless, their overall level of training is a good measure of their genuine commitment to ITIL. The big vendors generally excel here. The small players often pay lip service. Or worse they have no field support at all beyond one product tech at the local distributor. ITIL is about process not tools: you need process people on the ground to help you implement it.

12. Specifically for Service Desks:

    • Are Incident and Problem and Change all separate entities? I.e. an Incident does not morph into a Problem: it spawns a Problem. The Incident must continue to exist (and be resolved) as a distinct entity from the Problem. Changing the type of a record from Incident to Problem is not ITIL.

    • Do they provide Incident Matching OOTB? Incident Matching does not mean simple keyword searching - it is a clearly defined process (*Service Support*, p 102).

- Do they support Known Error and Workarounds as entities with associated workflow OOTB? Many tools have never heard of these. Some have them as categories of Problem, which is probably OK though strictly they should be another entity spawned from the Problem. Service Desk Level 1 staff need to be able to look for Known Errors and find the Workaround.

- Do they assess impact and report it meaningfully? Displaying the CMDB tree in a pretty GUI is not impact assessment. If this device is removed will the service still function? How many servers can be removed from the farm without degrading performance past SLA bounds?

- Do they provide Forward Schedule of Change OOTB?

- How to support a CAB? E.g. what reports when preparing CAB minutes and briefing papers before meeting? How to help them collaborate without having to physically meet, for minor changes that still need a ruling?

...The same list published as an internet article provoked a response from Pink Elephant. See page 359.

There are varying degrees of point-stretchedness, with so many products that claim to "deliver" or "support" or "monitor" ITIL. I've done it [in a past vendor life]. "This RFP wants Financial Management. Quick, how do we support Financial Management?" "Asset Whizz stores the supplier name and purchase cost, so say it does". Who's going to prove you wrong? In fact, you're not wrong. Asset Whizz is one part of FM. Not a very important part, but a part. Not a part that actually manages or supports or automates or delivers any process function, just a source or store of data, but a part nonetheless. Just. Kinda. [In the same way that a hair is part of an elephant] Ronald over at *Thinking Problem Management* [blog] has copped flak from vendors for suggesting that some software manufacturers do this.

A Service Desk tool (Incident, Request, Problem, Change, Release, Asset) is nearly indispensable for ITIL (though Post-It notes work, even if they do so badly). Real SLA measurement and reporting is very useful. Project Portfolio tools are great for those venturing into the rarefied heights of Service Strategy. Oh alright, and a bloody CMDB then, if such a thing exists. Then there are a whole bunch of monitors and explorers and reporters and data stores that come in handy for IT people to do their jobs, but they don't particularly pertain to ITIL process as such. You can't tell the vendors of them though, especially their marketing people (and their lawyers).

Business case

Recent correspondence suggests that ITIL3 struggles to articulate a useful value statement. Since anyone can play, the IT Skeptic has a crack at defining one.

A reader recently wrote to me (please everyone feel free to write to me at skeptic@itskeptic.org):

> I've just listened to a two hour or so long webcast featuring current star names in the ITIL universe...and as far as I can understand it all they are claiming is that what ITIL 3 brings to the table is a view of services that "add value to the business".
>
> All well and good, but I remember ...early advocates of ITIL such as Ivor Evans, Michael Hill and Bryan Dennis, who said that, with a passion, twelve years ago.

Everything adds value to the business, from McKinsey consultants to paperclips. Well, at least the paperclips do, but you know what I mean. Heck even I add value when I rouse myself enough to go earn a buck. ITIL has always struggled with a value statement. If that's the best they can do for V3 then it only means V3 hasn't advanced any on V2 - it doesn't mean it has gone backwards.

For what it is worth, here is the IT Skeptic's value statement for ITIL. Note that in line with current thinking, I dislike the concept of "IT and the business", as in "aligning IT with the business" or "adding value to the business".

We don't talk about "Finance and the business". [We might talk about "HR and the business" but that is just because HR people are a bunch of tossers living on another planet, and usually acting contrary to the interests of the very organisation of which they purportedly form a part.]

IT is part of the business. In a desperate attempt to avoid referring to "the business" I am trialling the name "not-IT" for the rest of the business other than IT.

So the IT Skeptic's ITIL value statement for the "not-IT":

- In the worst case, the not-IT will see ITIL as IT getting its house in order. Reactions will range from a disinterested grunt to "Why are we paying extra for you to do what you should have been doing already?"

- In a reasonably well-done ITIL shop, the not-IT will see a better focus on quality and service. They will see IT talk about the service delivered instead of IT's own internals, and they will see a recognisable Deming Cycle making that service better over time. IT should not expect the not-IT to get excited about this; it is perfectly normal good management.

- Best case, in an excellent ITIL shop, the not-IT will observe IT talking in business language, will see them operating off the same strategy [what the heck is an ISSP? Why should IT have a distinct strategic plan?], and will get some transparency into why IT makes decisions and how it spends money. They will say "Welcome to the table, brothers (...at last)"

The value statement is that in the best of ITIL adoptions you can expect IT to start performing as if they are a normal part of the business.

An insightful remark at the IT Management Forum[1] set off today's train of thought:

> when an organization is allowed to pick and choose what [parts of ITIL are] implemented, what gets left out are the more difficult pieces to implement--which often are the pieces that would do the heavy lifting. What gets used are pieces that already fit into the way the organization does things. When the way you do things is fundamentally broken, sticking as closely as possible to the status quo just won't cut it.
>
> IF those implementing ITIL have experience with it and IF that person/team can be objective, then and only then is it a good idea to pick and choose. Usually, though, a halfway implementation of any framework is a fast road right back around to where you started.

If the decision on which processes to reengineer is driven by a business case then it seems to me that the "right" ones will be chosen: those where ITIL will yield an improvement.

It might be that adopting ITIL in a capability where it "fits right in" does have a ROI, e.g. less training of new staff, better contracts with service providers, off-the-shelf training...

In that case doing these "easy" bits first isn't wrong. It just means the "heavy lifting" bits are still there to do and doing the "easy" bits has laid the foundation for the project that is still to come. And if it is "fundamentally broken" then the business case for doing it should be easier. The thing that is probably holding it up is the size of the decision to fix it.

On the other hand, what happens in IT is often that decisions are NOT driven by business case, in which case the result described is exactly what

---

[1] http://forums.datamation.com/showpost.php?p=2960&postcount=7

will happen. The path of least resistance is taken and investment sunk into projects that return little benefit because some manager thinks (or has been convinced) it is a good idea.

I'm tempted to say "what is it about IT and its inability to base business decisions on business cases?" but I suspect HR, Marketing, Sales and others are just as bad in many organisations. If you are part of a business then you should run it like a business and that means having a business case.

"Business case" is another one of those long-suffering terms that gets knocked around. I think I'm using it properly. I mean a reasoned and structured document, with supporting evidence and references, that justifies a project on either financial or strategic grounds in terms of the overall strategy and plans of the business, and which has been reviewed and approved by sufficiently senior management.

Of course the public service is not so constrained with our money, but one hopes they would still build a case for every project, based instead on how it delivers budget and/or policy compliance, but still focused on the outcome justifying the investment and the outcome contributing to overall strategy and plans.

For too long we have made many decisions in IT based on whether something will be "better" (faster, more flexible, more space, cooler) without asking the real question: "Show me the money". If the return does not exceed the investment, don't do it.

Let's get down to the nitty gritty: where is the value in an ITIL project?

The keys to a strong ITIL business case are some basic things:

- There ought to be low-hanging fruit. If there are no real short-term gains you will never hold the attention of either grass-roots participants or senior management.

- There ought to be real money. If you are not saving dollars somewhere to pay for at least part of it, you will be dependent on a "religious decision" (i.e. a leap of faith) by a senior manager who supports you. When that person moves on, the support is gone. Without demonstrable ROI you are back to square one with their successor. A Pink Elephant person posted[1] an excellent rule of thumb for ROI:

> ...you set your maturity target for process improvement at CMM3. You then analyse the incident data and determine what percentage of incidents would not have occurred with a CMM3 level of process implementation. From this, you can calculate the ROI

Thankfully the operational side of IT tends to have strong metrics to support business cases, and to involve repeatable processes where efficiencies can be made. Nevertheless, the dollars will seldom be enough, so make up the "shortfall" in the business case with risk, compliance, and strategic advantage.

- Risk: the easy one if management are at all risk sensitive. Reducing risk can be a compelling argument if (a) there is focus on that risk right now due to scrutiny or a recent embarrassment and (b) the person who owns the money owns the risk. Find the Audit Office, Risk Manager, or Chief Security Officer, and find out what concerns them about IT. Get them needling your decision-maker, or at least threaten the decision-maker with them. If you are a bank, use Basel II. Security is the obvious domain to talk about risk, but do not neglect the other ITIL domains. Reducing production outages or speeding mean time to repair can have a dollar value, but they also reduce risk.

- Compliance: really easy once a compliance requirement has been slapped on the business. SOX, ISO9000, and coming soon ISO/IEC 20000. Also look for a big customer contract that has some process or quality SLAs in it. There may also be internal requirements: a much-talked-about example is "transparency" or "business alignment". If this is a genuine formal requirement on IT from the business, good: use it. If it is just words then it is not an argument. There must be a real pain.

- Strategic advantage: this is much harder for back-room stuff like IT operations but you can argue increased flexibility and responsiveness, and faster time to market with new IT systems. Well, you can try: the Skeptic is sceptical and so are many managers. The best argument the IT Skeptic has seen is that improved processes mean less fire-fighting, thus freeing up resources for more strategic projects, but this is still drawing a long bow. The exception is IT Service Providers, and other

---

very IT-intensive organisations. If IT is the business, then there are real strategic advantages to making IT slicker and more robust.

Make sure the way the case is explained does these things:

1) Take away pain or fear. SOX compliance is a common one right now. Managers just want to make it go away. There are managers too who just want to tick the ITIL box and move on. The bunker-buster is a "This Must Never Happen Again" decree from the Board. One of those and you will be including a new staff canteen as part of the project scope.

2) Deliver on key people's personal agendas. What new CIO can resist being the one who ITIL-ised the department? Here is a radical concept: go ask the decision maker what they want from the project. If you can never get an appointment to talk about what you need, try this topic for a change.

3) Align with key business initiatives. A quality drive is a good one. Throw on all that "continuous process improvement' and "Deming Cycle" stuff that is there in the ITIL theory and so seldom in the practice. SAP implementations are a gift too. They over-run so badly no-one notices an extra million to ensure the IT infrastructure can cope with the flood of support calls and the deluge of changes.

4) Use the right buzz-speak. ITIL is not necessarily the right buzz-speak for your organisation and the decision-makers in question.

If you think about these four points, there is one final simple rule: don't call it ITIL (unless the decision-maker wants to hear "ITIL"). Call it "IT Operational Support for SOX Compliance", "IT Transformation 2010 - Exciting Times for IT", "Customer Oriented Services", "Projected Operational Enhancements for 2007", or "budget item 17".

There you have it. You know you can succeed. Look around at all the ITIL projects where you think "How on earth did they get that through?"

Possible future

In preparation for the release of Microsoft Service Manager (previously known as "Service Desk"), Microsoft made a surprise joint announcement today with IBM.

SAN DIEGO, April 1st /PRNewswire-FirstCall/ -- At the Microsoft Management Summit 2007 (MMS 2007) today, Arden Laws, newly appointed Vice President of Infrastructure Methodologies for Microsoft (Nasdaq: MSFT) said "In partnership with our good friends at IBM, and in support of the upcoming beta release of Microsoft System Center Service Manager, Microsoft are pleased to announced the release of Infrastructure Library 20000, scheduled for May 30th 2007. Both our organisations have been concerned for some time by the excessive control and influence wielded within ITIL and itSMF by Hewlett Packard. The ITIL Version 3 Refresh has brought this to a head and left us with no option but to make a competitive response. IBM created ITIL and Microsoft evolved it to a much higher level with Microsoft Operating Framework (MOF) so we decided we were uniquely positioned to create an equivalent ISO20000 Infrastructure Library together. By combining MOF with a number of IBM publications, we have created a library that covers all aspects of ISO20000".

Briar Jenning, IBM Director of Operational Practice (and also recently appointed), said "The ISO/IEC 20000 standard documents the "what". We have documented the "how"' with five books of practical advice, based on a Deming lifecycle of continuous process development. Now businesses can implement a process framework across all aspects of their IT operations instead of the limited scope offered by ITIL; they can benchmark themselves against an internationally recognised standard; and they can access practitioners and products certified to the same standard. Due to the rigorous quality assurance cycles we have already applied to this content, the first release will be IL20000 Version 3. Starting on June 1st we will run a Version 3 Road-show in 30 cities across 14 countries with joint presentations and training from IBM and Microsoft staff. There will be free breakfast seminars and free three-day IL20000 Fundamental certification in all locations, along with executive retreats in the Cayman Islands, Boracay, the Azores, Monaco and Goa. "

Copyright in the books has been gifted to an independent Foundation Institution on Service Management , whose Board of Trustees - we can exclusively reveal - includes an ex-President of the United States, a Gulf War veteran general, a former UK cabinet minister, several board members of Fortune 50 companies, and a French academic. The FIoSM is reputed to have a marketing war-chest of $14M and a permanent full-time staff of nine. In a surprise move, Sharie Tailor has resigned her current positions to take the role of International President of the FIoSM. Said Tailor: "My work on my past project is done. The IL20000 presents far greater opportunities and far greater resources with which to bring those opportunities to fruition."

When asked to comment, an OGC spokesperson, who asked not to be named, replied "We are not amused. This is a tawdry attempt to buy the market. This will have no impact on the ITIL Version 3 Refresh Roadshow which shall soldier on. Or very little, other than possibly resheduling it once we find replacements for some of the key players".

A Microsoft spokesperson strongly denied that the new group are "buying the market", responding that "We consider it a great opportunity for our organisation to give back to our loyal customers and future customers by including the eBooks at no charge with every copy of Windows (desktop or server), along with free training and certification to the first hundred thousand practitioners. So as not to disadvantage existing clients, copies of IL20000 will be available for free download from June 1st from the Microsoft website for existing Windows users."

When asked to comment on the OGC remark, Jenning added "IBM do not seek to profit from IL20000. We will demonstrate our commitment to the open source community by publishing the IL20000 books under the GNU licence for download in OpenDoc XML format from the IBM Linux website".

The two organisations have also commissioned a print run of 100,000 complementary bound sets of the books for distribution to "valued clients, prospective clients, libraries, tertiary students, and attendees at all major IT conferences in 2007/2008".

The practitioner's body, already incorporated in the USA and UK, is known as the IT Service Management Guild. "Local start-up chapters of 25 members or more will receive seed funding of $25,000 each" says Laws, Chairman of the Board of Trustees of the itSMG. "Nominations are open for interim positions of International President and committee. These will all be salaried full-time positions. Remuneration will be in six figures, and extensive international travel is required. We would prefer candidates with prior experience from similar organisations. Election will be held in May to assume the positions from June 1st."

In related news, the Chinese government has announced a free public domain version of the ITIL books based in Mongolia. Apparently a pirate pdf copy of the ITIL Version 3 books has been posted on a server in Ulan Batar along with the message "The forces of capitalism shall hold this wisdom enslaved no longer. The glorious People's Revolution has set it free on a website in the Autonomous People's Republic of Mongolia, far beyond the clutches of capitalist pig-dog lackey lawyers and their decadent copyrights or trademarks. It shall be known as the Autonomous People's Republic Infrastructure Library and the practitioners' body will be the Foundation Organisational Operations Liberation Service". The URL for the pirate copy is april.ch and the practitioners' body aprilfools.ch.

...Note the dateline. At the time Aiden Laws had just left itSMF, Brian Jennings was the Chair, and Sharon Taylor was just steering ITIL V3, the Refresh, to its release.

Several people commenting privately to the IT Skeptic are worried that ITIL has taken over itSMF. ITSM is ITIL: get over it. Of course, it won't always be thus.

That might change in future as some other movement or body of knowledge gains ascendancy, e.g. ISO20000, but right now ITIL is the only significant IT Service Management game in town.

If that does change, then a few newly emergent power players in the ITIL world might have too much emotionally invested in ITIL for them to see the writing on the wall. This does not concern me. It will be bad for them personally but not for itMSF. If the landscape changes they will be seen as less relevant and rolled at election.

As for itSMF itself, I have argued that itSMF is driven by commercial considerations not any attachment to members or to ITIL per se. The moment the market moves somewhere else, so too will itSMF (faster than a robber's dog, I'd suggest).

The almost total domination of itSMF by commercial interests is actually a positive in this regard (there had to be one). They will be entirely unsentimental about dumping ITIL the instant they see the money moving away.

Meanwhile, I think the itSMF has the mix about right (in terms of reflecting the interests of the marketplace): massive emphasis on ITIL, a few exploratory ventures into ISO20000, and completely ignore SM-CMM, FITS, MOF...

Here is an excellent article by Noel Bruton[1] on how ITIL has peaked, that I commend to your attention. But not just for that concept, though it is a lovely skeptical read. I particularly enjoyed his take on CMDB:

> As a process, configuration management has its own problems, largely stemming from four schools of thought - one that has begun its configuration management programme but is yet to complete it, another that is confused about the difference between configuration management and asset management, a further one that does asset management but calls it configuration management because, well, you do don't you, and a fourth that believes configuration management to be so complex and fluid that as to be fundamentally non-doable.

"...because, well, you do don't you". LMAO. And some killer criticisms of ITIL:

> Survey after survey shows that ITIL adopters have had to add other processes to make up for the gaps in ITIL... The refresh was a chance to bring more specific IT service management topics into ITIL to plug some of those gaps - yet they passed it up...

> Because it offers no real means of benchmarking itself, nor can ITIL really ever prove that it is successful in operation...

> No longer can IT managers utter the vicariously decisive sentence "We're going down the ITIL route" with solemn confidence, because ITIL has shown itself to have no particular route in mind.

Perhaps I am a little less apocalyptic than Noel, but I feel the signs he sees [read the article] for ITIL being "peaked" are not signs of its demise so much as signs we are now hurtling down the slope of the Gartner Hype Cycle. Noel sees the wreckage of ITIL at the bottom. The Gartner model sees an eventual recovery to a calmer steady state after the hype wave, i.e. ITIL may not go away, just settle into whatever is its rightful place without all the hysteria. I have myself predicted ITIL's possible displacement by something else, and I'm not saying that isn't going to happen: just that Noel's portents are more related to disillusionment than demise. We shall have to wait and see...

---

[1] http://www.bruton.win-uk.net/articles/current/thatwas.htm

Visions of the future

On a freezing Southern midwinter solstice night last month, beside a driftwood bonfire on wild Pukerua Bay beach, New Zealand, the IT Swami gazed into the future to give us his "Southern New Year" predictions for the IT Infrastructure Library.

I was shivering as I wrote so some of my notes are a little illegible but here is the first of his visions that I recorded:

> Let us consider what is to be coming for the ITIL on the endless wheel of life: for now, at the end and what will come after. Firstly there are those present earthly perturbances that cloud the future view, second we are looking at the most likely end that will come for the ITIL in this life, and at the last we will be looking into the further distances of time to be seeing what will rise up for all the nice people of Service Management.

> So to begin I must clear my sight of the visions that arise from today. I see a crowd in a desert, wandering lost. There is a city but it is not for them.

itSMF members are dissatisfied. Some practitioners don't join and vendors don't sponsor. In the USA, participation and dues payment are low [7000 out of 350 million is woeful and don't ask how many of those 7000 actually pay up or show up].

The IT Service Management Forum (itSMF) exists to advance Service Management, a function it performs well. It does not exist as a professional body to represent its members, though most of those members labour under such an illusion, hence the dissatisfaction.

The Institute of Service Management (IoSM) fulfils this role in the UK but is struggling to establish in the USA, and will continue to do so until the role of itSMFUSA is clear to the general population. Worldwide, the IT Skeptic believes having two organisations will only cause confusion.

The professional body should be itSMF by broadening the organisation's aims or having two arms. That is what most members think it is for and they stand ready to make it so globally overnight. itSMF International just has to say the word but of course they can't now as they have given IoSM the franchise. Overall the constituency's need for representation is not being addressed.

This is his Second Vision:

> I am seeing ... oh most unpleasant! ... a gorilla strangling a pig. This tells to me there is a powerful, greedy force overpowering a better cause. The pig speaks to me of digging truffles of knowledge but the gorilla roars "gold". In other lands I see pigs and monkeys foraging together, but here in the largest area I see a killing.

Not that I want to call vendors monkeys - except the vendor who once called me that on this blog - but the delicate balance between the interests of those who practice ITIL (foraging, digging for truffles of knowledge) and those who commercialise ITIL (hunting and gathering) is one that requires constant vigilance, else the forces of commerce will grow too powerful and kill the very industry that feeds them.

The bigger vendors (the gorillas) wield enormous power that must be carefully policed else they could easily (and even accidentally) crush the very industry that feeds them by forcing it to serve their own interests instead of those of all members of the ITIL community. There are those who think this is happening in "the largest area" now, the USA. There are strong signs of it happening in ITIL V3 certification.

Actually the two visions link up, because if the monkeys rule the farm (getting all Orwellian now) they have no interest in representation for the pigs. That is, if itSMF dances to the vendors' tune then promotion of ITIL will only increase in emphasis and services to members will decline further. Actual representation of members would be counter to their aims.

As an aside, one can enhance the metaphor to explain what the pigs do to produce gold as by-product for the monkeys, but it would be in bad taste.

This is the Third:

> There is a king who does not reign, a castle closed and dark. Rogue knights roam the countryside, pillaging and brawling. The roads are unsafe, boundaries undefined. Dukes and princes levy their own taxes. The people cry out for law and order, guidance, and unity.
>
> One group of knights from all corners of the kingdom has formed a Round Table. It is not the King's table – they answer to no-one. They ride up and down the highways levying their own taxes and feasting in far away towns. They govern nowhere and defend no-one, but they ride on in the morning before the people can rise up and lynch them.

The rightful ruler of ITIL is the UK Office of Government Commerce (OGC) but it either outsources or abdicates authority over most parts of the ITIL domain, choosing to be heard only in the areas of the brand and the books. Even then, most proclamations are delivered by its lieutenants: the itSMF, TSO and now APMG. See my recent article The Pillars of ITIL. When was the last time the king appeared in public, let alone toured the kingdom? Do you know the king's or queen's name, i.e. the ultimate "boss" of ITIL at OGC? If you answered Sharon Taylor, you are wrong. Sharon is a "hired gun" to manage the creation and delivery of Version 3 (and what an excellent job she has done of it) but she doesn't wear the crown. A king can neglect his kingdom only so long and then one day the people will rise up.

In the meantime, power structures rise and fall all over the place, unmitigated by any central authority.

I leave it to readers to guess who "the Round Table" is referring to ... and no it's not Rotary :-).

This is the Fourth:

> These then are my visions of today: the crowd in the desert, the gorilla and the pig, and the closed castle. Now that I have freed my mind of them, and with some difficulty restored my inner balance, let us be examining the fate of the ITIL...
>
> Goodness gracious! This current agitation is making it very difficult to find only one vision of the future, so I can see three fates awaiting the ITIL: one pleasant, two not so.
>
> First fate: the ITIL walks the road of knowledge, seeking enlightenment. I see the ITIL achieving that and rising up into the light to be born again as something better, fuller, more powerful. Many similar bodies rise together and whirl around to become one, the One that comes after. I see it doing greater good for greater numbers. Crowds come to its doors begging for help and many are healed. How great is the joy and the glory!

Certainly the potential is there for a synthesis or at least a greater consistency and synergy of ITIL, ISO20000, COBIT, CMMI, SixSigma, PMBOK, Prince2, ASL, ISO27001 and/or many other bodies of knowledge. Much is the waving of hands and nodding of heads. Little is the progress.

Here is the Fifth Vision:

> But there is a second outcome: a stubborn ITIL, fighting those it meets on the road. It refuses to see the greater vision, remains locked within its earthly self, brawling and bickering with others on the same path. In the end the ITIL is dying, quickly and brutally, slain by one that is stronger, kicked into the ditch.

Certainly ITIL should not get too confident about being top of the heap. ITIL Version 3 is cause for some concern, with the way it makes only token acknowledgement of others such as ISO20000 and COBIT then ignores them throughout the V3 core books.

Now here is the sixth:

> There is a third fate coming to me, of an ITIL that settles, living quietly where it has always been. It renovates the house for a second time, into five nice new rooms. It grows old slowly. At first it has many friends but the crowd moves away and soon it is alone in the silence. It dies slowly, lonely, embittered, ignored and forgotten.

It would be easy for those who control ITIL to see Version 3 as the last word, the ultimate investment in the framework. They can settle back now and cash the cheques for many a year.

Here is the ultimate seventh Vision:

> Goodness me! These are chilling me, the three deaths of the ITIL: one a glorious fusion with similar seekers; one a quick and violent casting aside; and one a slow decay. Let us be moving on. I must seek deep within for the final prophesy: That Which Is To Come.
>
> I see... I see... I see... oh well actually I see an office chair.
>
> But wait! there are words emblazoned on it. They say... um... "RollaSeat®".
>
> I must see deeper!
>
> There are three castors, yes, three castors and The ...Three ...Castors ...Of ...The ...Seat ...Of ...IT's ...Future ...are ...are ...Governance, Service and Compliance!!

He fainted.

The IT Swami's final prophesy shows us the way the IT world is heading. IT will roll on governance, service and compliance: these will be the main demands on IT from the business we serve. First we must deliver governance of the business: visibility, accountability, control of risk. Second we must manage and deliver services to enable the business. Lastly, we must ensure compliance with external requirements through standardisation, audit, and reporting.

ITSM supports one third of the chair. We in IT need to lift our sights and see the other two thirds as well. We must integrate The Three Castors - Governance, Service and Compliance - else we will end up sitting on our ...er... floor.

Update: As a result of his latest research, the IT Swami has apparently "dissipated the clouds of uncertainly discombobulating my prognostications" and can now say "most certainly indeed, my goodness" that the Three Castors Of The Seat Of IT's Future are Governance, Service and **Assurance**.

It is early days in the IT Skeptic's investigation of the implications of this insight. One thing that is clear is that Compliance is but one aspect of the broader term Assurance. Assurance can be seen to cover all the operational activities that track the organisation against governance directives, take step to rectify divergence, and provide feedback to the governors.

These Assurance activities include

• Compliance (to standards and regulatory requirements)

• Risk

• Security

• Audit

The frenzy around Service Management is transmuting into BAU (business as usual). There is rising interest in Governance and Assurance. The Assurance area is more fragmented and less hyped but look for this to come together soon.

The ITIL hype

Jaded observers of IT could be forgiven for wondering if ITIL is "just another Y2K". There certainly are some strong similarities.

Y2K became an industry in its own right. As momentum gathers, that very momentum becomes a powerful selling tool that few can resist. In other areas of business, I have told people a certain solution will take effort to do properly, or they should not undertake it at all, or even that it is impossible, only to watch less scrupulous vendors commend the outcome and take the business. If you can't see some consulting firms and software vendors fanning the ITIL flames you need to stand back and look again.

The Y2K industry raised the art of FUD[1] to heights not seen before. Nor will we see them again, as the world is wiser and more cynical as a result. But they whipped the business world into a frenzy of spending. Everyone did it because everyone else was doing it. You were mad if you didn't. Worse, you were negligent.

Does ITIL feed on FUD? No, but it feeds on a different momentum founded on the implicit assumption that everyone should do ITIL because everyone else is. Is it a bandwagon? Absolutely. Are the vendors and consultants jumping on? For sure. It has become an industry, and the industry's marketers learned a few techniques from Y2K for creating momentum.

So there are some interesting parallels with the Y2K phenomenon: the wave, the marketing frenzy, the "why aren't you?" mentality. Hopefully we have learnt something from Y2K so as not to repeat our mistakes. Hopefully we have learnt not to get stampeded into anything.

We in the ITIL community must thank Y2K for generating the wave of interest in ITIL in the first place. It was the Y2K-induced budget blowouts that triggered much of the interest in transparency and business alignment that led us to ITIL, that and the collapse of change control systems when the Y2K freeze came off.

Equally we must beware the mines that Y2K has set for us. People are cynical about any IT project that has no clear ROI; that appears to be IT fixing stuff that should not have been broken in the first place; that sounds like it should be simple; that looks like this year's big thing.

---

[1] Fear, Uncertainty and Doubt: a sales technique reportedly pioneered by IBM

Do ITIL when you can see the benefits, when it delivers something tangible to the business, when you feel you ought to.

Gartner[1] has a most useful model for considering the waves of irrational exuberance that regularly sweep across the IT industry: the hype cycle[2]: a peak of enthusiasm followed by a trough as reality sets in, then rising to a steady state. The reality of most hype cycles is that the phenomenon in question settles down to a sedate middle age and eventually fades away from view (but in IT things seldom becomes obsolete, just another layer of complexity to be paid for and managed), while a new kid in town takes all the focus and glory.

ITIL is somewhere around the peak, though it varies around the world. It is not in the trough yet anywhere: it is still greeted with acclaim and enthusiasm and often inflated expectations. But progress down the slippery slope is beginning. Hopefully a little objectivity now can reduce the height of the peak and the depth of the trough, and ease the transition into a more stable maturity.

The IT industry is certainly prone to its fads. This is a reflection of the immaturity of the whole industry (as compared to say most branches of engineering. You don't see civil engineers coming up with cool new ways to build bridges every few years, especially not cool new ways that turn out to be more expensive and less safe than traditional techniques).

One of the big dangers ITIL faces is being taken for a fad due to the wild enthusiasms it is generating. OK the word "wild" hardly applies to service management professionals but you know what I mean. Hopefully forums like this one can restore some decorum.

Those in the know are aware that ITIL has been around for a couple of decades, which is seldom true of fads. But for most Americans (which is a third of the world, economically speaking), in fact for most non-Europeans (there's another third), it appears to have burst onto the scene recently.

Really, it **has** burst onto the scene recently. It has gone from an esoteric idea used by back-room geeks in the helpdesk in eccentric countries like the UK and Holland, to centre-stage in the thinking and conversations of CIOs worldwide. Of course this has been driven by the attention being paid Service Management, which we will show later is a Real Thing. So ITIL must be real too, right?

Wikipedia has a fad as "a fashion that becomes popular in a culture (or subcultures) relatively quickly, remains popular, often for a rather brief

---

[1] Gartner is an IT industry analyst firm: www.gartner.com
[2] See Wikipedia: en.wikipedia.org/wiki/Hype_cycle

period, then loses popularity dramatically." A fad can be based on solid foundations: it is people's response to it that makes it a fad.

Certainly it is fair to say that after a decade of very quiet growth, ITIL's acceptance by the mainstream has been a curve that rose very sharply. We are somewhere around the peak right now. If and how we descend again will characterise ITIL as a fad or not.

Referring back to the Gartner Hype Cycle, the curve is much shorter and steeper (up and down) in a fad. I would also add that fads often come back again after an interval. Those of you with knowledge of systems theory will recognise this as an unstable or at least under-damped system. It oscillates to eventual stability or it slams wildly against whatever boundary conditions it has (until perhaps it self-destructs). This blog is trying to be a feedback damper to get us to the former result instead of the latter.

Those of us who have been around a while remember the fads. If you are not from an IT background, forgive me while I reminisce for the next page or so. Read along and see if you recognise some of the IT madness that you have observed. There is a point to it.

For those who were there, remember[1] how all data was in flat files but relational databases were coming and they were going to fix everything? We followed "the one true Codd[2]". Once we had all our data in one place, referential problems and inconsistencies would vanish. With SQL all programming would be easy, and we wouldn't need many programmers anyway because users would write their own queries.

I got my start programming and teaching 4GLs[3], the end of COBOL and other crude 3GLs for ever. Once again, the end of programming was nigh as end users could learn to write such simple languages. They said the same thing about COBOL, the "business-oriented language", when my Dad learnt about it in the 1970s - but this time it was really true. Really.

Then we all built vast corporate data models. Once we got all our definitions in one place, and achieved third normal form[4] across the organisation, then all the answers would just fall out. I worked on one project that had four and a half thousand beautifully normalised tables. Boy that really helped those end users write their SQL. Slowed those 4GLs down too, and hardware hadn't gotten cheap yet – we were still running IBM 370s.

---

[1] Yeah yeah I know: "If you can remember...."

[2] Dr Edgar J. ("Ted") Codd, IBM researcher; "inventor" of relational database and normalization; creator of the sacred Codd's 12 Rules.

[3] 4GL: fourth generation language

[4] Third normal form or 3NF is a sacred state of data purity

Next, CASE[1] tools were going to transform programming. Once we generated code in one place, end-users would draw pictures and finished applications would burst forth automatically. Twenty years on that one still hasn't laid down and died.

Structured programming, modular programming, object-oriented programming (once we get all the methods defined in one place...), information engineering, repository (once all the meta-data is defined in one place...), RAD[2], JAD[3], directory (once all the data is indexed so it looks like it is in one place....), data warehousing (once we have a copy of all the data in one place...), EAI[4] (once we glued it all together automagically so it looks like it is in one place...), MIS[5] and then EIS[6] (once the executives have all the key data in one place....), CRM[7] (once all the customer interactions are kept in one place...), extreme programming, content management (once all the documents are in one place...), HTML, ERP[8] (once we have the whole damn business in one place...), Web Services (once all the APIs are dynamically linked, and the UDDI lets us look up everything in one place...), and of course e-commerce [embarrassed silence while we all blush].

A decade ago it was PCs, client/server and three-level architectures to decentralise everything. Now it is browsers, thin clients, blades and virtual machines to centralise everything. Every one of them has added a little value and a lot of complexity to IT. Not one has been the silver bullet the vendors and consultants had us believe. Every one cost more and delivered less than promised. Is it any wonder the business is cynical? Not that they have a right to toss too many stones about. While all this was going on in the data-centre, over in the boardroom we had Quality Circles, BPR[9], zero based budgets, TQM[10], 6sigma, MBOs[11], KM[12], coaching, the one minute manager, centres of excellence, intellectual capital, ISO9000, outsourcing and off-shoring, triple bottom line, and of course e-commerce ...

---

[1] CASE: Computer Aided Software Engineering
[2] RAD: Rapid Application Development
[3] JAD: Joint Application Development (as in together, not as in reefer)
[4] EAI: Enterprise Application Integration
[5] MIS: Management Information Systems
[6] EIS: Executive Information Systems, presumably more refined than mere Management Information Systems
[7] CRM: Customer Relationship Management
[8] ERP: Enterprise Resource Planning, as in SAP
[9] BPR: Business Process Re-engineering
[10] TQM: Total Quality Management
[11] MBO: Management By Objectives. In traditional IT mangling of English, one can have "an MBO" that one is measured by.
[12] KM: Knowledge Management

Every now and then innovation comes along which really does change the game, disrupt, introduce a paradigm shift, create a sea change (even the language of change has fads). These were real "tectonic shifters": the computer, the compiler, the PC, mice, the hyperlink, the internet, the virus, email, project management, supply chain management. In the hindsight of future decades, Service Management will prove to be one of these.

The early IT shifts were in technology. Later ones were in software. More recently, IT step changes have been in process and methods. As it matures, IT is following the same path as manufacturing (technology, then control systems, then process) and other disciplines. In fact as we will see, IT is adopting much that has been learnt in other sectors.

ITIL the Cult

We have seen that the ITIL movement has distinct overtones of a fad. What about a cult? A group that defines its own measure of good and bad by comparing against its own internal reference books then declares that those books hold the key to getting from bad to good sounds mighty like a cult to me.

Alan Mayo[1] gave me a model that I shall call the Skeptical Maturity Model for Technology Adoption. It has four phases

- Idea
- Product
- Wave
- Religion

His central tenet of course is that as a new innovation moves up the Gartner hype cycle, objectivity goes out the window. That is the central tenet of this blog too.

There ought to be a fifth exit phase to that model. What would it be? Disillusionment? Obscurity? Yet another technology layer?

So is ITIL becoming a religion, or at least a cult? Consider this:

What defines "bad" process that "needs" ITIL? Getting a low score on a CMM-like maturity model.

What is that model benchmarked against? The ITIL definition.

Who defines the model and then measures it? The consultants who stand to profit from "fixing" the processes.

Kind of circular reasoning don't you think? What if we measured existing processes against assessable metrics on usefulness to the business or value returned on investment or quality, or whatever the organisation cares about? We might find the existing processes don't fit the ITIL model but

---

[1] http://www.linkedin.com/pub/3/159/8bb

they work (more on that another day). That is, we might find there is no business case for changing.

Anyone who has been accosted in the street and offered a personality reading by the nutters-who-shall-remain-nameless-because-they-play-too-rough knows the trap that is being set here. Tell someone they are broken and then offer the secret to fixing it.

A group that defines its own measure of good and bad by comparing against its own internal reference books then declares that those books hold the key to getting from bad to good sounds mighty like a cult to me.

The first step to reforming is often ITIL awareness training, for if they wallow in ignorance they cannot be saved. Never mind what they call their processes now; they have to know to call them the one true process. "Because you are ignorant of my framework, that makes you ignorant".

The next step is executive sponsorship. First rule of missionaries: if you want to convert the populace, try to convert their ruler.

Then we have to work out how to effect cultural change, which is a nice name for overcoming resistance. In a recent survey "72 percent claim the biggest barrier to ITIL adoption in their business is organizational resistance." Well, hello. What makes you right and them wrong? Several billion people find it disgusting to blow one's nose then store it in one's pocket.

OK, much of this is overstated and deliberately provocative. "You made that up". "That doesn't make it wrong". [1]

But the ITIL community should beware the onset of cultish behaviour. It is especially prevalent in the born-again ITILists. Who has encountered the happy-clappy evangelical zeal of those who have been freshly sheep-dipped? (Sheep-dipping = ITIL Foundations training) The Skeptic admits guilt on that one.

---

[1] Scott Adams (Dilbert) http://www.dilbert.com/

The more mature practitioners tend to get it bashed out of them by reality. The very experienced original authors of ITIL knew this when they made "adopt and adapt" a basic principle (the one completely omitted from ISO20000 – there is a topic for another day).

You can measure effectiveness with metrics like incident counts, but most metrics are not good measures. For example a GOOD service desk process improvement would result in an INCREASE in incidents, at least initially, as people make more use of a better service.

So usually the baseline is an abstract figure called maturity. And maturity is nearly always measured against ITIL as the benchmark. The logic is you rate poorly against ITIL so you need ITIL to fix it. And lo and behold after you implement ITIL, your ITIL maturity improves, so ITIL was the right solution and ITIL delivered.

This is the same circular reasoning as cults use: to measure you against their answer. It is also similar to the trick the Scientologists play when they accost people in the street and offer personality readings. Surprise! the readings come up with broken personalities that only they can fix.

The March of ITIL Zealots

We discuss the lack of decent empirical evidence for ITIL later [see p170]. Vendor surveys are a poor substitute (I know, I worked for one), but when they are all we have then we should at least listen to them.

...I later changed my mind: no we shouldn't....

Sadly I don't think I can include Evergreen in my Circle of ITIL Skeptics, but they undoubtedly take a mature and rational approach to ITIL:

> Which industry standards are relevant to my organization and which are redundant? How do I get started?
>
> ... Evergreen Systems can help you ....to deliver value in your business.

Now that I've been nice to them, let me quote extensively from their survey results[1]

> • 72 percent claim the biggest barrier to ITIL adoption in their business is organizational resistance. At a very distant second, 34% are not sure where to start.
> • ITIL is quickly becoming visible at the enterprise IT level, with 36 percent of respondents working on re-engineering enterprise IT service delivery, and 29 percent planning to leverage all 10 ITIL discipline areas.
> • Most ITIL programs are living in a potentially dangerous vacuum. While 95% selected ITIL as a framework they are using to improve IT Operations, less than 20% even showed awareness of CobiT or CMMi.
> "While visibility with CIOs continues to rise, the alarming combination of a lack of effective planning, organizational resistance to change and the enterprise level of change required for success in ITIL is very troubling. A large number of initiatives will fail to yield any value, and insufficient planning will be the root cause for failure to establish senior management support and funding," said Don Casson, President and CEO of Evergreen.

Now, Evergreen are highlighting these facts because they want to help fix the symptom, while I would like to examine the underlying cause. These numbers scream out to me that people are embarking on ITIL projects because everyone else is.

They don't have the support of the organisation, they haven't looked at alternatives or context, and about a third are launching in holus-bolus,

---

[1]

http://www.evergreensys.com/campaign/itil_benchmark_2006/blog/index.html

without proper planning, hacking away at everything. A third of these organisations have processes broken in all ten disciplines to such an extent that there is a good business case for fixing them? Puh-leease!

Yes the processes are inter-connected. In fact, one of the greatest strengths of ITIL is the way it defines the interactions and divisions of responsibility instead of considering the areas in isolation. But people implement chunks of it every day. It works. For heaven's sake, start where the pain is, do a bit, show benefit (or not) then decide what next. In the stats above I hear the march of zealots, sweeping aside reason in their quest for ITIL purity.

It gets worse: From itSMF USA's own research newsletter of April 2006[1] (bit of an own goal, this one):

> Compass then asked the companies how well they actually measure their ITIL process maturity. Only 4 percent of respondents felt able to say that all of their ITIL processes were fully measured for maturity and fewer than one third of respondents had maturity measures for all ITIL processes. Compass also asked people to define how well their organization is able to relate process maturity to performance improvement based on measurement. Only 9 percent of respondents felt able to say that the relationship was based on full measures, fully linking process maturity with performance. A staggering 72 percent felt unable to acknowledge any linkage at all between process maturity and performance improvement.

How on earth do they get the money? and how do their managers keep their jobs?

---

[1] http://data.memberclicks.com/site/itsmf/Research_Newsletter_-_April_2006_Issue.pdf

The chosen one

Those who say "COBIT is the what and ITIL the how" either haven't read COBIT, are oversimplifying or are being excessively polite to ITIL.

Everyone is tiptoeing around the fact that COBIT offers a significant competitive body of knowledge (BOK) to ITIL. Sure ITIL goes into more depth in places, but to say COBIT sits over the top is to grossly understate the overlap. COBIT extends a long way down into the "how" and it does it with an intellectual rigour that ITIL lacks. I haven't done or seen a detailed mapping but my guess is that COBIT is as comprehensive a description of the how as ITIL in some areas. And of course it covers areas ITIL (even ITIL V3) doesn't, such as information architecture (PO2), manage HR (PO7), educate and train users (DS7), ensure compliance with external requirements (ME3) or provide IT Governance (ME4).

I feel COBIT suffers a bit from the ITIL V1 and V2 problem of too many books: it is a fragmented BOK with multiple perspectives. This is great in terms of being able to find a view of the BOK to suit any situation, but it makes it more challenging to find the right view (book). Funding those consultants again.

Take a look at my favourite: *COBIT Control Practices*. Add to it the *IT Assurance Guide* for assessment, the *IT Governance Implementation Guide* for business governance, *Val IT* (now 2.0) for measurement, and what looks to be a great book, the upcoming *COBIT User's Guide for Service Managers*[1]. "The guide will contain ... the key governance tasks for the role aligned to the ITIL 3 processes and COBIT 4.1 control objectives" What a shame ITIL V3 wasn't quite so cooperative in the reverse direction! Put them all together and you have a hefty BOK on the "how" that I think easily rivals ITIL.

And take a look at what is coming down the pipeline from ITGI/ISACA[2]. This is starting to look very like ITIL V1's 26 books!

But it's not considered polite to say so and spoil ITIL's day (or decade) in the spotlight.

Here's hoping the upcoming (any day now, apparently: "the first quarter of 2009") *COBIT User's Guide for Service Managers* is closely followed by a

---

[1] Rob was a reviewer of this book

[2] http://www.itgi.org/Template.cfm?Section=Home&CONTENTID=19907&TEMPLATE=/ContentManagement/ContentDisplay.cfm

certification. Imagine "COBIT Certified Service Manager". Wouldn't that put a cat amongst the ITIL pigeons?

I think the Manager in the Street wants one answer-in-a-box to their process problems and that answer is - according to everything they hear - ITIL. 90% of the IT community are not party to our broader knowledge of other frameworks and complementary systems. If they have heard of COBIT at all it is as some obscure audit thing. And none of them have the leisure of picking and choosing or mixing and matching - only expensive consultants do that for the small proportion of organisations that pay for a tailor-made solution.

If the wind changes and all the talk is about COBIT, it will need only a little meat on the bones to provide much the same guidance as ITIL does now, only over a broader range. So I say "why not?" and so do others. There is more in-depth guidance to COBIT arriving all the time.

It has the components that ITIL lacks such as prescriptive criteria for assessment but I think it is as loosely aligned to ISO20000 as ITIL is.

Personally I think the world is moving towards more professional formal systems such as COBIT, and the amateur ITIL days are numbered. Big numbers but numbered.

COBIT is wooing. ITIL is playing hard to get.

I think ITGI and ISACA are exceedingly polite, given the brash upstart that is currently posturing all over their front lawn as if it owned the place.

In their own genteel way I think they are getting quietly even, what with the mapping paper and now the Service Managers guide. All in good time... ITIL will be put firmly (but politely) back in its place any year now.

Gating ITIL

We can do without all this angst about "Should we do ITIL?" That is the last question we should ask ourselves.

- The first question: is anything actually broken? (Just because it doesn't comply with ITIL doesn't mean it isn't working just fine: if IT ain't broke don't fix it)

- The second question: is it worth fixing? Will we get a decent ROI? ITIL is irrelevant to this question. The ROI is measured by what happens before and what happens after, in business terms.

- The third question: is this something the business wants us to fix? Is it in line with strategy and plans?

- The fourth question: is this the best possible use of the money, given limited funds? Where does this rate in the overall portfolio of proposed projects?

Only once you have an affirmative answer to all four of those questions should you then look at: how are we going to fix this? As a SMALL subset of that discussion, the question comes up: should we do ITIL? It is only a small part because engaging the people who perform the processes, looking hard at the processes, and making changes are the key activities that bring the results. How does one distinguish ITIL process improvement from process improvement? I reckon you could use astrology as your framework for process review and improvement and you'd still show a significant result. What framework you use for that transformation is of less importance than what experts you get in to help, what cultural change methodology you use, what executive support you get, how real the project is, and so on. All those decisions will help determine whether ITIL is useful or not in your case.

...For a whole book on this topic see this author's *Owning ITIL®*

ITIL vs. placebo

If there is an eccentric company owner out there who would like to contribute to business science by conducting a controlled experiment on your company, please contact me. I would like to trial ITIL versus a placebo.

Instead of using ITIL as the framework or guidance for process improvement in IT production, I would use a placebo body of knowledge. Examples might include:

- astrology

- today's process is brought to you by the letter "A"

- Madonna's lyrics

I think astrology is the most mindless example there, so it would serve admirably as a placebo. We would

- assess the organisation's maturity against astrological principles

- train all staff in the basic principles of astrology

- review existing processes and categorise them using the twelve zodiacal signs

- hold workshops and interviews with key stakeholders to understand how processes are not meeting current business needs, and how they might be improved using the principles of the assigned zodiac sign. For example Libran processes need to get better at decision-making

- use experienced worldly external consultant astrologers to advise on process redesign

- reorganise the IT department assigning people to process areas based on their birthdate

- run an organised funded program to get everyone enthused about the potential of astrology and to ensure everyone knows how the processes work and what their role is

All the steps but the last are just ritual practices with no more real meaning than throwing I-ching or dealing tarot or polishing a crystal ball or reading a zodiac chart. Just as a reading is really performed based on someone's experience and wisdom and a cold read of the subject, so too the astrologer's advice to the company would probably make a fair bit of sense.

But the doozy is the final step. We could use Texas boot-skootin' as the framework for all it matters. What matters is that we actually pay attention to staff, ask them what they think, get their buy in, fire them up, and run a concerted program to get everyone to understand how things really work and to get everyone on the same page, i.e. we build a new consistent culture.

I contend that is the real value of an ITIL program and it doesn't have a danged thing to do with ITIL. Most companies are too humour-challenged to use any of my proposed bodies of knowledge as the basis of a change program, but they could certainly use MOF or SM-CMM or ITSMBOK or eTOM and get much the same results.

ITIL will still win most beauty contests just because it is a standard which gives it an inherent advantage, but my point is there is nothing mystical about ITIL that couldn't be replaced by something else tomorrow.

If IT Aint Broke Don't Fix it

Perhaps the saddest sight in the ITIL world is organisations that adopt ITIL processes when the old ones were working OK. Don't tell me it doesn't happen.

IT Operations is a domain that tends to attract perfectionists. Damn good thing too when sites are aiming for three-, four- or five-nines [99.999% availability]. The unfortunate aspect of perfectionists is that they can't leave well enough alone, especially when a fad like ITIL sweeps through, or they get indoctrinated into a cult like ITIL.

Others make changes because change is power. As that genius business commentator of the late 20th century, Scott Adams, said in the Dilbert Principle: "change is good for the people who are causing the change. They understand the new information that is being added to the universe. They grow smarter in comparison to the rest of us".

Then we have that phenomenon The New CIO. You know the one: brought in to make some changes. Or because they are new they feel the need to make some changes. Good managers find what works and leave it alone, but good managers are rare in IT. And of course they are rare, because there are no professional qualifications or accreditations for IT people: not real qualifications and accreditations like, say, for engineers or doctors. IT gives anyone a go. And some companies give anyone who can speak geek a go at CIO.

I have watched with fascination one guy who bluffed his way into a small company X as CIO, stayed long enough to look OK on the CV but not so long as to blow his cover, then used that experience to get a job at a much bigger organisation Y where he bluffed and bullied for a couple of years until he couldn't get away with it any longer, then quickly left. For quite a while he was appearing in the press and at conferences as the CIO of Y and then the ex-CIO of Y until that got tired, then he scored a job as country manager for a vendor (vendors respect a master of B.S.). So many CEOs and Boards are IT-ignorant that it is easy for these guys to pull it off. The sooner we have a proper professional body the better...

OK a quick nip of Wild Turkey and a walk round the garden and I have calmed down again. There are a few things other than ITIL I'd also like to take pot-shots at one day. As I was saying, plenty of CIOs and Ops Managers change things because they need to be seen to, or they feel they want to, or it isn't perfect, or they like change, or they really have no idea what they are doing.

I worked for a software vendor, a big one. I was present when our CIO was interviewed by a journalist for the IT press, who asked if we used ITIL ourselves in-house. Now you need to know this is a big shop: mainframes, huge storage farm, worldwide network, tens of thousands of users. And they sell a service desk. A PinkVerified one, so there. My breathing stopped as I waited to hear his answer because I knew we didn't, and I had often whinged about the fact (to colleagues who like me didn't matter): how could we sell an ITIL tool and services when we didn't even use ITIL ourselves? (though we used the tool and very well). He replied no we didn't, because our processes were very good and delivered effective service to the business (all true). When they needed fixing he would look at the business case for ITIL.

Those guys I worked for cop a lot of flak but they run a tight business: the political pressure on him to be a showcase ITIL shop must have been immense, but his job was to run IT on a budget and he wasn't going to blow it on the fad du jour. I told that story with pride when challenged. If IT ain't broke don't fix it.

I have been discussing ITIL ROI with the Spanish ITIL community, via Antonio Valle's blog with the magnificent name "Gobierno de las TIC. Conocimiento Adquirido". I was asked the question "How is the relationship between an architectural project and a house?"

Unless one is setting up a data centre from scratch, I don't think the architect analogy fits. An ITIL adoption is usually more like renovations.

I have renovated three houses now. In all cases they were fit for habitation already. It was not money well spent: the house didn't leak, the doors were secure, it was sanitary and there was no fire risk. So renovation was just for our own satisfaction. It was overcapitalising - we would not get a good ROI when we sold the house.

(In two countries now I have seen the fiscal illusion where people see a rising capital value on their home and use that "free money" to renovate it. It is no different to renovating a house that has a falling value. Unless the renovation further increases the value of the house by more than you spend, it is money you could have had but now you don't.)

Now if I want to squander my money changing the way my house looks it is my right: it is my money. ITIL project money isn't mine. So often, adopting ITIL is like ripping up perfectly good carpet so you can polish the floorboards: it is very satisfying but there is no business case for it.

No proof of efficacy

Where is the evidence for the benefits of ITIL? There isn't any. Not the kind of hard empirical evidence that would stand up in, say, clinical trials. There is more evidence for quack alternative medicines than there is for ITIL.

There is certainly more solid evidence for the application of CMM in solutions development[1], an analogous methodology in a closely related area.

Granted there is some research around the benefits of aligning IT with the business but not around quantification of ROI and nothing (that I can find) specific to ITIL.

The itSMF themselves make a few outrageously unsubstantiated claims in *An Introductory Overview of ITIL* [version 2]

- Over 70% reduction in service downtime

- ROI up by over 1000%

- Savings of £100 million per annum

- New product cycles reduced by 50%.

Send no money now!!

The Best Practice Research Unit is associated with the ITIL 3 refresh [Updated: It was. The site has disappeared]. After 20 years it is about time there was such a unit. It is just a shame this is not an initiative of either OGC or itSMF (at least itSMF USA is doing something, in fact several things focused on research). The BPRU website explicitly recognised this problem.

> Much of the material published on IT management, including IT service management, has been normative or prescriptive in flavour. Few rigorous, academic studies have been undertaken to evaluate how tools, techniques, methods and management approaches have been selected, adapted, implemented and measurable benefits achieved.
> There is a danger that new approaches arise out of the practitioner community with little empirical validation.

"Few rigorous, academic studies"? Don't be nice, Tony. The solitary piece of academic research I [could] find [in 2007] carries a bold and, I think, unproven title "Evidence that use of the ITIL framework is effective".[2] It is

---

[1] E.g. www.dtic.mil/ndia/2004cmmi/CMMIT4Tue/goldenson.pdf
[2] www.naccq.ac.nz/conference05/proceedings_04/potg_itil.pdf

from Dr B.C. Potgieter, Waikato Institute of Technology (New Zealand), J.H. Botha, Oxford Brookes University, Dr C. Lew, Damelin International College.

It opens by saying "Very little academic material exists on ICT Service Management Best Practice..." and concludes its own research with:

> We found that both customer satisfaction and operational performance improve as the activities in the ITIL framework increases. Increased use of the ITIL framework is therefore likely to result in improvements to customer satisfaction and operational performance. Although the study was limited to a single research site, claims made by executive management of the research site and OCG as to the contribution the ITIL framework seems to be justified. More definitive research delineating the nature of these "relationships" is however needed, especially regarding each process in the ITIL framework.

The data base is poor: "research site was a large service unit of ICT in a provincial government in South Africa during 2002/3." One site. More importantly, the two things measured to support this brave conclusion were (1) customer satisfaction (the three surveys they conducted only included management in the final survey so all we can say is that non-managerial staff were happier) and (2) "objective service improvement" by measuring "the number of calls logged at the Help Desk" because "we can rather safely conclude that the number of problems logged would be a good reflection of objective service levels". I expect that last statement leaves this research with zero credibility with anyone who understands ITIL and ITSM. No cost/benefit analysis.

Not a single valid objective metric. Sure if you throw enough government money at anything and launch an aggressive enough PR campaign you can make the users happier. That proves nothing. And the fact that calls to the Service Desk went down over an initial nine month period would to me be a cause for concern not celebration. But you can bet this paper will be quoted all over the place as evidence of the effectiveness of ITIL.

But since we've started, here is another 'sponsored survey'[1]: "Did you make a business case before decision? (Base: 62 European firms): No 68%" TWO THIRDS had no business case!!! And "Don't know 11%". Who on earth was answering the survey that didn't know if there was a business case? But wait!! There's more! "Did you observe the expected ROI? (Base: 20 European firms). No 50% Don't know 30% Yes 20%." Good lord! If less than a third built a business case, one would guess the ones that did represented a sample biased towards those who had a good case, and yet

---

[1] i.i.com.com/cnwk.1d/html/itp/Front_Range_ITIL_Beyond_Goals.pdf

only ONE FIFTH of them achieved the expected ROI. This is best business practice? I think I need to go lie down.

Before I do though, here is one more. If you are willing to make major decisions based on amateur research by vendors (as everyone adopting ITIL does), here is an interesting one to ponder[1]:

> In a survey carried out by Bruton of 400 sites, about half of the 125 organizations which were found to have adopted ITIL made no measured improvement in terms of their service performance or the rate at which they were able to close helpdesk calls. "Some helpdesks can way outperform a site that has adopted the best practices of ITIL," said Bruton. "Best practice does not mean superior performance. It is beginning to sound that ITIL is the only way to go. It isn't. It is only one way to go."

A man after my own heart.

I would like to see some solid scientific research on:

- Quantified cost/benefit analyses across a statistically significant number and diversity of organisations of adoption of ITL vs. other BPR methodologies, or vs. a simple process review and reorganisation, or vs. implementation of a service desk product.

- Quantified cost benefit analyses of organisations that have only done ITIL without concurrent Six Sigma or CMMI or other quality improvement programs.

- Analysis of the proportion of organisations that would actually benefit through adoption of ITIL.

The really delicious irony in all this is ITIL's own emphasis on the importance of a business case and ROI. But the facts are that few organisations even bother to examine the business case before embarking on ITIL; even fewer measure results; and the few that do are building their business case in the absence of any solid research to justify their estimates. The Emperor has no clothes.

The fact that ITIL itself is not based on scientific research is not the issue (in this blog entry), but the business decision to invest funds in its adoption should be. That is to say, I'm not looking for evidence to support why ITIL does something a particular way, I'm looking for evidence that doing it that way returns a benefit to the business (financial or other) sufficient to make adopting ITIL worthwhile.

---

[1] www.computerwire.com/industries/research/?pid=8673D122-721B-4450-8C57-30A9665D4BA2

To return to the CMM analogy: the CMM evidence that I respect is not evidence that 5 maturity levels is the right number; it is evidence that companies that moved from maturity 2 to 3 in software development saw an average x% reduction in errors and a y% reduction in costs. Likewise the evidence does not have to be related to adopting all of ITIL. In fact I'd love to see some evidence relating to the benefits of adopting fragments of it, since that is what the majority of sites do.

I never said ITIL has no value: I just said that before embarking on an ITIL project we have almost zero evidence that it WILL have value. More subtly, we also have no evidence that ITIL makes any more difference than any other shakeup of process, though once again it might.

Research on ITIL ROI would be a useful thing for the general information of the industry, but if you are considering whether or not to adopt ITIL, any ROI information you can find now is useless.

Your ROI will be entirely dependent on how broken your organisation is. So the fact that organisation X got $7.43 in ROI by implementing ITIL incident management is of zero interest to your organisation, unless they happen to be remarkably similar organisations.

ITIL isn't some new and magical thing that doesn't already exist in your organisation. ITIL is a transformation of existing processes from one maturity to another (hopefully higher) maturity. So the return depends totally on the current maturity levels of your organisation - how much room for improvement there is.

The average weight-loss on a particular diet is not a predictor for what I would lose, especially if I were already underweight (which I most certain am not but work with me here - it is just an analogy).

If there were tables available of average ROI in moving between any two maturity levels, and if you went to the expense of taking a read on your current ITIL maturity levels, THEN that generic ROI information would be useful in predicting your return.

But the only data available currently is all this anecdotal drivel that comes out of the analysts and vendors about how one organisation saved a million bucks. This is (a) not a predictor of your own results and (b) usually bullshit anyway.

ITIL V3

ITIL V3 has shed the down-home, amateur grittiness that provided ITIL's appeal.

Its new commercialism might help ITIL's appeal in some sectors but it diminishes it in others. While the largest organisations and the Service Management zealots have all embraced ITIL V3 with fervour, many of the less obsessive are lukewarm in their enthusiasm for V3.

Why is this?

Several factors are at play, from the dauntingly monolithic nature of v3 to fatigue having just come to terms with version 2. Another factor is the image of v3. ITIL v1 and v2 were seen as independent, impartial, folksy and real. ITIL v3 has lost some of that: it is a little too glitzy, commercial, clever, remote and ambitious for some consumers.

The nostalgic, the Luddite and the just plain old amongst us pine for a simpler time when ITIL was wholesome, down-home common sense from some no nonsense Pommy codgers (once again let us not confuse perception with reality). Of course, in some ways this isn't fair. ITIL grew beyond a certain threshold where it did attract the attention of the money engine and then nothing was going to be the same, no matter what OGC or anyone did. But that doesn't excuse the unseemly haste with which ITIL was tarted up in a shiny suit, given fashionable new songs to sing, and shoved out on a stage in Vegas.

At the US Pink Elephant conference [2007], Sharon Taylor, the Chief Architect and Chief Examiner of ITIL, listed five common myths about ITIL V3. I thought I'd make it clear that none of them came from this blog.

I may be bombastic at times but I'm careful that the facts are right and I'm willing to correct when they are not. So I was a bit worried that any of the myths might be pinned on my door. But as she went through them I was relieved to cross them off.

Let's look at them from this blog's perspective:

1) I have to recertify everyone

We know that isn't true. All agencies involved have bent over backwards to get the word out that V2 certifications will continue to be "recognised". What is just now emerging is that they won't be recognised as prerequisites for further V3 qualifications without an "upgrade" course first.

You won't need to re-certify everyone, but once you get around to upgrading to V3, everyone is going to need some upgrade training obviously. This is especially so for those who want to go on to further qualifications but everyone who needed training when you adopted V2 ITIL will likely need upgrade training when you adopt V3. I'm not complaining: this isn't a scam - it is just common sense.

So needing to recertify everyone is a myth. Upgrading everyone is a high probability. People are talking about upgrade training being just one day. We shall see. The training vendors must be salivating.

2) All the processes I know will be gone

Also not true. All ten processes and one function from V2 will be there in V3. So too will be a number of new process and functions: at least 13 by my count. These are Demand Management, Service Portfolio Management, Strategy Generation, Seven Step Improvement Process, Service Catalogue Management, Information Security Management, Supplier Management, Knowledge Management, Transition Planning, Evaluation and Early Life Support, Event Management, Request Fulfilment, Access Management, Common Service Operation Activities. My information is imperfect so I may have missed some or got some wrong.

So all the processes you know will be there. You just won't know all the processes.

3) I have to buy new tools

You never have to buy any tools. But they help. Not only has ITIL expanded into new processes, but it has also expanded in another dimension: along the service lifecycle. Think of it as not only has functionality got longer but it has got wider too.

If you are lucky enough to have picked a vendor who will include all this new functionality as an upgrade and you are current on maintenance, then you will only need to go to the expense of rolling out a new version when you adopt V3.

Having worked for an ITSM vendor, I'm betting that (a) some of the new functionality will be extra cost options and (b) parts of it will go outside the comfort zone of some vendors and they just won't cover it - think Service Strategy.

So nobody needs new tools but there is a fair chance you'll be paying for options or additional tools.

4) Processes I use won't work in a service lifecycle

Of course they will. The lifecycle extension of ITIL is orthogonal to process - it is a new dimension. Existing processes fit into the lifecycle just as any new processes do.

But your lifecycle processes may need change: how you do what the service lifecycle does. Just as V2 changed the way you do service management, V3 will change the way you do service lifecycle.

5) V3 is an addon to V2

No it's not: as Sharon says it is a replacement. Saying it is an add-on is like saying a Chev Corvette is an add-on to an LS1 V8 motor, or Windows is an add-on to MS-DOS. Sure V2 is still in there somewhere but not so as you'd notice.

So I'm happy to say that this blog does not endorse or spread those five myths (or any others I hope).

People are starting to realise how different ITIL v3 ("The Refresh") is from ITIL v2, and how much more extensive the scope and ideas are. There is no doubt that the re-engineering has been extensive. A bit like a DOS-based command-line-driven utility being rewritten as a Windows GUI with workflow. The original routines are still in there somewhere but the manuals sure look different! Saying it is an add-on is like saying a Chev Corvette is an add-on to an LS1 V8 motor, or Windows is an add-on to MS-DOS. Sure ITIL2 is still in there somewhere but not so as you'd notice.

Even though OGC are trying to make ITIL3 more integrated than ITIL2, it is a good bet that users will concentrate on the Service Transition and Service Operation books (at least initially), in the same way as we focus on the red and blue books in ITIL2, so that ITIL3 will have its own "lost processes", as I call them. If true, this will serve to mitigate the increase in scale considerably.

You can see a diagram of the transition from ITIL V2 to ITIL V3 at http://www.itskeptic.org/scale-itil-v3. The key ideas this diagram tries to impart are:

- ITIL2 is still there in ITIL3

- Not only has ITIL3 expanded ITIL2 along the same dimensions that V2 considered (made it "longer" by over a dozen more processes) it has also expanded it in a whole new dimension (made it "wider", changed it from a line to a plane).

- There was actually much more to ITIL2 than the ten processes in the red and blue books, but often you wouldn't know it to hear folk talk. Some of the processes making ITIL3 "longer" are these "lost processes" being brought back into the core. Others aren't - they are specific to running a lifecycle.

Sooner or later it is going to dawn on people that they do need to retrain (upgrade), they do possibly need to change the way they do things (service lifecycle), and there are more than twice as many processes to learn and implement.

Personally I think it is a good move - there had to be a quantum step and one assumes it is aligned with the majority of the feedback. People hate change so there will be much howling and gnashing of teeth, but in a few years I think we will view V2 as quaint. It might be quite a few years though, and in the interim I believe we will see two streams of ITIL: the big boys and the top guns doing ITIL version 3, and the lesser mortals and beginners doing ITIL version 2.

OGC and TSO think they are going to sunset ITIL2 round about end of 2008. I think they don't have a snowflake's chance. Pink Elephant say[1] the ITIL2 Practitioner certifications will survive at least "until late 2008".

...2009 and ITIL V2 is still going strong: as at February, ITIL V2 Foundation exams still outnumber ITIL V3 Foundation. The following was published in 2007 and it all still holds true in 2009...

ITIL Version 3 has the IT Operations world abuzz. People are asking questions, worrying about the impact, revising plans, and hurrying off to do training that sounds like it may not be quite finished yet. There is no rush to go to ITIL3.

Chill out:

- There is nothing much wrong with ITIL2

- ITIL3 is too big with no help available (yet) on getting there

- ITIL3 is too raw and nobody understands it properly yet

- ITIL3 certification isn't even ready yet, and

- Only a small proportion of the ITIL community are advanced enough to need ITIL3

ITIL V3 was "Yank-heavy". I'd count David Cannon and Majid Iqbal as honorary Americans. Let us not confuse national origins with current political alignment. David Cannon [is South African but] has been resident in the USA for a long time and works for HP. Majid Iqbal [is Indian but] was at Carnegie Mellon, on of the great bastions of the American empire, and is now at Gartner. I am a Kiwi but for years I worked in Australia and represented Australian interests within my employer. I didn't like being called an Aussie any more than David(s) or Majid like being called a Yank but I wasn't there representing NZ.

So I'm counting six out of 11 authors from North America including the Chief Architect. (and David Wheeldon works for HP so some would count that as another half). Given the mix that wrote ITIL 1 and 2, I'd say the balance had shifted trans-Atlantic.

We've discussed the relative influence of the various contributors already on the blog. From those who were there in ITIL V1 it seems it was indeed international, but with a strong input from the UK and Europe. Where the origins of the ideas was is anyone's guess.

It is generally felt that there was a certain element of the "Not invented here" syndrome around the slow adoption of ITIL in the USA, and only the championing by HP (and Microsoft's pushing MOF perhaps) that changed that. So the throttling happened in the past due to America's own xenophobia and we are past that.

It is inevitable that ITIL get dominated (or else pushed aside) by the biggest and most aggressive economy on earth. It is happening in certification and training despite APMG - a British company - retaining control. But that should happen in a controlled manner, with the consent of the rest of us, and without losing the international flavour (spelt with a "u"). There is nothing unprofessional about keeping an eye on the power politics of ITIL to ensure it does not become captive to vested interests. Somebody has to do it, and OGC and itSMF and APMG don't.

I am delighted to see other cultures contributing at an international level, in books and in itSMFI. I wish there were more. I think some countries pull above their weight. I'd expect to see more participation from other European and Asian countries. India is showing rising interest and activity. I expect China to loom large in a few decades just like it did in manufacturing. China is the sleeper.

Right now ITIL is still the property of Her Majesty Queen Elizabeth II.

The IT Skeptic argued [previously] that ITIL is not best practice. Now Version 3 is upon us, has anything changed?

Back then I said best practice is one of those terms where the meaning gets gradually eroded by constant misuse, especially by vendors, analysts and consultants—the phrase gains currency and pretty soon everyone uses it. By now, "best-practice" has been so abused perhaps it does only mean "we wrote down a way of doing it." But ITIL is two decades old so let us assume that when ITIL was first created they really meant best-practice.

OGC [still] defines best-practice as "Proven activity or processes that have been successfully used by multiple organisations. ITIL is an example of best-practice."[1] This strikes me as evasive: What has this to do with "best"?

The itSMF has in the past defined best-practice as "the best identified approach to a situation based upon observation from effective organisations in similar business circumstances." Now itSMF have wimped out to something just as limp-wristed: "A Best Practice approach means seeking out ideas and experiences from those who have undertaken similar activities in the past, determining which of these practices are relevant to your situation, testing them out to see if they work, before incorporating the proven practices in your own documented processes."[2] What do "relevant", "if they work" and "proven" have to do with best?

Wikipedia (the Skeptic's favourite source of the Zeitgeist) defines best-practice as "a management idea which asserts that there is a technique, method, process, activity, incentive or reward that is more effective at delivering a particular outcome than any other technique, method, process, etc."[3] Yes, that is what "best" means, isn't it? "More ... than any other ..." Calling something best-practice is (or was) a brave statement. It led with the chin. "This is superlative. There is no better way of doing it."

So why are OGC's and itSMF's definitions nowadays so wimpy? Because ITIL isn't best-practice. It is good practice. It is generally accepted practice. But it isn't "best." There are good arguments why ITIL is not the ultimate approach to IT operations:

1. It is still improving. Optimal process does not need a refresh.

[1] http://www.best-management-practice.com/gempdf/ITILV3_Glossary_English_v1_2007.pdf, still there at December 2008
[2] http://www.itsmf.org/bestpractices/what_is, now gone
[3] http://en.wikipedia.org/wiki/Best_practice

2. We could not know if it were the best, as we have no objective measure of efficacy of ITIL against any other approach.

3. ITIL is not based on any rigorous research so there is no proof of efficacy, and there can be no evidence-based process of optimising it.

4. ITIL is designed, created, edited and reviewed by individuals, acting as a committee. Although they are highly knowledgeable, experienced professionals, they are still people with opinions and personal biases, and they still need to reach a consensus among several diverse positions. It is hard to imagine this process ever reaching the best result (something about design of camels comes to mind).

5. [Some of ITIL is unproven blue-sky good ideas. See p215.]

Even if ITIL were best, it is best as defined by a narrow group of people drawn from consulting firms and a university, all from the Western European culture and all working with major corporations.

The IT Skeptic is not anti-ITIL V3. ITSM View suggests[1] "There are plenty out there that are seemingly wanting to derail ITIL v3". I'm not one of them. Nor can I think of anyone who is. That blog post has the heading "Where is the love?" Let us not confuse reluctance to leap immediately into bed with active animosity. Once upon a time people grew up together, and falling in love was a gradual process of getting to know those best suited. Wise heads knew that falling in lust is not the same thing. The brilliant Australian cartoonist Patrick Cook offered the advice to potential newlyweds "Try to get to know each other before the sex wears off".

Just because people are not dumping ITIL V2 like a Vegas bride and running into V3's arms does not mean they want V3 to go away. It is just too much too soon.

We need time to get to know V3. We want to assess compatibility, take time to grow together, and to find out if it has any less endearing personal habits.

> The IT Skeptic is now collecting everything we can find out about ITIL Version 3 on one reference page, at
> http://www.itskeptic.org/ITIL_version_3

---

[1] http://blog.certification.info/2008/10/where-is-love.html

Processes

There has been discussion on this blog of ITIL's loose use of the word "process". I believe the ITIL authors use "process" and "practice" and "function" (and even "domain") interchangeably, as they did in ITILv2.

Since the release of ITIL v3 there is much "Ding! Dong! The Process is dead!" but I don't think so. There is a burgeoning market for third-party process charts for v3. Authors are interpreting the new "v3-speak" back into the process-centric frame of reference where most users are still comfortable. We just got over the wrench away from techno-centric to process-centric with ITIL Version 2. Many people aren't ready for service-centric yet.

While, v3 certainly is trying to move away from process, there is still debate about just how many processes there are in v3. The five core books never say. The official introduction says 27. itSMF says 26. There are many more "functions" in v3 that v2 would probably have called a process. The v3 Qualification Scheme offers 35 "subject areas".

Originally an official v3 process model was promised (for example "ITIL Process Maps" worked on by Jeroen Bronkhorst of HP and Sharon Taylor, Chief Architect of ITIL, were in the June 2006 scoping of v3) but it seems to have quietly disappeared, or is at least taking a while. Quite a while.

So, v3 is trying to bury the idea of process in favour of the new improved concept of service. ITIL has always only had a vague concept of what constitutes a process. ITIL authors have never felt constrained by the tighter definitions of "process" used by say process re-engineering or business analysis.

The ITIL V3 Glossary does define a process as:

> "A structured set of Activities designed to accomplish a specific Objective. A Process takes one or more defined inputs and turns them into defined outputs. A Process may include any of the Roles, responsibilities, tools and management Controls required to reliably deliver the outputs. A Process may define Policies, Standards, Guidelines, Activities, and Work Instructions if they are needed."

The five core ITIL V3 books have a different definition of process:

> "Processes are examples of closed-loop systems because they provide change and transformation towards a goal and utilize feedback for self-reinforcing and self-correction ... "

The ITIL V3 core books go on to say that processes are measurable; that they deliver a specific result "individually identifiable and countable";

deliver their primary result to a customer; and respond to a specific trigger.

Amusingly four of the five core books go on to say that functions are often confused with processes and use capacity management as an example where "it is a mistake to assume that capacity management can only be a process ... with discrete countable outcomes", whereas the one book that owns capacity management, Service Design, says nothing of the sort, and does not even mention capacity management in this section.

Dissent amongst the ranks?

Squabbles aside, the definition in the glossary and the definition in the core books differ somewhat. What they have in common is that many of the 24 or 26 processes listed by the official introduction or by itSMF do not fit them. Four out of five books agree that capacity management is one example of a process that by either definition isn't. The official introduction calls operations management a process, the Service Operation core book calls it a function (along with other functions that don't get called a process in the introduction).

A number of activities defined as processes do not fit well with the concept of a clear sequence of looping tasks that respond to a trigger to take inputs and turn them into countable outputs: IT financial management, service continuity management, configuration management, availability management, strategy generation, etc.

Let us accept that v2 was sloppy about what constitutes a process and used the word to label all the domains or functions or activity areas of ITIL. Despite brave attempts to introduce a crisper, more generally accepted usage of the word in v3, the historical legacy has lived on and the word still gets a rough ride. When ITIL talks about process, they mean defined people doing defined stuff in a defined area—nothing more. (Except in some instances where they mean a process.)

ITIL V3 shies away from the whole concept of processes. They are avoided and obfuscated, sometimes called elements, jumbled up with functions. And most of all, the "complete" lists are all different! In an effort to get a grasp on this, the IT Skeptic has cross referenced them all and the resulting IT Skeptic's Unofficial List of ITIL Version 3 Processes (ta daaah!) can be found at http://www.itskeptic.org/node/690

Incident Management

Why do most incident priority systems go from 4 (low) to 1 (high)? What does zero mean? What does 5 mean?

Real ITSM[1] does things differently to, say, ITIL.

Because Real Priority (also known as Care Factor) is measured by the number of metaphorical fans that are being hit by effluent, it starts at zero and goes up. What do you think of that idea?

This is much more logical than other systems where 1 is highest. Just when you thought you had seen the worst thing that can go wrong, something comes along that makes all past priority 1 incidents look mild. How can you communicate this? With Real ITSM, you simply assign it a priority that is one higher than any previous incident.[2] Just like fire brigades with their "three alarm" fires.

Change Management

I believe ITIL has aspirations beyond its station. ITIL is an operational framework for IT production environments. So long as it knows its place and sticks to it, all is well. But every now and then it gets an inflated view of its own importance and starts poking into the development aspects of IT, or worse still the strategic ones. This is an example of the latter, where the book is hopelessly confused between operational and strategic aspects of change. The forums (fora?) are littered with confused postings. Sometimes a RFC is something that fixes a problem, at other times it is something raised by an end user, e.g. a request for application enhancement. The two are totally different things.

I'm holding off on this one until I get my hands on the V3 books, to see if they systematically address business change as compared to operational change. Or put another way, ITIL V3 can do either of two things to clarify this: (1) grow to properly cover more than production operations (2) pull its head in to only cover production operations. If it does either, then issue solved. If not, I'll be having a go at it.

...It didn't but I haven't yet.

---

[1] www.realitsm.com

[2] Extract from Introduction to Real ITSM. See www.realitsm.com

There are differing perspectives of Change. In order to further muddy the waters, here is the IT Skeptic's Change Model which attempts to draw those perspectives together.

1. Change has four major views: Organisation, Project, Development and Operations. But these are only views: the underlying change entities exist as a single set. Note also that these are not IT terms. That is, IT Operations is a subset of Operations, IT Development is a subset of Development. Other groups to have a development area include Marketing and R&D. But we will talk mostly from an IT point of view, because IT is the thought leader in this area, and because it is what I know.

2. Changes are managed by view. Process and ownership of the process occurs at the view. Overall ownership of the change is trickier: there could be a Chief Change Officer that owns all, or ownership could be passed like a baton as a change moves through processes.

   Personally I favour an über-manager ("manager" meaning owner, roles, processes and tools) that tracks all changes, even if a sub-manager manages the details of one view. So there is a central portfolio of all change, but the detail of the change management is handled below it in

   - demand management (user and management requests for change)

   - project portfolio management (holistic, strategic deployment of people and money across projects)

   - project management (tactical control and forecasting of people, tasks and timelines across inter-related projects)

   - software development lifecycle or SDLC (versioning, changes, defects, builds and staging)

   - service desk (changes generated by incident and problem management, and "casual" requests for change)

   - configuration management (tracking what is happening to the production environment; understanding the implications by relating the change to the impacted objects and services)

   - operational change management (controlling the implementation and deployment of changes into production environments)

   E.g. The central process shows a status of "with development", while all the techie details are managed in IT Development's geeky process and tool, with occasional updates flowing back to the centre as the change passes development milestones, until the change is passed back from Development.

Then some other process gets control of the change with occasional updates flowing back to the central controller (where Development can check on progress).

Others will prefer a federated model - it seems to be in vogue right now (sunrise, sunset...).

3) A change goes through its lifecycle from an idea to a proposal to a project to a production system, and as it does so it appears and disappears from views as it moves in and out of their scope of interest.

4) In theory a change may appear in any one view and not appear in any other. For example:

- a business change may never make it to the project stage

- many IT operational changes will never appear on any other view

5) But most changes will flow through multiple views:

- An operational change requires business process change

- A new product needs changes to operational systems, e.g. Warehousing

- A business-initiated change initiates a project which requires new software developed which has to be implemented ...

6) And many changes need to at least appear on all other views so that they can be examined for impact:

- Operations departments need to have advance warning of proposed changes entering demand management

- One function of the CAB (ITIL Change Advisory Board) is to facilitate this for the Business view, so they are aware of upcoming production changes.

7) An underlying tool might be the repository and engine for one combination of views, and another tool for some other combination. There is not a one-to-one mapping between tools and views. For example

- an IT Service Desk will almost always manage IT Operational change and might manage some or all general Operational change and some of IT Development change

- SDLC is a specialist function (think bug tracking, copybook management, builds...) that usually has its own tool

- A Change Manager would use CMDB to check change impact, and an operations technician would update the CMDB or notify the Configuration Manager after they have made the change so that the mappings to services and other logical entities can be updated.

- the business executive will want to manage project portfolio in yet another specialised tool which usually integrates with the project management tool(s)

- try telling contract project managers to use a tool other than MS-Project to manage project changes.

I see lots of problems when people try to force a square tool into a round view. People have seriously proposed JIRA as a problem management tool in my hearing.

Recently I saw CVS+Bugzilla being promoted as an IT Operational change manager. Wrong. There is an overlap (release, software distribution, staging...), no more.

More subtle is the fact that tools evolve from one view to encompass more. I think we need to be careful to ensure they actually fit the requirement at hand when applied to other views. E.g. powerful toolsets that come from an IT Development background for modelling, RAD and CASE are now proposed as a more general repository: a CMDB.

Not wrong, but not necessarily the best solution unless the environment is Development-heavy.

People come from diverse backgrounds too, and they bring with them preferences and mindsets that also skew planning and designs. Personally I think a CMDB needs an IT Operational bias, but that is my own background showing. People from project or business experiences might suggest another toolset as CMDB, perhaps a financial asset tool that has grown up.

When selecting tools, each situation must be assessed to decide which aspect is most important, what skew is appropriate.

8) How the views relate hierarchically is an organisational decision. I often draw them as Venn subsets, i.e. nested circles: Development within Operations (yes if I ruled the world Operations would manage Development change) within Project within Business. But I think there are several other valid ways of arranging them:

- four peers under an umbrella view

- business managing the other three

- Development and Operations within Project within Business

- "group hug": mutually cooperating peers (yeah, right)

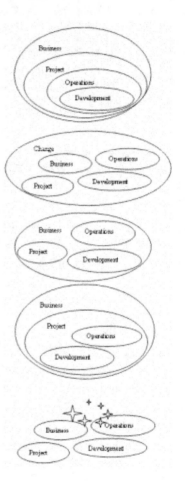

In the IT change world, ITIL has a lot to say. Most of the time, ITIL Change Management (and Release and Configuration Management) is about service desk and operational (production) change management. Unfortunately ITIL has aspirations above its station: at times the ITIL books try to expand "Change" into demand, project, SDLC and even portfolio management.

A lot of debate stems from definition of terms or scope. If we have a clear mental model of all the aspects of change (the IT Skeptic once mapped about twelve, not the four here), then we can be clear what we mean when we talk about that much-debated word "Change".

Configuration management

As it becomes clearer that CMDB is a flawed concept, I'm seeing occurrences of folk talking about CMDB as a process rather than a thing. It isn't. CMDB is the (nutty) thing. Configuration Management is the perfectly sensible process associated with it - and often forgotten. Take for example (and it is only an example - there are more but this is the most recent I saw which reminded me of this phenomenon) this report[1] from Forrester. Apparently we need a CMDB Manager. Is this over and above a Configuration Manager, or have they just forgotten that role?

> it encompasses people, processes, and technology to gather, manage, and link information vital to every ITIL process discipline. Enter the emerging role of CMDB manager, which is a vital component in the process of managing and maintaining the CMDB.

Sounds to me like the latter, but let's give the benefit of the doubt and assume the former: that we need a CMDB manager in addition to a Configuration Manager. Oh my, CMDB isn't getting any easier is it? It gets worse:

> As an I&O executive you should institute CMDB managers

Managers plural????

This report is of course only available to the analyst's hosts/clients, but according to this article from Network World

> ...if the service management effort grows significantly, IT shops should consider creating a team of CMDB managers to enable subroles with distinct responsibilities, Hubbert writes [in the Forrester report]. Lastly, the CMDB manager should report to the head of infrastructure and operations.

Reports to head of infrastructure and operations? Maybe they have forgotten the Configuration Manager after all. The Network World article confuses technology and process too (this may be a quote from Forrester - it is not clear):

> the CMDB is not about rolling out a single product but more about shifting best practices to support a collection of up-to-date and inter-related configuration and change metrics about IT infrastructure and applications

No it isn't. That is Configuration Management process.

1

http://www.forrester.com/Research/Document/Excerpt/0,7211,44798,00.html

Application Management

ITIL attempts to establish authority over Application Management. Does ITIL V3 have what it takes? No. As bodies of knowledge go, it is scrawny and under-developed.

This blog post came about in response to a couple of excellent comments about the problems faced in the interface between Development and Production. See also the post about how ITIL V3 failed to get it together with a leading body of App Mgmt knowledge called ASL [see p264]. Heck they didn't even make much use of another body of App Mgmt knowledge called ITIL V2.

Everyone agrees that production handover is a weakness in lots of organisations, that there has to be something better than chucking the dead cat over the wall. That's not the question. The question is whether ITIL is the answer, as it were. Does ITIL's idea of App Mgmt even come within pissing distance of what is really needed to get the Development geeks under control? (Development/solutions may run a tight ship when it comes to version and build management, requirements gathering, parallel development, RAD, JAD, RUP, JUP... but they typically don't know jack about interfacing with the real world. Actually they could know if they wanted to, they just don't care: "My work here is done. Operate this.") Or is it but a token effort to tick the box? A paltry five pages to cover what used to be a whole book in ITIL V2, and still is in ASL.

ITIL V3's section on App Mgmt is nearly as embarrassing as its Information Security. It would be bad enough to muscle in on other domains with something powerful in hand. To barge in there with these emaciated bodies of knowledge - when in both cases established substantial BOKs exist - will make us a laughing stock.

P.S. the photo is Astro. He's the reason I haven't had much sleep for the past few days - my son's new puppy. Somehow he made me think of ITIL V3's section on App Mgmt.

How does IT Operations get control of "the other half"? How do we stop them chucking dead cats over the wall for us to own? It is pretty straightforward. We have recently been discussing Application Management, and there have been several comments about getting those developers under control. IMHO, it is pretty simple to get some basic control.

- Define a "production readiness" standard (does ITIL offer any help at all here?)

- Get it included in the architecture: in design specs, in requirements gathering, in deliverables, in required infrastructure. The Architects usually go along with this readily - they are mostly non-partisan on the Dev/Prod divide.

- Get CIO mandate for: "no Operations signoff on production readiness, no production change". This is the hard bit but it is easy to make a business case for this: cost of failures and degraded service, cost of manual support processes, cost of re-working apps to make them supportable

- Push in to dev project-start-up meetings and make it known this is how things are from now on - nicely. Then help.

- Try to get as much as possible retrofitted into in-flight projects - lots of coaching and sleeves-up help required here. Be seen to be helping.

- Get a "head on a pike": make a project late by refusing signoff. The more fuss and debate the better. Whether you win or lose this fight in the end does not matter. Project managers like a smooth ride. They'll take note and get readiness engineered in to their other projects.

As one comment said, it is all about communication. This is a People issue not a Process one. (Nor a technology one: "we need better lifecycle tools"). Go along to project meetings, especially in the early days and especially those projects that make you nervous.

- Explain why we need this stuff to make a project into a successful service.

- Explain how much of it is design thought and documented information and only a little of it is actual engineering in the system.

- Explain how Operations wants to work with the project team to help design it and document it (then deliver on that promise).

- Explain what will happen if it isn't there. Tell the story of the project that didn't play nicely.

It's a bit like training a puppy (sorry folks it is all puppy analogies round here for a while). You just gotta keep saying "No" and putting them on the newspaper. And you can't train them until after they have made a mess so that they make the connection. The ideal time to initiate production acceptance is right after Development's failure to provide a ready system has cost money, reputation, property or - god forbid - lives. Music to my ears is a Board or CEO saying "This must never be allowed to happen again". So don't make it about what it has cost "my people", make it about what it has cost "us". As for the career, it is the same as introducing Change Management. It is all stick and little carrot. There are few friends to be made. So my preferred model is hire a contractor in for 3-6 months to do the dirty work, then they can leave and take much of the negative baggage with them. It's worth the money (said the consultant).

I think developers have got away with this in the past, but these days end users are as likely to want a smooth transition, customers to see better service for their money, and management are sick of developer cowboys. I believe exhibiting a little professionalism in defending the service levels goes down well with most audiences. Only for so long, but you can't win them all. Even if you eventually get steamrolled the people who matter are the PMs. They don't like roadblocks even if they eventually crunch them into speed humps. Next time they plan ahead for a smooth transition.

Risk Management

Is Risk Management the "lost process" of ITIL V3? The ITIL V3 syllabus refers to an 'element' called Risk Management that students must learn. It is also defined in the ITIL V3 glossary.

Service Operation will own up to "management of risk", but not to describing a process called Risk Management. And of course every book has a section on "risks". But no book explicitly covers Risk Management.

..this is despite the fact that OGC provides an entire BOK about risk: M-o-R. But then they provide Prince2 too and PM is another lost discipline in ITIL3...

Project Management

Why is Project Management all but invisible in ITIL V3?

PM is the engine that moves much stuff (hopefully just about everything) from Development to Production, which is pretty important now that ITIL has muscled into Application Management. PM should interlock with Change Management and Testing. PM should provide most of the Early Life Support. Release and Deployment shouldn't move without PM: if it is big enough to be a release it should be a project. And so on.

So why is it no-one tells you how ITIL aligns with the Project Management bodies of knowledge PMBOK or PRINCE2.

Service Operation gives Project Management two paragraphs (p165), and not as part of Application Management.

Service Transition gives Project Management passing mention on pages 40 and 62 and 200, and page 180 of *Service Transition* that explains how important it is NOT to ignore it!! To be fair, it also explains how PM is something done by those people over there, not IT Services (and hence out of scope). *Service Transition* also duplicates all of PMs functions in the Service Transition plan (p40).

Service Design spends time on it (p31-32) but only vague directions to keep the project honest, not details of how the interface might work between Service Design and Project Management, and never once mentioning PMBOK or PRINCE2. The diagram on p31 is just wrong. It shows the project team's job is done at the start of the pilot or warranty period. This is "dead cat syndrome" which must be avoided at all costs. A project team should retain ownership through the warranty period until acceptance has been signed off.

The Official Introduction gives a cursory nod to assorted BOKs in the Complementary Guidance section.

What happened to Project Management when ITIL V3 was put together? Did someone get bitten by a project manager? Have the PRINCE2 people got all the good carparks at OGC and everyone hates them?

The fact that PRINCE2 got snubbed is one thing, but a Yank-heavy team doesn't explain it really because PMBOK suffered just about as rough treatment too.

In fact the whole domain of PM got short shrift. Along with Risk and perhaps one or two others, I think it is a reasonable expectation that project management would have got more attention, and more detail about how it interfaces with ITIL (not how to do it).

BTW, the fault in the *Service Design* diagram mentioned is not a distortion due to flattening. The big fat arrow labelled "Project (Project Team)" stops one phase too short. It is old entrenched thinking that Operations has to pick up the baby at the start of a pilot and clean up any messes it makes going towards production.

Progress Management is an important subset of [Real ITSM's] Workload Management, where the progress of projects is closely monitored and – if necessary – slowed, to ensure minimum rate of change in the production environment, reduced pressure on project staff, and plenty of time to prepare the target infrastructure during normal work hours (9:30 – 15:30 Monday to Thursday)

IT departments should establish a Progress Management Office to centralise skills and knowledge of project retardation, to prioritise across project portfolios to identify those most in need of braking, and to provide common templates and tools for progress slowing.

One of the most effective mechanisms for slowing a project is the RFC (a.k.a. Request for Chains) which allows IT Operations a range of opportunities: requests for further information, postponed CAB meetings, requirements for further documentation or testing, and outright rejection for incorrect just-about-anything.

Another important tool is the Cant Chart, which tracks interdependencies between tasks in a graphical way, in order to show why certain tasks can't be done yet.

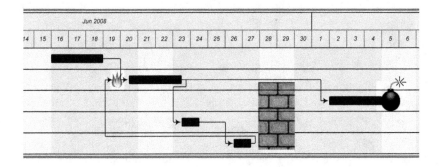

The meta-lifecycle

Writing a presentation today, I was reminded again of the biggest hole in the ITIL content, even ITIL3. ITIL3 now describes the lifecycle of a service, and does an excellent job of it. But where is the guidance on how to implement the ITIL process machinery to manage that service through its lifecycle? Where is the lifecycle of the lifecycle, as it were - the meta-lifecycle?

ITIL2 had the very good *Planning to Implement Service Management* which was a start - sort of an orientation course before one set out. But nobody has done a Route Guide on the Road to ITIL or a Phased Approach to ITIL Maturity.

ITIL3 only makes the need more pressing. ITIL3 has - quite rightly - raised the bar. As I discussed in the latest *Skeptical Informer* newsletter, ITIL3 looks a long way away for someone just starting their ITIL journey, and the core books only really describe the destination.

The complementary guidance books are a handy catch-all answer for any deficiency in ITIL3, but a guidebook along the path to ITIL maturity is a stand-out candidate for the first book off the block. If I didn't already have one book long overdue and assorted other projects on the boil, I'd have a crack at it myself.

The cynic in me wonders if this gap is too big a revenue generator to all the consulting firms for OGC to ever rectify it.

How can we speak of implementing ITIL or measuring the results of ITIL if ITIL ought to be an ongoing (unending?) process of continual service improvement?

ITIL is indeed not about implementing something new - it is about improving the maturity of existing processes. They exist even if the level of maturity is so low that everyone is unaware of their existence.

However experience shows that ITIL improvements cannot be introduced in your spare time, that any ITIL initiative that is run as part of BAU (business as usual) is generally doomed to fail. ITIL initiatives are more successful if the investment is initially packaged as a project to plan, design and make the changes required to get things going. This makes it easier to fund, it ring-fences resources, and most of all it gets the attention so as to effect real cultural change (hopefully).

Only once this has been done can we move from a capex step-change to an ongoing opex activity to maintain and improve our newly matured processes.

In order to do this there ought to be defined success criteria and measurable ROI (even if this rule is often breached).

It is this sense that we talk sloppily of "implementing" or "doing" ITIL (I'm as guilty as any). We are referring to the completion of the initial measurable body of work to set the organisation on the path of ongoing self-improvement.

I too prefer an incremental approach, addressing the pain spots. But I don't think "viral" works. I believe people need to understand that we don't do things the way we did any more. Formalising dysfunctional process areas works. So does defining the interfaces to other areas and clearly delineating ownership and accountability.

So does introducing a standard language and mindset to the organisation. None of those work well virally. Get in with an allocated team of people, fix the broken stuff (yes assess/plan/architect/implement), and start an ongoing process to keep it alive and make it better over time. And if that CSI process is not formally defined and measured with ownership then anything you changed will be gone in 24 months.

People say:

You can't "do" change without config, or release, or...

You can't "implement" incident management in just one area or team or...

What they really mean is "You can't get to maturity 5 in ..." Sure. But you can move existing process up a notch on the maturity scale in one or two process areas in one part of an organisation. But if it isn't approached with rigour and commitment, it's just dabbling.

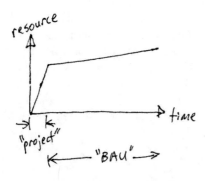

Even the most gradual of approaches needs some initial step to assess the situation, decide the best course, create some sort of roadmap forward, and create the cultural change to make it possible (acceptance, agreement, commitment, education, support).

On the other hand even the biggest of bangs is a waste of

money unless it signals the start of an ongoing process of maintenance, consolidation and improvement of what was achieved in the bang.

So in either case the graph is the same shape - it is just the scales that vary.

The world has forgotten the ITIL principle of "adopt and adapt". And ITIL suffers as a result.

You don't "do" ITIL. ITIL is not a plan to be followed. Instead, you should design what your organisation needs, taking what fits from ITIL and other sources. You can check what you come up with against ITIL (and others) to make sure you are headed in the right direction. You can even assess your maturity against the ITIL reference model. But don't start at book 1 and implement until you get to end of book 5.

If only people saw it this way and used it this way I would be less fiercely critical of concepts like SKMS and CMDB. They make more sense if seen as some idealised infinite-maturity reference point rather than a blueprint for contemporary "good practice".

But people don't. "We are ITIL-compliant", "we do ITIL", "we are going ITIL across the board"... With Version 3, ITIL is "good" rather than "best" practice (yeah I know, I know: I just might be one of the reasons they changed it). No vendor that I'm aware of provides an ITSM course rather than an ITIL course, reviewing multiple bodies of knowledge and the strengths of each. In popular perception, ITIL is how you do it.

People like it that way. They want the decision made, the rules packaged, the path simple.

I think on this point we are pissing in the wind. The world (and V3) long since forgot "adopt and adapt". ITIL is The Way. In effect, in practice, it is the implementation model.

Publications

The tangible part of ITIL is a set of books.

There are several versions of ITIL. In 2007, Version 2 (in this book "ITIL2") was "refreshed" by the new Version 3 ("ITIL3").

ITIL1 is still in print and there are those (a dwindling band of diehards) who swear by the original Version 1 books.

Core

There are a number of *core* books (about nine or ten in ITIL2, five or six in ITIL3 – depending on who is counting) that are the "official" set. These describe the processes that are the "best" way of doing IT operations. They go into a detail about roles of people, activities to be performed, how the processes link together, and so on.

In ITIL2 there was even a "core within the core". Many people mistakenly think that there were only two ITIL2 books: the "red book" *Service Delivery*[1] and the "blue book" *Service Support*[2].

Contrary to popular belief, ITIL is not in the public domain. The books are copyright the OGC, published by the British Government Stationary Office (TSO), now TSO a private for-profit company. Copyright is owned by Her Majesty the Queen (though I doubt she has read them). The trademark is defended by OGC – well, so they say although there are a large number of products using the ITIL name without license.

The books can be bought as old-fashioned books, or as single- or multi-user CDs (ITIL2) or e-books (.pdfs) and online subscriptions (ITIL3).

ITIL books are not cheap.

The minimum ITIL2 set of "the blue book and the red book" will set you back a cool six hundred bucks on CD ROM or half that on paper. The other books tend to run to about the same or a few for about half that much each. So a full set of ITIL2 would not leave much change out of a thousand British pounds on CD or a thousand US dollars on paper.

The main five ITIL3 books can be had as a set for three hundred pounds. Alternatively you can take out a single user annual subscription to ITIL3 for about the same price as the hardcopy books are to buy outright, and corporate online licences are open for negotiation. This is still less than

---

[1] *Service Delivery*, OGC, TSO 2001, ISBN 978-0113300174
[2] *Service Support*, CCTA, TSO 2000, ISBN 978-0113300150

some of the proprietary frameworks and methodologies peddled by consulting firms, but certainly more than the free open content emerging from the Internet MOF, COBIT and FITS are all free.

In addition, *The Official Introduction to the ITIL Service Lifecycle*[1] is often treated as the sixth core ITIL3 book.

Complementary

Then there are **complementary** books that provide supplementary advice and different perspectives. A popular example is the ITIL2 introductory pocketbook on ITIL[2]. They are published by a number of sources, and tend to be priced more like typical business books.

In ITIL3 there are official Complementary books approved and integrated with the core, as distinct from third party publications such as this one you are reading. The first Complementary book is *Passing your ITIL Foundation Exam*[3], and the second is *Building an ITIL based Service Management Department*[4] (about organisational structure, not about the process of getting to ITIL). Coming in 2009 is *Delivering IT Services using ITIL, PRINCE2 and DSDM Atern* (DSDM Atern is not an Irish soldier: it is an obscure methodology that everyone is pretending they had already heard of).

itSMF International has the contract from OGC to produce an ongoing series of translations of ITIL3 into a wide range of languages.

Also considered part of the ITIL3 Complementary Publications is the ITIL Live™ portal[5], a website owned, operated and copyrighted by TSO as a commercial enterprise. And it shows, with individual subscriptions costing £2500 and concurrent commercial user subscriptions costing twice that. What the value is and whether anyone will pay these prices remains to be seen.

Worth a look are the "alternate" ITIL books, not considered officially Complementary, owned by itSMF International and published by van Haren, known as the ITSM Library. Especially notable is *Foundations of*

---

[1] The Official Introduction to the ITIL Service Lifecycle, OGC, TSO 2007, ISBN 978-0113310616

[2] An Introductory Overview of ITIL, Rudd, itSMF, 2004

[3] Passing your ITIL foundation exam: the official study aid, Nissen, TSO, 2007, ISBN 978-0113310791

[4] Building an ITIL based Service Management Department, M. Fry, TSO 2008, ISBN 9780113310968

[5] www.bestpracticelive.com

IT Service Management Based on ITIL V3[1] which is an excellent in-depth coverage (not summary) of the five ITIL core books, but without all the duplication and fragmentation.

Finally there are a lot of third party ITIL books such as this one. Look on Amazon.

Which format to buy

You can obtain the ITIL v3 books as PDFs, i.e. downloaded softcopy Adobe books. Before you buy be aware that the PDFs, although searchable, cannot copy and paste text when quoting an extract from a book, which for me defeats one of only real advantages of softcopy. According to itgovernance [2]

> "PDFs are not networkable, can only be printed once and cannot be copied, cut or pasted...any attempt to copy, cut, paste or move the PDF may result in its corruption...They can only be viewed using Adobe Acrobat 6.1 or 7 (not 8.0) and will need to be activated by visiting the Adobe DRM Activator website."

Strike one.

The other advantage of softcopy is usually portability, but the ITIL v3 PDFs can only be installed on the one machine, which means they are only as portable as your laptop, as compared to the portability of a CD. Van Haren Publishing's itilbooks[3] site says

> "Once downloaded the PDF is permanently stored on your PC. It can be used on another PC provided Adobe reader 6.01 or Adobe 7 has been installed, and by setting up a .Net Passport from the DRM activator site."

Strike two.

Despite the massive reduction in production costs they don't cost any less than a printed book. Strike three.

And even though they are digital, ITIL v3 PDF buyers don't get automatic updates. Strike four... no wait, you're already out. Skip the PDFs.

You can also subscribe to online access to ITIL v3. The online subscription will also give you "Dynamic content, Easy navigation, Bookmarking,

---

[1] *Foundations of IT Service Management based on ITIL V3*, van Bon (editor), van Haren 2005, ISBN 978-9077212585

[2] http://www.itgovernance.co.uk/page.contact

[3] http://www.itilbooks.com/

History, Cross-linking between chapters, Pop-up glossary of terms" and 50% off a hardcopy set of the books. Now for me the only benefit of the online service that I can see (as compared to cool geek features that I don't need) is "dynamic content", i.e. any updates to the text (so far as I am aware there haven't been any yet, and BOKKED shows very few important errors in the texts). This subscription service will cost you almost as much per annum than the books will to buy. Let me repeat that: you can buy a new set of hardcopy books every 18 months for less than the cost of subscribing online. So much for dynamic content. Strike one.

Another thing about online subscription (for me anyway) is that it is less convenient to read in bed or ... er.... other places of deep thought. Strike two.

And I for one would still much rather read paper than pixels (maybe it is just my aging eyes). Strike three.

Which books to read

Which leaves the five books as books. Actually there are six books in ITIL version 3, including *The Official Introduction to the ITIL Service Lifecycle*, written by Sharon Taylor, as a summary of the other five. I think it is pretty good. Certainly a good place to start for those who are not keen to fork out more than five hundred green dollars for the five books.

Actually, as good a place to start with ITIL - and half the price - is *Passing Your ITIL Foundation Exam - The Official Study Aid*. It's cheap, and the first edition has a couple of errors that luckily the IT Skeptic has tabulated for you.

In fact, if you are really on a budget, start with the free *An Introductory Overview of ITIL V3*[1].

The ITIL V3 *Key Element Guides* are now available. These make a good "bluffer's guide": a quick intro to the terminology and concepts. These are the pocket versions of the five core books. Thirty eight quid for the set of five. The V2 books produced by itSMF were good - so are these.

For those who want to start with something with real meat, look at *Foundations of IT Service Management Based on ITIL V3*. It is a condensation of the five core ITIL V3 books not a high level summary. It contains most (if not all) of the content of the Five in just one book and at an eleventh of the price! It achieves this in a number of ways:

- smaller font, more densely formatted

---

[1] http://www.itsmfi.org/files/itSMF_ITILV3_Intro_Overview.pdf

- eliminates all the tedious duplication in the five books (not to mention inconsistencies)

- simplification of some explanations

- omission of some material? I haven't found any yet

After all that you will just have to read the five ITIL books. Don't start with *Service Strategy*, that could lead to internal injury. *Service Design* is a good place to start.

IPESC have endorsed all five ITIL v3 core books (with one country holding out on one book). For those who are wondering, this means that itSMF International now approves of the books and gives them their official stamp, allowing the itSMF name and logo on the books. As if it was ever in doubt. Curiously IPESC did not get to review the *Official Introduction* but the itSMF logo got bunged on there anyway. So much for process. The ITIL V3 *Key Element Guides* did undergo IPESC review.

There have been a whole list of amendments to the five core ITIL Version 3 books. The IT Skeptic has gone through these for you, cross referenced them to the BOKKED database, and listed the ones that are worth knowing about.

Go to http://www.itskeptic.org/node/490

Now here's a thing. A reader uncovered a most interesting deletion from the ITIL V2 Service Support book. Antonio Valle Salas pointed us to an interesting article on his blog[1], entitled "the mystery of the 1.1.1 deleted". So as to save you, gentle reader, from wrestling with translated Castillian Spanish, I hope Antonio will forgive me if I repeat the essence of it here.

In the original edition of ITIL V2's Service Support copyright 2000, which I have a copy of, there is the following text:

1.1.1 Public domain framework

From the beginning, ITIL has been publicly available. This means that any organisation can use the framework described by OGC in its numerous books. Because of this, the IT Infrastructure Library guidance has been used by such a disparate range of organisations, local and central government, energy, public utilities, retail,

---

[1] http://gobiernotic.blogspot.com/

finance, and manufacturing. Very large organisations, very small organisations and everything in between have implemented ITIL processes.

In my more recent edition (Tenth impression 2005), it reads (you guessed it)

1.1.1 Deleted

Isn't that interesting? As Antonio says, I think, perhaps somebody doesn't like the term "public domain" being used now that OGC is on a mission to enforce the Crown copyright. Clearly it never was public domain in the strict sense: it has always been copyrighted, but it obviously was once public domain in spirit. This is an indicator of the changing approach to ITIL as it becomes more aggressively a commercial industry and less a service to the IT community.

My colleague Ross has suggested a technique for dealing with the density of the new ITIL version 3 *Service Strategy* book: read the diagrams, then work your way back into the text sufficient to understand them. For those of us who are graphical rather than textual it makes a lot of sense (and the older I get the less patience I have with text). I tried it and it works for me. Just as soon as he gives me the book back I'll test it all the way through. Tell us how it works for you....

The IT Skeptic does not support infringement of intellectual property rights, but there is a way to access the ITIL Version 3 books (and many others) online that the IT Skeptic believes is legitimate. And free. It is Google Book Search. The number of pages you can view is limited, and text is presented as an image - no copy and paste, but if you want to know all about say Incident Matching or E/CAB, then you get more than enough pages to read up on the topic. It is conveniently on the Web so you can access it anywhere. For links to ITIL books, see http://www.itskeptic.org/node/1076

Certification

There is no OGC-ratified certification of organisations or software in ITIL, but there is certification of individuals and accreditation of trainers and training organisations.

The basic certificate is the ITIL Foundation. A large proportion of staff get ITIL Foundation certificate as part of many ITIL implementations. This is referred to as "sheep dipping". It is often overdone, but it does produce a few zealous project supporters.

There are a number of ITIL Intermediate (called Practitioner's in ITIL2) certificates to train specific ITIL roles in the organisation.

An ITIL Expert (previously ITIL Manager's or Master's) certificate is currently the top qualification.

A higher ITIL3 Advanced level of qualification, confusingly now called an ITIL Master's, is under development.

All of these qualifications provide a useful indicator of basic knowledge, but be aware that they are based on a few days or at most a week or two of training, followed by a multiple-choice exam.

They require no practical experience, no practical or written examination, no peer review, no ongoing professional development, no re-certification, and certainly do not include the level of study of a tertiary degree.

...I try to keep this information current on the blog at http://www.itskeptic.org/node/535, along with the following info too...

Most readers of this blog know this stuff but certainly not all so here's the IT Skeptic's shaky understanding of the world of ITIL V3 certification. I welcome corrections and elaborations.

Your certification for ITIL version 2 was either issued by EXIN or by ISEB - there were two competing schemes. EXIN are a commercial Dutch-based operation with deep roots in ITIL's past. ISEB are run by the British Computer Society. Both seem well-meaning but V2 certification was a mess and needed cleaning up.

V3 certification is managed by APMG, a commercial British operation who [updated: are contracted to the OGC to provide services for] ITIL (and Prince2) accreditation and certification (beating out EXIN and itSMF and others? in a tender). Now ISEB and EXIN have to pay tithe to APMG, and APMG are bringing them all into line on a single certification scheme.

APMG are somehow advised and assisted in policy by the murky ITIL Qualifications Board. Don't be fooled by the word "Board" which implies some sort of independence: the Board is closed to all but the vested-interest training industry.

Under APMG there are now six or seven Examination Institutes (I can't keep up) not just the two, but they now all deliver the same exams and theoretically the same syllabus to the same (I think low) standards.

Those Examination Institutes in turn accredit Accredited Training Organisations, ATOs, who have to pay tithe to the EIs.

The ATOs deliver training to the masses. The exams are delivered online by APMG via their website.

Foundation exams are also available via Prometric (and EXIN? and ISEB?) without an associated (official) training course. Unfortunately APMG have decided that only V3 Foundation will be available this way.

The fact that there are a number of providers of unaccredited training materials or online courses who rely on Prometric to deliver the final certification may have something to do with this.

We have spoken at length on this blog about the unseemly commercialisation of ITIL. Many firms feed at the trough right now, but the IT Skeptic predicts the trough is about to get higher and harder to reach.

ITIL V3 drags the big picture back to the centre instead of conveniently marginalising it as in V2. Now ITIL implementation is business strategy and process implementation. What do any of the ITIL service providers know about

- business value networks

- governance of outsourcers

- reorganising the business with IT as an integral part

- feedback systems

- pricing models

This is really going to open the ITIL market up the consulting giants that have been sniffing at it for some time. It is no accident that one author is from Accenture.

Especially in large, complex organisations, emptors should caveat: purchasers should check closely the references and qualifications of consulting providers. They need to bring pure business consulting to the table to play in large ITIL Version 3 implementations. I put it to you that all but one or two of the current ITIL consulting firms, including the big software vendors, can't.

Secondly, ITIL Foundations training has already become commoditised. People do it over the web. The market has discovered that anyone with a few brains and a bit of self-motivation can pass without paying for expensive training. The entire training market is fiercely competitive - I would say verging on over-supply – and Version 3 is not going to help matters, despite the fervent hopes of the industry.

Sure there will be a feeding frenzy of "bridging" training, but then the party may be over. Not only will the broadening of ITIL bring more big players into the market (see above), but there is the little matter of the Advanced [now called Masters] layer.

I predict the Advanced training, yet to be specified, will be designed for delivery by "real" training institutions: universities and colleges. It is only a matter of time before some offer a Batchelor of Service Management. Then all the existing V3 diploma qualifications (the old Manager's and Practitioner's) will be offered as year one papers, only with more prestige.

So ATOs and ITIL consulting firms better eat up now while the trough is still low enough for them to reach it.

It is high time the IT industry in general and ITIL in particular had some robust qualifications beyond some facile multi-choice at the end of a few days lecturing labelled as training.

Oh wait, that's what they've turned the Manager's into isn't it? I had a lot of respect for the fact that the old Manager's exam was one of the few real exams in the industry. Now we've dumbed it down to the illiteracy levels of the new market: the USA.

So if they dumb the Advanced down too that would be tragic. On the other hand, what am I thinking? No way are Pink and Fox and HP and others going to let them hand it over to universities, for reasons described above. Guess we'll have a half-baked Advanced too.... sigh.

When I did my V2 Foundation - from Pink Elephant - it was 3 days. It is only in recent years it has been shortened to two by some providers in some countries. Since this seemed to coincide with the expansion of the US market, the cynic in me says this is because Yanks have the attention span of a TV commercial. (Ever notice how American TV programs -

especially the "hard" ones like documentaries - explain the story so far all over again after a commercial break. Why is that?)

APMG and the ITIL Qualifications Board are insisting on using multi-choice exams to certify ITIL V3 competence for Intermediate and Expert level qualifications. We have discussed this already across the blog but allow me to summarise the arguments against it here.

As argued elsewhere on this blog, by me and others, multi-choice:

- might be wrong, or open to debate (the examiners are not perfect), but there is no forum/medium for arguing a better answer. It is extremely patronising to assume that the examiners always know better and are always completely right in a complex domain like ITSM. There are anecdotal reports of people arguing with the orthodox position in their V2 Manager's exam essays and getting a pass because of it

- should be crisply back or white. The V3 exams reportedly have a very right answer and a less-right answer. This sort of subjectivity indicates that the answers are opinion-based not fact-based

- test the ability to recall sacred texts or guess eight correct letters. This is not a test of somebody's ability to communicate complex ideas, to write articulately, or to argue subtle multi-faceted positions, all of which I would regard as essential in Expert and probably also Intermediate level roles

Multi-choice is good for testing basic facts with one clear right answer. How many questions can you come up with in the ITSM domain that meet that criterion, especially questions suitable to test above Foundation level?

Here is a Real ITSM[1] exam question:

7) For which audience are multi-choice questions best suited?

        a) kindergarten

        b) primary school

        c) trade apprentices

        d) gossip magazine sex questionnaires

I see your point [in a comment] about being able to "understand and leverage the concepts in their work" - if that is all the certification is for

---

[1] www.realitsm.com

then just grasping the concepts is enough. To me an OSA [Operational Support and Analysis] Intermediate qualification should indicate someone is fit to operate a Service Desk or to be an internal expert/champion or the owner of related processes. I'd say a process owner needs to be able to document, teach and promote the process.

At Expert level I think the expectation is that it qualifies someone to be a consultant or an internal expert/champion of all of ITIL and there is most certainly an expectation that they can communicate concepts to others articulately.

In both levels, the real world will present complex situations which will not be as clear-cut as the multi-choice, where subtle decisions have to be made. The ability to argue and reason and weigh factors is just as important as a grasp of concepts. Multi-choice does not test this. Essays do.

If the certifications only indicate that the person has a basic grasp of core concepts then multi-choice is probably enough. I'm not sure that is how they are perceived, especially the Expert one. We need some sort of professional certification and obviously APMG and co are not out to provide it. But in the absence of anything else I think the ITIL certifications are being used for more than certifying basic facts.

In most countries a driver's licence consists of a multi-choice, an eyesight test, medical certification and a practical driving test. The licence indicates you are able to operate a car. And yet for ITIL they only have to pass the multi-choice, no practical exams, no test of basic capability, before they are let loose on the "roads".

Passing any kind of exam is a developed skill. If you are skilled at writing essay answers I think you are better equipped to write proposals, process descriptions, promotional newsletters etc than if all you know is how to tick one of four.

Multiple-choice exams test how well someone can do multiple-choice exams. Depending on how well written the questions are, they might also test some understanding of the topic ... or not. With good technique you can get a pretty good score with limited knowledge.

We had this sample question discussed here recently:

19 Which is the first activity of the Continual Service Improvement (CSI) model?

a) Assess the current business situation

b) Carry out a baseline assessment to understand the current situation

c) Agree on priorities for improvement

d) Create and verify a plan

...which is ambiguous at best.

And buraddo made the comment that

> ...multiple choice (which when written in ambiguous form as per this blog entry example or using the classic, which answer is more right than the others trick) is still a test in english comprehension and not understanding... Its not whether they make you think, but whether they make you think about the right stuff. I have no doubt that they are challenging, but an accomplished student can always win over an accomplished subject matter expert.

I long ago learned effective multiple-choice technique:

1. Analyse the question:

    a. What is it actually saying?

    b. What is the Boolean logic? Sort out all the NOTs/ANDs/ORs to find out what they are really asking

    c. Any tricks?

2. Eliminate the obvious wrong answers. Usually you are now down to two

3. Look for a subtlety in the wording of one that would eliminate it

4. Now make a value call to pick from any remaining options

5. When all else fails, guess. Usually you are down to two so you have a 50/50 chance. Even if they penalise wrong answers [which I don't believe ITIL does - anybody know?], you might still like those odds.

...so multiple-choice tests your ability in Boolean logic, English comprehension, subtlety of meaning, and judgement calls. Some basic understanding of the terminology is required to also understand the questions. Equipped with those skills and this process you should scrape a pass in most multiple-choice exams.

But only the very best-written multiple-choice questions actually test competency in the subject.

My pet hate is examples such as the #19 discussed above. This question does not test knowledge. It tests memorisation by rote of the list in the book. Which one comes first? Depends on where you start: CSI is a circular process. In the book the process starts with one particular point, but knowing that has more to do with treating the ITIL books as holy writ to be memorised and less to do with understanding what service improvement is all about.

Other examples of memorising the sacred texts are:

"Which of the following is NOT described as a function but as a process..."

"Which of the following is NOT one of the 7 Rs that must be answered for all changes..."

ITIL V3 is big business now. An ITIL certification counts, and people pay good money to get one. Questions require expert writers, rigorous quality assurance and - an IT Skeptic hobby-horse - effective feedback and review.

After a wobbly start that I think arose from having the vested interests in control, the exams seem pretty good now. Feedback on this blog was about 50% positive. But there are still some bad questions out there. So far I'd give OGC a C pass for preparing the exams.

Certifications in the IT industry are so wimpy that ITIL Manager's looks tough. But stack it up against any undergrad or postgrad IT degree and it is just a test. Perhaps one day soon there will be plenty of ITSM-related degrees for it to compete against and it won't count for much any more.

A comment from Michiel talked about "ITIL is more and more part of the curriculum of universities and colleges". There is one more step for the tertiary institutes to take: from teaching awareness and general knowledge about ITIL to providing industry-recognised certification.

I'd love to see tertiary institutes emerge as accredited competitors for Expert and Advanced level training. Foundation and Practitioner are so short as to hardly count as a tertiary qualification but the higher two might - should - have enough meat to perhaps amount to one undergrad paper.

The alternative scenario is probably more likely: The existing training vendors keep their grip on governance of the qualifications and shut the tertiary institutions out. The tertiaries create their own Bachelors and Masters degrees. The industry finally realises that a year or three spent studying ITSM counts for far more than a commercial Expert or Advanced certificate and these become irrelevant or relegated to entry-level.

I can just see the university prospectus:

> Batchelor of IT Operations Engineering
>
> 12 credits required
>
> ITIL Advanced Certification: 1 first year credit.

Approved practical experience: 1 credit per year, max 6.

As someone who spent six years getting my own (non-IT) degree I've never quite understood the respect accorded an ITIL Manager (sorry folks). Folk say "it takes weeks of study and the exams are really hard". People who think ITIL Manager's is tough (or expensive) have either never been to university (common in IT but very rare in other engineering disciplines) or forgotten what it is like.

I for one would prefer to employ someone who studied for more than three weeks and knows more than one idealised model. There is a lot of context here, and ITIL3 has massively raised the bar by introducing strategy and design. Since ITSM is a people problem not a process or - god forbid - technology one, I'd be very happy to utilise someone who had a PhD in Organisational Behaviour - I see that as very relevant.

I also see it as very threatening to the computer geeks who so often consult in ITSM, with less people skills than the Soup Nazi.

I am in wholehearted agreement that ITIL certifications should be based on practical experience. They aren't. Anyone can sit the ITIL Manager's cert. Pink can bluff all they like about the "intended audience" - I've never heard of them turning down anyone's money.

Decent professional qualifications don't look like ITIL V3 certification. It is better than nothing but worse than many alternatives.

We don't need all graduates. The current ITIL certification program provides "cannon fodder": people who go in to battle. What it does not provide is the experts to do the high-level planning, or for the training. I think the friendly neighbourhood ATO should have someone who has a decent qualification and/or some real experience, instead of the "kids in suits" we sometimes get now, one page ahead of the students.

So the current system and a tertiary system both have their place.

But just as those who build a bridge are not all engineers, I wouldn't have anyone but an engineer design the thing. And I'd prefer that they were all trained by an engineer. Right now ITSM has no qualified engineers.

The IT Skeptic provides links to free ITIL Version 3 practice exams to help you on your quest for ITIL V3 Foundation certification. The IT Skeptic has not worked through them so we make no comment on the quality of the questions, but evaluating that yourself is a useful exercise. See http://www.itskeptic.org/node/542

10 things

...they don't want you to know about ITIL Version 3. Some time ago, in response to a fairly inane "10 Things You Should Know About ITIL" on the internet, the IT Skeptic posted "10 Other Things You Should Know About ITIL". To save you looking they were:

1. There is no evidence for ITIL

2. CMDB can't be done, not practically, not as defined in the blue book

3. ITIL is the opinion of a select few

4. There is no public feedback or contribution mechanism for ITIL

5. ITIL may or may not be "best"

6. You cannot certify a tool or an organisation in ITIL, only individuals

7. Formal SLAs may or may not be a healthy way to relate to the business

8. ITIL tries to be more than it really is: a set of Service Desk practices

9. ITIL is not public domain, or free

10. There are a number of alternatives , some of which are public domain

Continuing the theme, it is time we had "Ten Things You Should Know About ITIL Version 3". The first thing you should know is that there actually Fifteen Things:

1.   ITIL Version 3 is only a Refresh. The intention was "to clarify the guidance and improve its relevance to business needs today, not to rewrite it". Changing from seven books to five, moving from a process-centric to a service-centric approach, slimming down the core and spinning off content to complementary books, introducing the lifecycle, adding business strategy, peeling off requests from incidents ... these things are not a re-write, they are just a refresh. So relax.

2.   Your certifications under ITIL Version 2 will still be recognised under Version 3. Whether they will be the least bit competitive in the job or consulting markets is another question. Right now the job and consulting markets are booming so it won't be much of an issue until the market starts to contract. Ooh, no, wait, some people think it already is. Two bridging courses are available to allow you to migrate your certifications across: The ITIL Foundation Bridging Certificate In It Service Management (ITIL V1/V2 Foundation to ITIL V3 Foundation), and The ITIL Manager's Bridge Certification In It Service Management (ITIL V1/V2 Manager to ITIL V3 Diploma).

3.   The V3 equivalent of an ITIL Manager is an ITIL Diploma, now called an ITIL Expert, and possibly to be renamed again [it wasn't].

4.   All ITIL Version 3 exams are being developed by APMG, a private for-profit company, the new outsourcers of ITIL certification and trainer accreditation. The governing body advising APMG is mostly made up of the biggest vendors (HP x 2, Pink Elephant, Fox IT, BMC, CA, EMC, IBM, ITpreneurs, Itilics...).

5.   ITIL books are published by TSO, a private for-profit company. TSO does very little marketing, relying on itSMF volunteers and other vendors. In fact the ITIL Version 3 worldwide launch was organised, executed and funded by itSMF with sponsorship that reputedly did not shave significant contribution from TSO.   TSO thanked itSMF by undercutting them in book sales to the biggest global organisations.

6.   The core is supposed to be "slimmed down" from version 2 and more will be put in the complementary books that go around the core. The original intent was that everyone will need the five core books. I suspect pretty much everyone will need one or more, but not all, of the complementary books too, though what is in the complementary set is not clear yet.

7.   There will be an online portal at www.itil-live-portal.com – it says so in the *Official Introduction* on page 150. This may or may not provide the longed-for official ITIL community. It seems to be owned by TSO but there is nothing there yet. No hurry I guess. [It didn't. It became ITIL Live™, which at £2500 per annum is a very exclusive community.]

8.   The books came out on May 31st 2007. Only the books. Only the core books. We are still waiting for the web portal, a full qualifications scheme, complementary guidance (other than the online glossary, *Passing Your Foundation Exam*, the pocket *Key Element Guides*, and a rewrite of *Small-Scale ITIL*), or the CMDB Federation's interoperability standard, so you could argue that ITIL Version 3 isn't fully out yet.

9.   There is no process model for ITIL Version 3. It has been suggested at various times that there would be one, but what has been published so far is nothing of the sort. Boxes and arrows do not make a process model. At a minimum one expects that each of the boxes is a process, with defined inputs, actions and outputs. This is not true of the diagram labelled "process model" in the *Official Introduction* p154 or the one on the OGC website (which is administered by APMG).

10.   There is no rush. Everyone is getting excited but think about it: complementary books not appearing yet; few certified in Version 3 beyond Foundations; nobody experienced in implementing Version 3 for some time yet. Although the core set of books are supposed to be stable, the

complementary set is intended to be revised regularly, and even the core set are intended to have "updates and amendments" (in fact there has quietly been one already).

11.   ITIL V3 represents "good practice", i.e. proven generally accepted practice. Except where it isn't. Parts of ITIL V3 are speculative utopian models untested in practice, e.g. Service Knowledge Management System. And other parts are hotly debated, e.g. value networks. These parts look the same as every other part – you need to know.

12.   itSMF International now owns a competing complementary body of knowledge called the ITSM Library. Even TSO sell it. There is no guidance as to which one should be used when. Even itSMF was confused enough to initially embargo the publication of the books after buying them. The ITSM Library originates out of the Netherlands, edited by Jan van Bon and published by Van Haren Publishing.

13.   OGC is publishing white papers to explain how ITIL V3 aligns with ASL, COBIT and ISO20000. The books don't tell you. The answers are:

- COBIT: not published yet [roughly ITIL is a subset – see p268]

- ISO20000: close but no cigar. The paper plasters over most of the cracks but can't cover up the lack of Known Error or SKMS in ISO20000.

- ASL: they don't. Described as "Living Apart Together". The IT Skeptic's interpretation: they have divorced but stay in touch occasionally.

14.   And no-one tells you how ITIL aligns with the Project Management bodies of knowledge PMBOK and Prince 2, which is pretty important now that ITIL has muscled into Application Management. *Service Operation* gives Project Management two paragraphs (p165), and not as part of Application Management. *Service Transition* gives Project Management a couple of paragraphs too, but appears to duplicate all of its functions in the Service Transition plan (p40). *Service Design* spends more time on it (p31-32) but only vague directions to keep the project honest, not details of how the interface might work between Service Design and Project Management, and never once mentioning PMBOK or Prince 2.

15.   Nowhere on or in the five core books, or the *Official Introduction*, or the *Key Element Guides*, does it actually say "Version 3". You are supposed to know.

Blue sky

At the request of a fellow skeptic, I am asking readers to name one, just one, example of an ITIL V3 Service Knowledge Management System, SKMS, in the wild. Not the beginnings of one or part of one, or a bastardised version of one. Just one fully formed, grown up, functioning SKMS. Name one.

I too doubt that there is even one real SKMS anywhere. To be a SKMS it should:

- provide full lifecycle management from acquisition to disposal for a 'complete' inventory of CIs ST [*Service Transition*] p65

- ...where those CIs include business cases, plans, management, organisation, knowledge, people, processes, capital, systems, apps, information, infrastructure, facilities, people, service models, acceptance criteria, tangible and intangible assets, software, requirements and agreements, media, spares... ST p67-68

- Contain the "experience of staff" ST p 147

- contain data about "weather, user numbers and behaviour, organisation's performance figures" ST p 147

- record supplier's and partners' requirements, abilities and expectations ST p 147

- record user skill levels ST p 147

- record and relate all RFCs, incidents, problems, known errors and releases ST p77

- group, classify and define CIs ST p72

- uniquely name and label all CIs ST p72

- relate all these items with multiple types of relationships including component breakdown structure, composition of a service, ownership, dependencies, release packaging, product makeup, supporting documentation... ST p72-73 including "part of", "connected to", "uses" and "installed on" ST p77

- integrate data from document stores, file stores, CMDB, events and alerts, legacy systems, and enterprise applications, integrated via schema mapping, reconciliation, synchronisation, ETL and/or mining ST fig4.39 p151

- provide tools against this integrated data for query and analysis, reporting, forecasting, modelling and dashboards ST fig4.39 p151

- take baselines and snapshots of all this data ST p77

- perffrom verification and audit of all this data ST p81

- be based on a Service Management information model ST p150

- measure the use made of the data ST p151

- evaluate usefulness of reports produced ST p151

...and so on and so on.

The IT Skeptic thought ITIL V2 CMDB was a silly idea but not everyone agreed. Surely a larger proportion of readers can see that ITIL V3's SKMS has gone to a new level of absurdity.

How many organisations blew a fortune trying to do data warehouse only to see little or no return on their investment. The idea of doing an equally ambitious exercise solely to service IT Operations is just daft.

This idealised techno-fantasy of the SKMS is so detached from practical reality as to be ridiculous. Anyone who embarks on this journey is squandering resources with an irresponsibility that is breathtaking... and destructive.

I think the word for the SKMS is "aspirational", something to aspire to.

Me, I aspire to twelve hectares of native bush, a Mazda MX5, and riding every railway on Earth with my son. Not unreasonable but there will never be a "business case", any more than there will ever be a business case for the process geek's aspiration to have everything nice and tidy, done right. Nice to have but nothing my wife is going to sign off on right now (actually she WOULD sign off on "nice and tidy, done right").

I would also like a deck round three sides of the house, and some concrete for the hillside behind the house so the hillside doesn't come join the house. Those would add value to the house but probably not a good return on the investment. And they are beyond any rational budget right now.

If you don't have a SKMS what will you lose? Well, you'll lose information. At times you'll make mistakes that could have been prevented with a SKMS, or have to rediscover information that could have been preserved in a SKMS. Will the mistakes cost more than the SKMS? I doubt it but that is up to the business case - occasionally maybe.

Then there is a second, less-often-asked question. Even if the business case stacks up, we live in a finite world. Is this the best use of limited funds? I would say even less likely than there being a good business case.

An aspirational object gives us an optimal model - something to steer towards, a final objective perhaps never attained but at least providing shape and direction to what we do.

Finally the book does not warn us about this. It does not say "Don't try this at work". No, it (*Service Transition*) just says "a consistent set of high-quality guidance", "world-class Service Management expertise", "The aim of this publication is to support ST managers and practitioners in their application of ST practices", "This publication supplies answers", "This publication explores industry practices", "document industry best practices". Nothing about "some of this has never been tried before". Section 4.7.5.1 and a few paragraphs elsewhere vaguely allude to SKMS as a planned implementation over time, but nothing about "WARNING: the next bit is a highly speculative future vision".

So, let us beware those who equate SKMS with Configuration Management Database (CMDB) or ITIL V3's superset of that the Configuration Management System (CMS) ["Are you the People's Judean Liberation Front?" "No f*** off, we are the people's Liberation Front of Judea"[1]]. SKMS is to CMS as Windows Vista is to MS-DOS. No, as Windows 2012 is to MS-DOS.

So SKMS is nice to have, but it is seldom a sensible decision to build it now. It gives us something to work towards so long as we don't see it as a blueprint for CMDB (just as Bill Gates' house gives me something to work towards as I plan my deck).

And as for CMDB, I think my views are clear. Just start at the top of this article and substitute "CMDB" for "SKMS": nice to have, seldom a good business case, almost never best use of funds.

Every so often discussion on this blog touches on something fundamental. Lately we've been examining how ITIL seems to have a bet each way: it wants to be proven and bleeding edge at the same time. This is dangerous for the very people ITIL is supposed to serve.

> There is a real danger in my mind that ITIL v3 can be seen as having moved away from being a practical guide into the area of theory...There is a legitimate case for ITIL to be ahead of the game in terms of suggesting novel approaches, but they should be sign posted as such. Conversely there is not enough sign posting of those things you must do if you are going to deliver effective services.

---

[1] Monty Python's *Life of Brian* – in the author's opinion possibly the funniest, most insightful film ever made.

A better term than "best practice" is "good practice" and an even better term is "generally accepted practice", like GAAP for accountants. Either ITIL is Generally Accepted Service Management Practice or it is providing thought-leadership for where ITSM should be going in the future. It says it is the former, and everyone thinks it is, but it behaves as if it is either, depending on the author and the chapter.

Here are some possible reasons ITIL has wandered off from GASMP and contains unproven bleeding edge ideas:

- the authors want to be clever

- OGC wants ITIL to stay current for another ten years without having to go through another Refresh

- ITIL is now a handbook for consultants not end users

- Parts of ITIL are there to generate new markets for the vendors and/or consultants

You pick, or suggest others.

There are no clear indicators in the books of which ideas are which. They should be colour coded; blue for safe proven GASMP; red for theoretical ideas suggested to the industry as a future direction [at least one of the books could just be printed on red paper]. But they aren't.

This is dangerous for the very people ITIL is supposed to serve: those who need guidance in ITSM. If they know enough ITSM to differentiate when ITIL is being pragmatic and when it is being blue sky, then they don't need the books.

CMDB

The IT Skeptic is probably best known for strident criticism of the concept of CMDB as described in ITIL, and of ITIL3's extensions of the concept to CMS and SKMS.

This is my Second-to-Last Word on CMDB. The IT Skeptic is over it now [Lies! He still gets all het up], but discussion continues and the Skeptic's understanding of this area does actually mature. So this may not be my last word on this topic, but it endeavours to summarise everything to date.

CMDB can not be done

A CMDB is a central database of information about all objects managed by ITIL, and their inter-relationships.

ITIL adopted the concept of CMDB from the start. It is the only technology concept required in an otherwise process framework.

ITIL2 was vague about whether CMDB had to be a single physical instance of all the data. ITIL3 is clear that it isn't, except in the places where it is vague.

Look carefully at any project proposal to see to what extent a Configuration Management Database (CMDB) is planned. The IT Skeptic maintains that CMDB can not be done as ITIL defines it with a justifiable return on the investment of doing it - it is such an enormous undertaking that any organisation attempting it is going to burn money on an irresponsible scale. Organisations that need to get their Configuration Management processes to a CMM maturity of 4 or 5 are probably going to have to attempt it; others will generally struggle to cost-justify the effort.

Put another way: a company could put a man on the moon. It would be great marketing. Whether that would be the best use of funds is another matter.

It should be disclosed here that this is a minority opinion, but not a lonely one. The CMDB engenders much debate (see www.itskeptic.org/cmdb).

In brief, the requirements are complex, especially the amount of data to be gathered and maintained, the integration of systems, and the compliance and audit requirements.

CMDB as ERP for IT

It has been argued that CMDB integrates data for IT in the same way that ERP systems do for the enterprise as a whole. Whether ERP is a justifiable project is in itself a fascinating debate - we've all seen ERP bring companies to the brink of ruin ... or over it. I never saw an ERP project run to business case projections. There are organisations big enough, diverse enough and screwed enough that ERP might just return on the investment. But to say it justifies CMDB is like saying that because DHL own their own jumbos, the ten-truck company down the road from me should buy one too. No, that is not right. It is like saying that because DHL use jumbos to move product, DHL should also use them to get the milk for the cafeteria. Just because a mega-gazillion software behemoth provides the ERP of a total organisation does not mean that something like it is a sensible use of funds just to manage the objects in the IT environment.

What happens is that ITIL convinces people they need a jumbo but they only have budget for a billy-cart. Then they get up on the roof and the inevitable happens.

Living without CMDB

Neither ERP, relational database, data-dictionary, repository, nor directory succeeded in unifying our environments. Nor will CMDB (nor Web Services nor SOA nor .NET nor ...). Lighten up and stop trying to find one repository to rule them all. Let our data be a little untidy. Let go of that old "everything has to be complete and correct" mindset. Live without CMDB. People are doing fine without CMDB now. In statistics for implementation of ITIL processes, Configuration Management is always one of the lowest percentages. One 2008 survey[1] said 30% of very large organisations (those who can afford it) claimed to have something they called a CMDB. The IT Skeptic estimates[2] that between 2% and 5% of IT organisations have a fully-implemented as-defined-by-ITIL CMDB. This raises the question of what everyone else does.

Incident-Problem-Change works fine on top of a single asset database. It is not that important whether Availability or Release or Continuity or Financial or other disciplines use the same repository – the perfectionists love it if they do but there is no great downside if they do not. It is nice to store those basic "depends on" links to show the key CIs[3] which services depend on. My experience is that most organisations can manually maintain these service mappings for about ten to fifty services. Yet most have two to ten times that many services. They all seem to end up pragmatically picking the top services to store the mappings in the database.

What happens to the rest? They wing it; they work it out on the fly; like they always did. It works. You can do without CMDB, so long as you are aiming at not too high a maturity level, say 3. If we aspire to a moderate level of maturity, then yes we can do without a CMDB. Plenty of people do. They may have an asset register, a systems management tool auto-discovering the network, a purchasing system, maybe even a service catalogue. But they don't have a CMDB as defined by ITIL.

---

[1] *How to Develop Your CMDB Project's ROI*, EMA, 2008, whitepapers.techrepublic.com.com/abstract.aspx?docid=386941
[2] www.itskeptic.org/node/732
[3] CI = Configuration Item, ITIL geek-speak for "thing"

On the other hand, if you are NASA or Boeing or Tata or EDS, ignore me. You want level 5 maturity and you'll need a CMDB to get there ... or rather you'll need to start working on a CMDB. The IT Skeptic is still not convinced you will ever get to the idealised model. It is going to cost you trying.

CMDB building.

We don't need one, but we have to have one. Everyone else is. The books say so. It would be neat. This is the area of Real ITSM worst affected by Excessive Technical Fastidiousness, or ETF (discussed further in *Categorisation*).

The best strategy is to decide to build a bespoke custom CMDB. The resulting project will happily run for years designing, data modelling, coding, integrating, extracting and reporting, best known as "the three D's": Design, Development, and Data.

Second best strategy is to buy one. Nobody can actually sell you one of course. CMDB is an aspirational concept, like holiness, or honesty.

The tools foisted on us by the vendors are asset databases with bells on, or network monitors with a whistle on top, or desktop managers with fluffy dice. This means you will embark on a customisation and integration project that is close to the effort required for the roll-your-own CMDB.

And then there is the data population exercise. If you have made the data model sufficiently broad and fine-grained (which is where they all end up) then you can keep several staff amused for years just finding, loading, labelling and inter-relating all the Stuff.

Either way, go for the full solution from the start: phased approaches might actually finish.

A critique of the concept of CMDB

A CMDB is sometimes compared to the wheels of a car. 95% of the cars on the road have no wheels or tires? I don't think so. 95% of cars have no GPS navigator, which is a far more valid analogy for a CMDB. A GPS navigator can be a very useful tool to high-intensity, mission critical drivers, such as emergency services or couriers. In the same way a CMDB shows benefit to the small percentage of sites that are so big or complex or critical that the tool is worthwhile. CMDB isn't essential like wheels. It is nice to have: a gadget like a GPS navigator that occasionally has a valid business reason for existence but mostly is there to appeal to the geek driving.

To understand the fundamental issue with a CMDB, consider the scale of the project. To meet the ITIL requirements, you will have somewhere between 10,000 and 10,000,000 objects in the CMDB. How will you populate the CMDB initially? The vendors' silver bullet solution is auto-discovery. It can find out something about many things, but not everything about all things. It won't help with disconnected devices, or financial information, or physical location. Ask how they go with finding UPS, PABX, embedded computing in factory machinery, or building security and cooling systems.

Maybe half the objects can be auto-discovered initially, but only half the data about them will be discovered. Warranty, contractual and other data still needs to be manually loaded. So expect between a few person-months and a few person-years to load the initial data, with or without auto-discovery (see below). The problem then is that any manually collected data is out of date before it is entered.

How will you keep it current and accurate? By good tight Change Management which ensures the CMDB is updated whenever anything changes. How will you know if an error is made or someone subverts the process? The vendors' silver bullet solution is ... auto-discovery and comparison with the CMDB. Most tools don't do correlation of discovered data with CMDB data out-of-the-box: you will need to develop audit jobs to scan and report on discrepancies. And then develop manual report-and-review processes to deal with all the conceptual and logical entities the auto-discovery processes don't know about.

So expect a significant development effort to build quality control processes and tools.

Let us turn our attention now to the core of the CMDB that distinguishes it from a simple asset database, the relationships, or links, that define how each CI is interconnected and interdependent with its neighbours. A single parent-child relationship is not enough. We have relationships such as "is physically networked to", "is responsible for", "depends on", "depends on but only at the end of the month", "depends on to meet a gold SLA but can manage without it for silver"...

Not to mention dealing with redundancy. Say we have seven web servers, equipped with load balancing and automatic failover. If one fails, what will be the impact on the SLAs? How many can we take out for maintenance without degrading performance? How to record that in a CMDB? How to define "broken"?

Consider the permutations between half a dozen relationships, with embedded business rules, and thousands – or hundreds of thousands - of objects. Capture those and keep them current.

If the whole thing could be automated then the problem might go away with enough hardware, but we are far away from having that kind of intelligence in the tools. The relationships are often conceptual and sometimes subjective: only humans can infer them. Any IT shop big enough to cost-justify someone maintaining those relationships is too complex for them to maintain them within reasonable cost. Or if they did manage, the cost would not justify the return. That resource would have been better deployed fixing problems or processing changes or answering calls or a hundred other tasks than maintaining an anal book-of-all-things.

We are not done yet. Let us crank up the complexity by another order of magnitude. The probability of the CMDB being one integrated database is virtually nil. No vendor has technology that can manage the whole environment from .NET objects to telephones, so all CMDBs will be a federation of multiple vendor repositories.

The problem is that many organizations have multiple discovery tools to glean information from the same components. A federated CMDB must prevent data duplication, as well as be able to understand that different pieces of data gathered by different tools--an IP address, patch level, a host name--all belong to the same component. This process is called reconciliation, and experts say it is critical to a successful CMDB.

There is as yet no standard for CMDB database integration[1] so all interfaces will be custom built[1].

---

[1] A standard is proposed. It is slowly evolving towards an official public standard. Some vendors are already demonstrating inter-operability using it.

The CMDB is in its infancy. There are no standard definitions of what information goes into a CMDB, no schema for structuring that information, and no standards for integrating data from disparate vendors. While the CMDB promises a host of benefits for the enterprise, it is horrendously complex, lacks implementable standards, and is rife with proprietary exploitation. At present, there is no standard schema for the data that's supposed to reside in the CMDB. Any CMDB implementation that aims to import and utilize data sources from disparate vendor tools will require manual integration.[2]

Vendors have rushed to fill that definition vacuum with their own implementations. For instance, Computer Associates created a data schema that is consistent across its own product line. This data schema populates the company's version of a CMDB. HP has been shipping a CMDB with its Service Desk that uses Web services to pull application information across HP's product portfolio. BMC Software's Atrium CMDB is shipped as a component of, or can be integrated with, eight BMC applications, including the IT Discovery Suite and the Remedy IT Service Management Suite.

However, all these CMDBs are essentially proprietary extensions to the vendors' own product suites. "There's no standard in the industry for how a vendor should build the data model inside the CMDB," says [Ronni] Colville. "There's a huge propensity to lock into one vendor for all of this." [3]

Some organisations will further multiply complexity by implementing a stand-alone "universal" CMDB which is a data-warehouse-style copy of all the other data, synchronised with the other vendor repositories.

(As an extension of an existing organisational data warehouse, re-using the infrastructure, this could be a useful approach for change management and other processes that do not need real-time information but it is less useful for incident management.)

If you want something that meets the ideal CMDB specification you are going to have to build it:

But it defines query semantics only: there is no standardization of the data model between vendors. www.cmdbf.org

[1] For you geeks out there: ask how many integration interfaces support two-phase commit protocol to ensure transactional integrity when changes are made.

[2] Demystifying The CMDB, Andrew Conry-Murray, IT Architect, 8/01/2005 www.itarchitectmag.com/shared/article/showArticle.jhtml?articleId=16640 0731&pgno=1

[3] The jury's in on the CMDB - or is it? CMDB adoption in the real world, Network/Systems Management Newsletter, Dennis Drogseth, Network World, 05/29/06 www.networkworld.com/newsletters/nsm/2006/0529nsm1.html?page=4

Every vendor claims to have a configuration management database (CMDB) or a CMDB strategy. Yet they are merely playing off Information Technology Infrastructure Library (ITIL) hype in this area and don't really have all the necessary functionality required for a true CMDB: reconciliation, federation, mapping and visualization, and synchronization. Rather, many are taking their domain-specific configuration repositories (such as for desktop or server configuration management, asset management, or help desk), adding one of these functions and calling it a CMDB. [1]

While the ITIL describes the processes associated with a CMDB, it says nothing about just how a CMDB gets built, how various tools are meant to feed data into the CMDB, how data should be structured inside the CMDB, and how various applications are meant to use that data. ... "Customers are just trying to get a handle on what a CMDB can do," says BMC's Emerson ... Enterprises that attempt to roll out a CMDB as a silver bullet for all their network management ills are likely to be disappointed. The difficulty of interoperability and the lack of standards mean a fully realized CMDB may be years away. [2]

My concern is that the convergence of architecture and process - and frankly often inflated vendor marketing - that now seems to be driving CMDB interest is complex and confusing. And CMDB technologies and standards are also very "early in the game." I am concerned that too many IT expectations are moving towards the notion of the CMDB as something that IT can simply buy to fix its woes. And this, of course, is both dangerous and false. While I am a big CMDB believer, I view it, like ITIL, as an enabler for more efficiency, improved compliance, better governance, etc. But it is not really a "thing." It is the beginning of a journey... [3]

So stack another development effort on to your estimates, to build the integration interfaces. Since these do not support two-phase commit, transactional integrity cannot be assured, so you will also need consistency reports, and repair policy and processes (mostly manual).

And now the sting: after all that, I don't believe CMDB is going to make that much difference to your ITIL processes. You won't be able to automate any but the most basic impact analysis (the sort of thing that vendors demo). The most sophisticated modelling tools on the market struggle to predict performance degradations, yet many SLAs put at least

[1] CMDB or Configuration Database: Know the Difference, Gartner RAS Core Research Note G00137125, Ronni J. Colville, 13 March 2006
mediaproducts.gartner.com/gc/reprints/ibm/external/article5/article5.html
[2] Demystifying The CMDB, Andrew Conry-Murray, IT Architect, 8/01/2005
www.itarchitectmag.com/shared/article/showArticle.jhtml?articleId=16640
0731&pgno=1
[3] The jury's in on the CMDB - or is it? CMDB adoption in the real world, Network/Systems Management Newsletter, Dennis Drogseth, Network World, 05/29/06 www.networkworld.com/newsletters/nsm/2006/0529nsm1.html?page=4

as much importance on performance as availability. Tools struggle to predict availability whenever IP networks are involved, especially if the internet enters the equation (though complex intranets are challenging enough).

So after all that time and money a human is still going to have to look at a proposed change or detected outage and make a judgement call; better informed than before, for sure, but still operating on imperfect information. Perhaps that money would have been better spent on a few nicer reports and exploratory tools, and another change management person, and a golf course for the staff.

In the past, companies wasted fortunes and diverted key resources for years trying to have one common relational database, and/or one common enterprise data model, and/or one repository of meta-data. They are doing it again trying to have one common repository of identity, or one repository of objects or Web Services... or a CMDB. The sooner technologists and vendors stop peddling this kind of magic fix the better off we will all be.

The problem is that CMDB is an inappropriate underlying concept for ITIL. It is fundamentally at odds with the basic principles of ITIL: pragmatic and conservative use of existing environments in better ways; fixing processes not technologies. CMDB is an alien intrusion in the ITIL world. It is a nice-to-have technologist's fantasy peripheral to core requirements.

ITIL is about fixing the people and the processes, and only then implementing pragmatic tools to help them. CMDB is the only major example of ITIL describing what-should-be rather than what-is-and-how-to-manage-it, and it fails the test of common sense.

We have devoted a whole appendix to criticising this one concept. No other aspect of ITIL receives this much attention in this book. CMDB is the least-thought-out part of ITIL so it presents the greatest danger of misspent funds, and requires the greatest awareness and vigilance from management.

To be clear: there is a distinction between having a repository of useful information and having a full ITIL CMDB. We need a good database under the service desk, and under the systems management and under the financials. But they are not the same as an ITIL-defined CMDB. We are not warning against collecting data. The IT Skeptic is against attempting to create the all-embracing, multi-relational monster that ITIL specifies. I try to use CMDB only when referring to that Hydra, and not the subsets of it which are generally useful (such as asset database, or network status monitoring).

Much of what we read about CMDB is actually singing the praises of asset management, network discovery or other simpler technologies. Other benefits attributed to CMDB actually come from process improvement and do not depend on the technology at all. When all you want to sell is a hammer...

I missed this article when it came out: *Strategies for justifying CMDB ROI*[1]. Forgive me for quoting extensively but I think the article is peppered with false assumptions about what a CMDB is and what it does.

> "Determining an ROI around CMDBs and ITIL is hard, because we're talking about productivity gains," said Jay Long, manager of IT service management at Forsythe Solutions Group Inc., an IT consulting company based in Chicago. "One of the big benefits of [CMDBs] is return on avoided outages, but that's tough to calculate because there's no empirical evidence available."
>
> A February 2007 study by Framingham, Mass.-based research firm IDC identified a potential pitfall of CMDB projects: organizations' difficulty in articulating the ROI that justifies the time, money and effort. In particular, the study noted that making the case for a CMDB's ROI tends to focus primarily on short-term cost savings. The problem, of course, is that many organizations will realize savings only in the long term -- that is, once a CMDB has been up and running for a while.
>
> Further such longer-range savings won't become apparent unless you invest the time and effort to develop process standards for change management. Then a CMDB can support improvements in service delivery, which can generate cost-saving benefits.

So is it the tool which is providing the ROI or the improved processes? Guess which one I think.

> All told, a large enterprise may spend several million dollars and up to three years to get a CMDB fully functional, according to EMA...
>
> IT managers who have deployed CMDBs cite several additional areas of savings:
>
> - Reducing or eliminating unnecessary servers and other hardware
> - Better license and maintenance contract management
> - Tighter management of outsourcing agreements
> - Labor savings

---

http://searchdatacenter.techtarget.com/news/article/0,289142,sid80_gci1 285976,00.html

No, that's asset management. All of these benefits focus on the better management of individual physical CIs, with no reference to their conceptual groupings (services) or their inter-relationships, the attributes that characterise a CMDB.

> "In terms of server management, our costs are primarily in resource time and manpower," Giblin said. Now information on the hospital's 100 physical servers, such as names of host bus adapters, are included in the CMDB. "We don't have to go out and physically touch the machines anymore," he added. "This takes our server management up a notch."

Asset management again.

> The real value of CMDBs comes from service excellence, and fostering a service-oriented culture," said Long. "Service resolution time, business alignment, customer satisfaction—that's what we're talking about at the end of the day."

No, that's cultural change. It needs no technology to be done effectively. If tools are involved, a Service Catalogue is a much more effective artifact for focusing minds on a service-oriented culture than a geeky inward-looking technology-centric CMDB.

> But the biggest payoff from CMDBs comes when organizations use them to gain visibility into configuration information to make better decisions about change management processes... According to Drogseth, one of the best ways to frame the ROI argument (at least in terms near and dear to a financial analyst) is to look at repair times. "The dominant metric for financial types is reducing the mean-time-to-repair," he said.

It is true that this is CMDB's biggest payoff. But change impact analysis is not a process under time pressure. The IT Skeptic proposes that just-in-time on-demand assembly of the configuration data is more cost effective [there is an article on this in the pipeline - look for more on this soon]. And the assumption that impact analysis is a major component of MTTR is highly debatable.

> most organizations don't have the luxury of investing in a CMDB and implementing it purely on the faith that a tool will lead to service management nirvana -- and thereby deliver a solid ROI. IT managers should look carefully at the immediate, short-term and midterm benefits they can deliver along the road to nirvana and determine if there's enough there to build a case for a CMDB project.

Go, sister! Finally we agree.

Asset management is not CMDB

Tighten up acquisition processes and you ought to have a good list of assets in the environment, but this will not address:

- all the stuff already out there

- in-house developed code

- database instances

- logical entities like services and owners- configuration (in the sense of "setting") info: e.g. web server config, routers etc etc- stuff that sneaks in anyway: e.g. rogue project servers and personal wireless hubs

- purchase clerks don't know anything about the relationships, which are what differentiates the CMDB from existing asset databases

- relationships and dependencies change over time

In short, an asset purchase register is not a CMDB.

A better place to tighten up the tracking is in Change Management.

If every change process includes a step to update the CMDB (where has it moved to? what was installed on it? what services depend on it now? what does it relate to now? ...) then in theory every CI should be properly tracked, and Change Management and Config Management staff ought to know the relationships better than anyone, and care about getting them right. By definition, if Change doesn't control it, Config isn't interested in it.

But even then, that still doesn't address:

- all the stuff out there already

- subversion of Change process (nobody can say it doesn't happen, deliberately or inadvertently)

Auto-discovery is not a panacea

For those who have never heard of "auto-discovery" it has nothing to do with navel-gazing. It is a software function that automatically examines a network and finds out as much as it can about what is out there.

Some tools just find the physical devices on the network ("assets"). Others go much deeper to examine hubs and switches for configuration, and servers for memory, storage and installed software ("inventory"), or even down to executing code, database objects, application objects, and transactions.

Most tools cannot auto-discover the software layer and the inter-relationships of software components across nodes. Web Services is making this almost impossible because it is so loosely coupled.

Few (if any) tools can auto-discover the logical functions (not counting demo situations). And no tools can automatically relate those functions to business processes. And no tools can automatically relate those processes to ITIL services. And no tools can automatically relate those services to business units and stakeholders. And no tools can auto-discover and relate SLAs or UCs or….

Using it to regularly and automatically populate a CMDB is a direct violation of the principles of Configuration and Change Managements. All such changes should go through change control for two reasons. First, when such automated tools get it wrong they do so either spectacularly or insidiously. Either way they should be subject to human review. Second, and much more important, the idea of Change Management is to know about changes before they happen, not to try to automatically detect them afterwards. Change is the chain-link fence to keep alligators out of the swamp, not the net to haul them out after they get in.

Even using auto-discovery to report what has changed or if new elements have been introduced should not be a business-as-usual function. We should know about them via Change Management. Auto-discovery is used as an audit tool for exception reporting to detect subversion of change control.

Audit is one valid use of auto-discovery. Another is to help populate the CMDB in the first place. The key word here is "help". There is no silver bullet. Auto-discovery can find out something about many things, but not everything about all things. It won't help with disconnected devices, financial information, physical location, UPS, PABX, factory machinery, or building security and cooling systems. This will require a team of people to capture and load the data. The result will be imperfect: any manually collected data is out of date before it is entered.

Maybe half the objects can be auto-discovered initially, but only half the data about them will be discovered. Warranty, contractual and other data still needs to be manually loaded. So expect between a few person-months and a few person-years to load the initial data.

Vendors like to talk up auto-discovery because it is sexy, it is technology (i.e. they can sell it), and it looks like a silver-bullet solution to one of the most intractable problems of CMDB: discovery. Of course it isn't but that doesn't stop them painting it that way.

P.S. We usually think of using the auto-discovery tool to validate the data, but how do we validate the tool's output?

Root Cause

What does Root Cause mean? I use a model of Direct Cause, Contributing Cause, and Root Cause. I'm not sure where it came from originally but it shows up often enough.

Some software tools are pretty good at finding Direct Cause because that is the easy bit and that is often defined in technology terms.

Contributing Cause is the old "it takes two mistakes to make an accident [incident]". We would have weathered the Direct Cause if not for the Contributing Cause.

If we fix the Direct Cause it is going to happen again until we fix the Root Cause. i.e. Root Cause = Problem.

The IT Skeptic loves to generalise and over-simplify. In my simple little world, the Root Cause is the one when you keep asking "why?" and there are no more (useful) underlying reasons. See the scenario below.

Root Cause is more often a process problem than a technology problem. The only way to find those is to have human(s) look at it, which means you won't do it for every incident. In general you'll only know Direct Cause for an Incident (if anything). You do RCA for Major Incidents and for Problems.

In order to keep us all entertained, ITIL v3 appears to use Root Cause only in the glossary. Likewise SFA appears only in the glossary (CORRECTION: ITILv3 discusses Service Failure Analysis in detail on pages 108-110 of Service Design – pages 397-399 of the PDF version).

SFA no longer means what I used to use it to mean ("Sweet Fanny Adams" is the mild version), but now means Service Failure Analysis.

In the books they refer to Kepner & Tregoe's "true cause" (V2 SS p 119, V3 SO p62).

To me

> root cause = true cause = problem
>
> usually = process error

Vendors are making a fuss about their Root Cause Analysis (RCA) features in their tools. People Process Things once again: who says Root Cause is in the technology?

The lowest level event message is often not the Root Cause, so drill down data is only a symptom ... Root Cause is often a procedural error [i.e. human not machine] and no software can detect it.

When geeks invent tools to fix technical problems it's great. When they try to invent tools to fix people and process problems it's not so great.

Root Cause Analysis requires a bunch of people in a room walking through what happened and building fishbone diagrams. The root cause is not necessarily technical. My belief is that it is almost never technical.

> The SAN crashed
>
> Why?
>
> The firmware update failed
>
> Why?
>
> We were missing a patch
>
> Why? Did we check?
>
> Yes we checked but the patch wasn't on the vendor's public support system
>
> Why not?
>
> They hadn't rated it critical
>
> Why not?
>
> Human error
>
> Did we contact the vendor to check required patches?
>
> No, we just looked for criticals on the system
>
> Will we check with them for all required patches before the next upgrade attempt?
>
> Yes
>
> And we want a letter from the vendor saying they've fixed whatever process failed to recognise it as critical

So the cool tools tell me Root Cause was the SAN. Crap. Root cause was a negligent vendor and a negligent engineer doing the upgrade.

Vendors make this song and dance about the RCA feature in their products, but it is only a gizmo. It provides one useful input to a RCA discussion, nothing more. There is no automating RCA.

Definition of a CI

The ITIL meta-data sucks. There is no good definition within the ITIL materials of what the data should look like (the best you will find is on page 164 of the blue book). So "officially" there is no answer to your question. As a result there is much debate.

Is the DNS name of the server an attribute of the server or the primary object name? Yes. Whatever. Your call. I would say that service management is about user-oriented computing, so using the DNS as the primary object name is unlikely to be meaningful to many users. Others will argue that doesn't matter as the user sees the service not the underlying CIs. More debate.

When the server's memory is upgraded or the operating system is upgraded is a new CI created? No, the properties of the server have changed. Unless of course the memory in the server is itself a CI, which is entirely permissible - but daft.

When a server is replaced with a new box completely -- is this a new CI? Probably, because among other things the CMDB should support Financial Management.

Does it have a historical tracking to the older technology box? Yes, because a CMDB maintains checkpoints over time. There is a physical CI which is the server ("HP Unix box A12745") and there is a logical CI which is the function the server performs ("webserver #1"). The current version of the CMDB relates the new box to the function. A historical checkpoint of the CMDB relates the old box to the same function.

A pragmatic approach

There is a boundary problem to CMDB: no matter how good your CMDB tool and processes, there will always be CIs that matter to your environment but are outside the reach of your CMDB: closed proprietary data-stores, service providers' networks, itinerant devices that attach casually, paper documents... So if you are going to have to interface from your repository to another somewhere, it does not matter where. If you have three repositories, each holding 33%, how is that worse than three holding 90%, 5% and 5% respectively? You will never get to 100% so settle for what you have, whatever it may be. CMDB zealots need to lighten up and learn to love mentally reconciling and integrating data from multiple sources.

It makes sense to automatically maintain dependency information where that can be automatically maintained. There are tools that crawl a network and discover the network connections, interrogate SNMP and Windows and ask all about what a device is and what is on it, and they will monitor said devices for status and performance. The good ones aren't cheap but the cheap ones aren't bad, so the business case stacks up.

Most tools cannot auto-discover the software layer and the inter-relationships of software components across nodes. Web Services is making this almost impossible because it is so loosely coupled (especially with UDDI involved). No tools can auto-discover the logical functions. No tools can automatically relate those functions to processes. No tools can automatically relate those processes to ITIL services. No tools can automatically relate those services to business units and stakeholders. And no tools can auto-discover and relate service contracts.

What shall we do with no single universal CMDB? What we always did, though ITIL asks us to do it better. Only people can really analyse impact. Only people can reconcile conflicting information. Only people can deduce how complex systems will respond to perturbation. No tool in the foreseeable future is going to have the smarts to do what ITIL asks of Configuration Management. The functions of Configuration Management that are defined or inferred in the process are people functions. Stop trying to automate them. ITIL is about improving process, not throwing technology at the problem.

Vendors will talk about the risk of having that analytical data and power in people's heads. It is true there is an exposure here to key people. It is a risk we recommend taking for the same reason we knowingly take so many other risks in business: because the cost of mitigating the risk is too high.

IT people also seem fixated with "one ring to rule them all" solutions: relational database, corporate data model, data-dictionary, repository, executive information systems, dashboard, portal, middleware, directory, and SOA. Getting everything in one place appeals to our tidy minds, but history shows the effort is usually not cost effective and falls short of the ideal mark.

Configuration Management is very appealing in concept: have a process that gathers together information about all the objects managed by IT and their inter-relationships. Provide views into the data so that staff can walk the relationships to understand the impacts (ideally the business service impacts) of changes or outages. The repository of all this data is the CMDB.

Make sure those working on ITIL understand the distinction between Configuration Management the process and CMDB the technology. You need Configuration Management the process. You do it now, at some level of maturity. People keep this data in their heads, in spreadsheets, in databases, inside tools.

Understand what level of maturity you need to get to with Configuration Management the process, and how critical it is to your organisation that you can access the data and how quickly you need it.

Only then can you decide whether you need to implement a CMDB.

Probably all companies that actually manage to get something working (many don't) will then benefit from CMDB. The real question is whether the benefit justifies the cost (often not) and whether it was the best use of the funds (usually not). For a small proportion of companies who are very complex or for whom IT is really critical, CMDB pays off.

CMDB appeals to the technoid's desire for a technical fix to a cultural and procedural problem. Technology does not fix process.

The IT Skeptic has seriously proposed[1] an alternative approach to keeping all the Configuration data centralised and current: assemble as much of it as you need *on demand* in response to a requirement.

Consider if we created the configuration data when we needed it in response to some particular situation instead of trying to maintain it all the time in a CMDB.

This is nothing new; it is what we do now. We create data ad-hoc anyway when we have to. If the data is not there or not right and management

---

[1] *On Demand Data and the CMDB*, ITSMWatch
http://www.itsmwatch.com/itil/article.php/3782211

wants the report, we gather it up and clean it up and present it just in time, trying not to look hot and bothered and panting.

How much better if we had a team, expert in producing on-demand configuration information? They would have formal written procedures for accessing, compiling, cleaning and verifying data, which they would practice and test. They would have tools on the ready and be trained in using them. Most of all they would "have the CMDB in their heads": they would know where to go and who to ask to find the answers, and they would have prior experience in how to do that and what to watch out for. Instead of ad-hoc amateurs responding to a crisis, experts would assemble on-demand data as a business-as-usual process.

They would understand basic statistical sampling techniques. When management wants a report on the distribution of categories of incidents, they would sample a few hundred incidents, categorise them properly according to what the requirements are this time (after all how often does an existing taxonomy meet the needs of a new management query?) and respond accordingly.

They would be an on-call team, responsive to emergency queries. "The grid computing system has died and the following servers are not dynamically reconfiguring. Which services are impacted and which business owners do we call on a Saturday?" They may not know the answers off the top of their heads but they will know - better than just about anyone - where and how to look to get the answers, and how long that is going to take.

Certainly we would need some basic CMDB data kept continually. This would be the stuff we discover automagically already, such as procurement-driven asset databases, or discovered network topologies and desktop inventories, or the transactional information captured by the Service Desk. Add to that the stuff we document on paper already (or ought to): the service catalogue, phone lists, contracts and so on.

The savings in not trying to go beyond that base CMDB data would be great. The price paid for those savings would be that "on-demand" does not mean "instantaneous". It might mean hours or days or even weeks to respond to the demand. So a business analysis needs to be done to find out how current the data really needs to be (as compared to what the technical perfectionists say). In some organisations the criticality demands instant data and they need to trudge off down the CMDB path. But for the majority of organisations this just isn't so.

Sure there is a cost when no-one can find Fred. There is a similar cost when everyone acts on incorrect information because it came from a computer so it must be right. To err is human - to really cock things up you need a computer. Personally, I'd be checking with Fred anyway which kinda renders all that fancy-work redundant in my eyes...

Go on, prove me wrong. Prove a tool can do CMDB functions as well as a person or better. Set up a complex environment of integration, reconciliation, synchronisation and whatnot to give a single virtual view over data from umpteen sources.

Then measure the amount of work invested to build and maintain that versus the work to manually do it ad-hoc as required.

Then propose changing something in the Citrix load-balancing and check the impact analysis from the tool against the impact analysis from Ralph the sysprog.

Use your new tool to drive automated notification and SLA impact reporting, then stand back at your next Priority 1 outage and see how much it gets right; who gets called, what turns red?

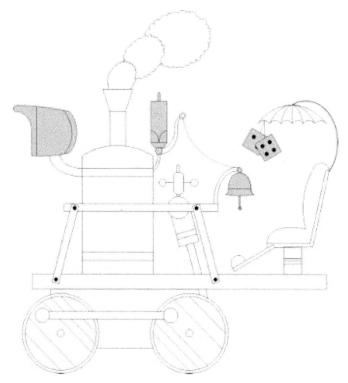

The illustration, Vendor CMDB, is from the author's first book, *Introduction to Real ITSM*

CMDBf

Cooperation between vendors over CMDB? I'd like to see that.

The major operations software vendors have released a white paper[1] describing how they plan to cooperate on ITIL CMDB. Don't hold your breath waiting for anything to come of it.

The CMDB Federation, a vendor consortium, has at last released a document describing their cooperation over CMDB. The good news is that CA and Microsoft are on board now, along with the original members BMC, Fujitsu, HP and IBM.

The original press release said a draft specification would be out by the end of 2006: The specification is still nowhere to be seen. Surprise. Getting these vendors to work together is like putting six cats in a suitcase.

The idea is a good one. This initiative is essential for the IT operations software industry in general, not just CMDB vendors. We need a fundamental common CMDB standard and this could be it. And proprietary lock-in is a big problem for consumers and this standard could go a long way towards solving that issue.

The document strikes me as sound, but not profound; documenting the obvious so they can all agree. It is not explicit in the document that the CMDB will include real-time status information. In places it is only implied: "Application (transactions) monitoring application ... Resource monitoring application(s) ...- Event analysis application ..."

In other places I get the impression the data is fairly static: "... performance records, event logs ... A federation service provides the interface to add, modify, and delete resource definitions."

Without status data it is hard to understand how incident management or proactive service level alerting can be supported. Without it this won't be the IT operations Babel-fish we seek either.

"Storing information that associates resources with services ..." is left to later. This is a cop-out. The exclusion of this issue supports my contention that deducing and tracking relationships between "real" CIs (configuration items) and abstract services is too hard for the current technology.

WARNING: Vendors may wave this white paper around to overcome buyer resistance to a mixed-vendor solution. For example, if you already have availability monitoring from one of them, sales people from the

---

[1] http://cmdbf.org/CMDB-Federation-white-paper-vision-v1.0.pdf

others may try to sell you their service desk and use this paper as a promise the two will play nicely.

Well they may — one day. Look at the timeline. It has taken the best part of a year to get the gang together and produce an in-principle white paper for comment. I would say it would be optimistic to expect a draft spec in anything less than another year since the devil is in the details.

I am still sceptical there is any real commitment by the parties to a result, as compared to be seen to be doing something. That need has now been fulfilled for a while.

One reason the big vendors may not want a standard is open source monitoring tools already threaten the growth of their markets. If the lower-cost tools can get past proprietary barriers, they can elbow their way into existing clients much more easily.

The main reason it will not happen though is politics. These companies have a poor track record of sticking together. The press rooms are littered with announcements of cooperative partnerships; Hollywood marriages last longer.

People outside the industry don't always realise just how viciously competitive it is and everyone will be playing games for maximum advantage. For example, who brought Fujitsu to the table? Any number of service providers could lay claim to having CMDB expertise (don't tell me Fujitsu claim status as a tools vendor on the strength of the internationally famous Systemwalker). Perhaps their presence gives someone two votes?

I hasten to add that this is not a reflection on the individuals involved in this project. The backroom technical people at these organizations tend to be the decent ones. I worked for one of the companies in question for a long time, though I worked at the sordid, pointy end.

I don't doubt the authors of the white paper are having entirely congenial discussions of honourable intent. When I refer to cynical or Machiavellian motivations I am talking about the companies as a whole, the executives who run them, and the games that go on between them.

In the event the specification gets done (and it hasn't all ended in tears first), a formal standard must be promulgated. This is what is needed, and it is the stated intent in the white paper ("adoption and standardization").

Standards gestate like elephants, so add another year or two. If we are lucky, some of the vendors will invest the millions required to support the standard in parallel with its development so they will release the software along with release of the standard. Look forward to that two or three years from now, best case.

What of the vendors not involved? Those already in the club probably figure the task of keeping the original six together is hard enough without encouraging more. Once they get to a standard then everyone else will follow along — they hope. They are taking a gamble. The risk is a competing proposal for a standard, or worse a competing standard. DCML, anyone?

I can't help feeling this initiative would have greater chance of success if it were itSMF- or OGC-driven. Both parties have been conspicuously absent when it comes to driving the ITIL software industry, though either party would have perceived right to do so.

Their hands-off approach is one cause of a peculiar phenomenon: the software industry and their parasitic analysts have seized on the only bit of ITIL that involves a new technology, CMDB, and run off with it. Look at the press release, or a recent ITSM Watch article and a fascinating pattern emerges: The vendors themselves never refer to ITIL in quotes, and seldom is it mentioned in article text. It is left to itSMF to make the linkage.

The consortium white paper mentions ITIL twice at the start and several times at the end, and not at all in the body of the paper. It does not once cite the ITIL books on what a CMDB should be or do (although to be fair the blue book is so light on this topic that such a citation would be there to show respect more than for anything useful).

The ITIL trademark is not acknowledged (other than with a "®"), OGC is never mentioned, and there are no references. ITIL is not defined at any point. There will be explanations for all of these omissions, but I am a great believer in the Freudian slip. You judge.

Finally, this consortium does not operate under the umbrella of any of the existing industry alliances: OASIS, OMG, DMTF, etc. or of a standards body or itSMF or OGC [it does now]. Apparently, this is so they can move quickly. If so, it isn't working, yet. Once you guys get past a jotting of notes by some friendly geeks, let us know, OK?

Way back when, the IT Skeptic said "I am still highly sceptical that there is any real commitment by the parties to a result, as compared to a need to be seen to be doing something. That need has now been filled for a while. "

We have crept up to version 1.0b of the draft specification, dated January 2008, so there has been some change since the first release of the specification.

More importantly the draft has been handed over to the DMTF. But don't expect that to mean a published standard any time soon.

Standards gestate like elephants: it will be even longer before a standard sees the light of day. My latest prediction is that by the time it does emerge blinking, nobody will give a flying fox anyway. CMDB will be, like, so 2007, and IT's chattering classes will be whipping some new concept to fever pitch, safely way out ahead of the possibility of actually building or delivering anything.

William Vambenepe points out[1] that

> I can't help noticing in the press release is that none of the quotes from the companies submitting the specification tout federation, but simply "integration" or "sharing". For example: "integration and interoperability" (BMC), "share data" (CA), "sharing of information" (HP), "view, track and change information" (IBM), "exchange data" (Microsoft). This more realistic assessment of what the specification does stands in contrast to the way the DMTF presents it in the press release : "this specification provides a standard way to federate management data stored in multiple different data models". At this point, it doesn't really provide federation and especially not across different models.

So, more hype and still no results. Nobody is mentioning any dates for the standard to emerge. When that fine day dawns [of a published standard] we'll finally have the ability to build heterogeneous IT management environments. The IT Swami predicts that this will give a tremendous boost to open source tools such as Zenoss. They will be able to displace vendor tools one bite at a time instead of a revolutionary overturning, thus making them far more attractive to companies who want to ease carefully into open source. No wonder there is no great rush to finish this.

Still waiting. Funny that.

The CMDB Federation standards initiative must be the most over-hyped vendor marketing smokescreen ever. Whenever anyone raises the bogeyman of proprietary CMDBs, the vendors wheel this one out as the future promise of interoperability. It is pure vendor double-talk. It solves little and is taking forever to appear anyway. It solves little because the standard defines only how management tools can pass data between them-nothing about what they do internally. I bet the much-trumpeted demos seen so far involved data massaging and informal backroom agreements beyond that dictated by the standard in order to get it all to work. I am

---

highly skeptical (surprise!) about the likelihood that this standard would enable or even facilitate anything useful in a real-world implementation.

It[1] explicitly does NOT define

- The mechanisms used by each management data repository to acquire data. For example, the mechanisms could be external instrumentation or proprietary federation and replication function. (Mechanisms will be redundant and will have no re-usability between tools)

- The mechanisms and formats used to store data. (The internal format, including the internal data model and the unique identifiers is NOT specified. I believe this means you CANNOT easily write a report drawing and consolidating data directly from two CMDB repositories in native fashion). The specification is concerned only with the exchange of data. A possible implementation is a relational database that stores data in tables. Another possible implementation is a front-end that accesses the data on demand from an external provider, similar to a commonly used CIMOM/provider pattern.

- The processes used to maintain the data in the federated CMDB. The goal of the specification is to enable IT processes to manage this data, but not to require or dictate specific processes. (There is zero commonality or consistency required in the concepts, skill-sets, terminology, tools, interfaces and workflows used by operations staff)

- The mechanisms used to change the actual configuration of the IT resources and their relationships. The goal of the specification is to provide means to represent changes but not to be the agent that makes the change. (i.e. the standard is read-only)

- What security mechanisms or protocols should be used (there is no commonality of identity, roles, or policy. Issues such as confidentiality, integrity, audit and privacy will all be dealt with independently and redundantly within each vendor island. Any interoperability will be outside this standard.) (line 1655)

No definition of acquire, store, maintain or change. Doesn't leave much, does it? In short this is once again a geeky technical solution to a cultural, organisational and procedural problem.

Vendors like to talk up auto-discovery because it is sexy, it is technology (i.e. they can sell it), and it looks like a silver-bullet solution to one of the

---

1

most intractable problems of CMDB: discovery. Of course ...vendors are busy painting federation/integration technologies the same way.

Probably because the world is slowly waking up to the hyping of auto-discovery so we need a new hot gimmick to pimp.

My favourite bit of the current draft (lines 483-494):

> A federating CMDB attempts to reconcile the item and relationship identification information from each MDR, recognizing when they refer to the same item or relationship. The federating CMDB performs this identity mapping using any combination of automated analysis and manual input... The determination of identity is seldom absolute and often must rely on heuristics because different MDRs typically know about different characteristics of an entity and thus establish different sets of identifying properties that characterize the entities they handle. Further, the determination may change as additional information is discovered and MDRs add, subtract, or change identifying properties as systems evolve.

There is no standard for the unique identification and reconciliation of objects. The reconciliation between repositories will depend in part on manual intervention.

Another good bit:

> The Federated CMDB operates in a closed environment, in which some security issues are less critical than in open access or public systems. (line 1652)

Tell that to Managed Objects and their MyCMDB.

Then there is the question of the pace at which this beast is moving. Although the document referenced here is dated October 2008 the changelog ends in January 2008, and it is certainly the only output we have seen this year other than one(?) multi-vendor demo. There are zero commitments from DMTF or from the vendors for any sort of timeline for delivery of anything.

The vendors have no interest in ever delivering this thing. Quite the opposite: it will generate a wave of support issues and negative sentiment if it ever sees the light of day. In as much as it does actually make some interoperability possible, it will also present a crack in the proprietary shell for open source management tools. Far better that it should exist as some vague promise of a rosy future.

The next time a vendor presentation implies that CMDBf or DMTF is going to provide seamless interoperability and/or a common data layer, throw something.

Top 10 reasons NOT to implement CMDB

OK I'll bite. One of the nice folk at Evergreen, Jill Landers, posted "Top 10 reasons to implement a CMDB[1]". I'll do the right thing and not quote it in full here so you need to go read that first. Then you can enjoy my "Top 10 reasons NOT to implement CMDB"

1. You would improve overall release, change and configuration management if only you could bring all configuration items and transactions under centralized change and configuration management control... but you can't. I've discussed the CMDB boundary problem before: No matter how much you store in a central CMDB repository, there will always be some data somewhere else.

2. You might automatically discover and map all key applications, computing and network IT infrastructure with sufficient technology and enough investment in its implementation and constant adjustment, but you won't autodiscover the most important information: the relationships of CIs to services and to people (ownership, key users, escalation paths...). That's manual.

3. Having all the data in one place is nice to have, but the actual improvements in efficiency seldom outweigh the enormous investment to get there. Geeks love tidy data, but geeks don't have to pay for it. We've been chasing this "one ring" myth of unification since relational database, through directory, repository, corporate data model, middleware, Web Services... Give it up.

4. Because the essential CMDB relationships (and much of the data) must still be maintained manually, CMDB is as error prone as any other source. After it gives the wrong analysis a few times people stop trusting the machine and go back to asking or at least checking with the guy(s) whose head was the CMDB before the expensive technology came along. CMDBs don't reduce risks, they just change them.

5. CMDBs have nothing to do with enforcing compliance. Auto-discovery will detect a few instances of non-compliance such as unauthorised devices connected to the network but you don't need a CMDB for that, just the autodiscovery tool that comes with most systems management tools these days.

6. Application Management is all about code. While Change Management may store its Releases and Changes in a CMDB, the code

---
[1] No longer online

entities are managed in specialist Software Development LifeCycle tools. CMDB plays little part in coordination across The Wall, the divide between development/solutions and delivery/production/operations.

7. Even Change does not need a CMDB. It needs its records of Changes so it can manage change, and report on MACs and other statistical information. It can do that in happy independence from any other system or process if you want to. Most sites do.

8. The only part of CMDB it is hard to do without is the view of a Service. Somewhere you need to document this. So do it. Use a handy tool such as a Systems management visualiser, or a Service Catalogue tool, or Visio or anything really, and document the relationships between Service and its important CIs. The best place is in the Catalogue (see below). It's manual to find this out, so put process in place so that all Change workflow includes updating it. Get someone to own it. Do everything else the way you always did. There. You have CMDB now. Happy?

9. It really is cool to be able to drill down on CIs via CMDB relationships to perform analysis. It is also cool to hold all your CAB meetings in a Lear jet.

10. You can do without a CMDB. You can't do without a Service Catalogue. This documents what the Services are, the impact on them of changes and outages, who the key people are. Once Catalogue matures beyond a "brochure" catalogue to a technical view for use within IT, it often also documents what the key CIs are for each Service. Just because you don't have a CMDB doesn't mean you can't write the important stuff down somewhere. You must, in the Catalogue.

Part 3:
The IT Industry

Castle ITIL

I didn't set out to be a trouble-maker. But as *the IT Skeptic* blog gained attention for being less than besotted with ITIL, people began posting comments voicing dissatisfaction with what was happening as well. Then the emails started. Whistleblowers came out of the woodwork. Some dodgy goings-on emerged in the ITIL world - in that nexus between the OGC and their agents TSO and APMG, the itSMF, and the vendors.

The whole thing veered into the surreal when a fake whistleblower blew the whistle on a fake fraud in an itSMF USA election. Well, the person was fake for sure and the fraud may or may not have been fake – we may never know.

In one year we had:

- the Institute of Service Management doing battle with Ian Clayton's IT Service Management Institute over USA trademark

- itSMFI flogging off deep discounts at the expense of local chapters to try to keep global members (read; big sponsors)

- A distinctly British government approach to consultation for ITIL3

- Microsoft trying to patent the obvious in CMDB

- backstabbing and pricing shenanigans between supposed partners in ITIL the moment the ITIL3 books actually went on sale

- the itSMF USA election saga with the mysterious vanishing Julie Linden

- itSMF USA's hasty exit of their executive director, James Prunty

- the US DoJ sniffing around the ITIL industry

- itSMFI's insistence on secret governance rules and cursory public financial accounting

- itSMFI's hasty and limited call for nominations for the new Board

- itSMFI declining a significant proportion of nominations for the new Board on what some would perceive to be a technicality

- the election results are then rushed out ahead of the planned announcement at the AGM

- the ITIL3 certification program, syllabi and exams degenerate to something close to fiasco under a barrage of criticism and complaints

- the ITIL certification owners lose their own accreditation from the UK government auditors

- Ivor Macfarlane elected Chair of IPESC when arguably not even a member of IPESC, just an invited representative from itSMFI. This one is questionable enough that rumour has it even some of the incoming Board object.

- Sharon Taylor's title as Board Chair mysteriously disappears. There is no explanation at all on the website but enquiries reveal that the full Board - i.e. all the chapter reps from around the world - decided they wanted the Executive Board to elect its own Chair and that the existing Board had no mandate to run the presidential-style election for Chair already executed.

- The Board calls for nomination for election of a seventh Board member - again without explanation ("never apologise, never explain", or is it "let them eat cake"?). Again the IT Skeptic goes enquiring. The explanation is innocuous: There already "was a co-opted, non voting directorship covering Chapter Services. The 'new' position is really a formalisation of that post [which could not be called for] during the original nomination, as it was not then a formal position." So why not tell the world that so there is some semblance that we know what we are doing?

- So far not so bad but then the new incoming Board, before they have taken up their new positions and before the seventh Board member is even nominated let alone elected, decides in its wisdom to hold a hasty vote for Chair and elects Sharon Taylor back into the position she vacated some days earlier.

- itSMFI finally lifts a moratorium on publication of its own investment venture, the Van Haren ITSM books, imposed because it seemingly hadn't occurred to anyone that buying the books might be seen as competition by their already contracted partner TSO.

About all we haven't seen yet is someone cross-dressing in order to meet their loved one's parents, and a custard pie being thrown.

And remember: this is only the stuff I dare tell you about! OK itSMFI, I surrender. If you stop doing it I'll stop writing about it.

...poor little IT Skeptic could hardly keep up. It is never a dull moment in the ITIL world. An extraordinary contrast to the genteel goings on over at ISACA.

Through 2008, things have calmed down somewhat. There is still a good quota of questionable happenings in the ITIL world but the more absurd excesses seem to have died away. Who knows what part the blog had in that – I suspect very little. On the other hand I know the IT Skeptic has been held up as a bogey-man at least once in emails.

Which is not to say that 2008 was quiet...

The crass over-commercialisation of ITIL has spread from the certification sector to the content itself. TSO is launching a website that provides process maps - something many of us thought would be part of the base product. They'll be clickable with stuff behind them including Visio and Word templates - something else that I for one fondly imagined might be generally accessible.

So what's wrong with that? Aren't we all - including me - in this for the money?

Well yes, but TSO are branding this as a site overseen by the Chief Architect and Authors of ITIL, as an "official" Live site. (It will be amusing to watch APMG and TSO fight it out for who has the real official ITIL portal promised by Sharon back around the launch of the books.)

That too would be OK. What has startled a number of people is the price. "Two and a half thousand fadurkin' British Pounds Sterling per annum" as I put it. Given the way the economy is going that will soon be the equivalent of about ten thousand US dollars. I resisted the temptation to make a joke about mis-spelling "per annum" but really this is too much. The ITIL core official products should be sold at prices that recover costs, give a royalty to OGC for working on the next version, and take a small margin for profitability. The corporate per-concurrent-user price for the TSO site is an eye-watering 5,750 pounds. Holy change control!

ITIL is turning into just another snake oil peddled by shiny suits. A snake oil that has curative properties for sure, but sold by those whose interest is the money not the resulting health of the buyers. We aren't in Kansas any more.

Most users won't care - they will get the boss to pay for the endless Intermediate courses and for the Live portal access. But a minority of us, those who pay for all this voraciousness ourselves, will start to look elsewhere for a less commercialised IP, like COBIT. I use COBIT more than ITIL now. I get the core for free, many of the books for free as an

ISACA member, printed books for less, and far more bang for my buck out of ISACA than I get out of itSMF.

Of course it won't last. The vendors are already sniffing round the wide green fields of COBIT but for now that is where I am headed. Here's hoping the upcoming COBIT User's Guide for Service Managers is closely followed by a certification. Wouldn't that put a cat amongst the pigeons?

I suggested a while back that the COBIT community was just biding their time before they put ITIL back in its place. I think the process has started. Certainly the recently released white paper aligning COBIT and ITIL was greeted with a stony silence by Castle ITIL, and not surprisingly as it was pretty blunt about ITIL's deficiencies in comparison. And the new Service Manager's guide won't help.

Now Microsoft have launched a broadside. It is as if Castle ITIL were watching the COBIT forces quietly gathering strength in the valley below when a flaming ball of tar popped over the back wall. That flaming ball was the release of MOF (Microsoft Operating Framework, a "competitor" to ITIL) under the Creative Commons licence. You can copy MOF. You can cut it up and edit it. You can paste it and build training courses around it and do what you bloody well like with it pretty much, without having to kiss anyone's ring. And you can do a Foundation Certification in it from EXIN.

Not a good month for Castle ITIL. Guess how much sympathy I feel when they are still up to the old games: five days between announcement and closing for ITIL users to respond to a survey on the ITIL Foundations course, for yet another review. I bet they are mystified by all the negative response they got to the last version. Maybe they should try asking the customer base. Properly.

...So for three years the IT Skeptic has hammered on the walls of the ITIL establishment calling for change.

If members don't mind the itSMF being the OGC's pet monkey or a carnival of prancing vendors, then they can just leave it to slide down its current slippery slope.

For the most part, my voice and the clamour of others have been mostly ignored. Which led to the IT Skeptic coining the term "Castle ITIL". Let us consider the attributes of a castle...

Closed doors

Congratulations to Sharon Taylor and all the people who have worked so hard to bring ITIL Version 3 to fruition. The task is by no means over, with the online offerings, the translation, the certification, the party in Sao Paulo, and all the complementary guidance still to be sorted out, but this is clearly a huge milestone achieved.

One ITIL V3 author told me I am a "terrier snapping at the heels of the establishment", and I know that hurts the owners of the heels.

On a personal level I'm sorry for those I hurt who act honestly with the best interests of the ITIL community at heart. I hope you can believe that I respect what you have done with ITIL Version 3 - it isn't perfect and I don't agree with everything, but it is a magnificent body of work. Again, congratulations!

For those who act with selfish or corrupt motivations, I have no sympathy. The blog's primary purpose is not to expose you, but I don't mind if that is a secondary effect.

A comment on the blog suggested I am obsessed with the ITIL Version 3 Launch. I replied:

> I don't think I'm obsessed. I am, in effect, a journalist. Not that I chose to be but that is another story. There is a huge vacuum of open discussion and debate around ITIL that this blog seeks to fill. The Refresh is the big story, the topic on everybody's lips right now, so I report it. Or maybe I'm obsessed. Let the readers judge.
>
> I'd like to get onto some other topics actually but OGC and itSMF keep alternately leaving this void and then providing me all this great material. I look forward very much to the ITIL world becoming so boring that I can look at other topics on this blog, and go do a few other projects that might pay better :-)
>
> You imply that I am delving into unimportant minutiae. Tell that to the Japanese and the Canadians. I for one would be interested in the reasoning behind the change [of countries for the launch roadshow] and I bet they would too. It's called "transparency".

That is this month's theme, transparency: whether it be transparency of the process of creating ITIL V3; transparency of the decision-making processes behind ITIL; transparency of the governance of the vested interests feeding off ITIL; or transparency of governance of the association which is supposedly owned by us, its members (even if it does not, by definition, exist to represent our interests).

For those who wonder what the hell I am on about, go see if you can answer the following seemingly simple questions:

- What are training vendors supposed to say to people who ask them for V2 training?

- What are the new consistent rules for accreditation of training organisations for V3?

- On what basis were the seven countries for the launch selected? Ask to see the minutes of meetings of the Board of your organisation, the itSMF, or of any other body running ITIL

- What is the formal commercial relationship between OGC and itSMF and between TSO and itSMF? On what basis is itSMF organising the worldwide launch of V3 instead of OGC?

- Why do the eight Global itSMF members (all poor, down-on-their-luck international mega-corporations) get deep discounts on V3 that go a long way towards paying back their subscription, while local branches carry the burden of servicing their staff without reimbursement from itSMFI?

- What are the allegations against itSMF USA's last Board elections? How long has the Board really known about them before finally being forced to act?

- What were the vote counts by IPESC for the V3 books, and what were the comments and discussions around them by the people who represent we itSMF members?

- How was the architecture of V3 derived from the 400+ submissions? Can we see the submissions to draw our own conclusions about what the user community wanted?

- What were the views of the reviewers of V3?

- Where are the annual report and audited accounts of itSMFI?

- Given that TSO is now a private operation owned by German banks, what is their contribution to the costs of the V3 Launch?

There is plenty more where that came from. The culture of ITIL's various organisations is trapped in the bureaucratic, secretive, patronising mindset of its origins. When ITIL is eventually displaced or absorbed by what comes next, one of the driving forces of the new model will be the open, inclusive, community-focused culture of the 21st Century. The new kids don't stand for that crap.

And the internet renders it impossible. I hope my blog will help prove that.

...This one got me so riled I had to apologise for the tone of this posting and moderate the language...

The ITIL establishment is still up to its old ways... itSMF International is having a Chapter Leadership Conference. Good. About time itSMF did something to mentor and support new chapters.

Perhaps you are a recognised expert in some area of managing or governing volunteer bodies, maybe a university academic. Perhaps you have worked with say ISACA for the last decade and feel you have learnt a thing or two. You feel you have something of value to impart to itSMF to help this obviously naive and struggling organisation mature. Can you present? No. Look at this:

> The itSMF International is seeking qualified, experienced faculty to present at the first itSMF Chapter Leadership Conference ("CLC")... the follow criteria must be met by selected faculty members.
>
> Required criteria:
>
> Current member of an itSMF Chapter in good standing
>
> A minimum of 3 years experience in Chapter leadership
>
> Evidence of service and commitment to the itSMF Community
>
> Desired criteria:
>
> Recognized industry advocacy, e.g., IOSM Fellow
>
> Extensive public speaking experience
>
> Manager Level ITIL Certification or equivalent (as indication of industry commitment)

Let me paraphrase: if you aren't one of the itSMF establishment you don't have anything useful to say to this organisation...

As I have pointed out before, we aren't in Kansas any more. ITIL is big $$$ and big power games are going on. The criteria for access to the CLC podium are not what a reasonable person might expect in a learning environment. I've my own ideas of where they might originate but I don't speculate on individuals here (unless there is a real good reason). To me it is clear they arise from some undisclosed political motive. The suggestion [in a comment on this post] that asking what that motive is would yield a straight answer is an odd one. I've sent emails asking similar questions and they sometimes go unanswered. If anyone on itSMF Board wanted to respond to my questions they can do so in the public forum on this site, as Peter Brooks and Alex Kist and Rob Stroud and others have done, or they can contact me in private, as a good many have done too :-D But the idea of asking this question seemed a very odd suggestion. No I do not expect that any political organisation in such a commercial environment would reveal the games going on, no matter how honest the individuals. They simply would not be allowed to say.

There are many good people in itSMF but the culture of the organisation as a whole is not a good one and I don't like many of the behaviours it exhibits, hence the "Castle ITIL" moniker. I go out of my way not to attack individuals. In the past I have refrained from revealing information that would impact on personal lives, and I've pulled punches just because I didn't want this to be about personalities.

So I stand by these comments but I urge readers to see them as reflecting on the entity itSMF not the individuals that make it up (mostly).

How to contribute to ITIL: you have several easy options to choose from:

1. Be an author. Wait 3-5 years for the next ITIL Refresh. Tender for one of the books. Be one of about a dozen people worldwide to win a tender. Devote a year of your life to writing a book.

2. Know an author. Get networking now: you have 3-5 years to guess who the next ones will be and get into their professional circle. Then persuade them your idea is better than theirs.

3. Contact OGC to tell them you have some content to contribute. There is no documented process to do this, not any advertised contact point, but OGC are British government bureaucrats so you should find them helpful and communicative if you just send stuff off to any old address you can find. Once you have their attention, they will put you in touch with the next authors. See 2 above.

4. Forget it.

A proposed question for the ITIL Expert exam:

Who of the following is the Queen of ITIL?

a) Queen Elizabeth the Second

b) Pippa Bass

c) Sharon Taylor

d) all of the above

Let me give you some background to help you answer.

ITIL is Crown Copyright. This means the copyright is property of the British Crown.

ITIL is a product of the UK Government's Office of Government Commerce. Pippa Bass was described, in a rare public appearance at the itSMFUK 2006 conference, as "the OGC responsible owner [of ITIL]". Ms Bass is Director of Knowledge Innovation, Standards and Skills at OGC. Or she was last time we heard: British government departments don't tell you who is in charge of anything. Talk to the hand, or rather the cold stone wall.

Sharon Taylor's current titles are:

- ITIL Chief Architect appointed by OGC

- ITIL Chief Examiner appointed by APMG

- Board of Directors of itSMF International, elected

- Chair of the Board of Directors of itSMF International, chosen by the Board

- President (and Board) of the North American Institute of Certified Service Management Professionals

- ITIL V3 author of The Official Introduction to the ITIL Service Lifecycle, in her role as Chief Architect

Who are the mysterious ITIL Qualifications Board? The definitive answer is given here[1] by LCS

> The ITIL Qualifications Board is the official group of ITIL stakeholders who are responsible for the creation and maintenance of both the v2 and v3 Qualification schemes including ITIL certification exam syllabi... The representatives include the official accreditation body APM Group, OGC, TSO, itSMF International, Exam Panel Chiefs for both v2 and v3, Accredited Training Organizations, Assessors as well as representative from each of the Examination Institutes. The only way to become a member is to be the representative for one of these stakeholders.

If you are passionate about certification and/or have expertise in this area and want to be on the Board, you can't. It represents only the money engine. We feel ever more deeply the lack of a body representing the ITIL users. Not the vendors. Not the promoters/marketers (itSMF). Not the practitioners (consultants). The users. The ones who make no money out of ITIL, they just bet their careers on it.

---

[1] http://www.lcsexams.com/pdfs/LCS_newsletter_sept.pdf

So now my question is, has this information ever been officially provided anywhere? And if not why not? Why is it so hard to get public information on the governance and management workings of ITIL?

Real ITSM is represented by the Real IT Service Institute, or RITSI. The Institute is incorporated in London[1]. Membership is inclusive: open to all vendors, consultants, trainers, examiners and publishers without exception (unless we don't like you).

The RITSI Board of Directors is elected by the RITSI Board of Directors. Nominations are open to anyone who we tell. In order to serve its international constituency, the Board meets in resorts worldwide.

RITSI and its agents do derive revenues from Real ITSM, but this income is used solely to fund the cost of operations, the ongoing enhancement and promotion of Real Practice, and the financial viability of the various organisations.

RITSI operates a number of programs for the benefit of the Real ITSM community[2].

DogmaITSM

The integrity of the Real Practice content is of course paramount to RITSI. The Institute retains a part-time unqualified career bureaucrat to govern the ongoing development of that content through the DogmaITSM program.

DogmaITSM keeps the core content up to the state of the art through reviews every seven to ten years. It employs a commercial tendering process to find the most knowledgeable authors. To ensure Real ITSM's relevance to the whole world, authors must be selected from vendors from more than one country.

---

[1] London, Tanzania not London, England
[2] The Real ITSM community is of course the vendors, consultants, trainers, examiners and publishers.

Cavalier

This post was headed "Dirty deeds done dirt cheap"...

The backstabbing and undercutting going on over the ITIL V3 book sales is good news for consumers, but less so for local itSMF chapters, or for those who'd like to see the ITIL world as a respectable place.

I can confirm that TSO sold direct to one or two of the Big Four vendors, causing orders with itSMF to be cancelled. The discount was reportedly 40%.

Now TSO doing the dirty on itSMF is good for consumers. With a bit of luck TSO might get into a price war with their own channels. It is not much sillier than what is going on now.

Of more concern to me is the news that itSMF International will enjoy somewhere around the same discount but is not passing it all on to the local chapters - they are taking a cut.

First this is divisive: any itSMF chapter with a good number of members (not thinking of any imperialists in particular) would be nuts not to join the general backstabbing by demanding the same deal with TSO direct.

Second, it is hardly working for the greater good of the itSMF community. The itSMF International discount was only possible by speaking as the voice of the worldwide membership. By profiteering in this manner itSMFI is clearly showing itself to be a body separate from the local chapters instead of one representative of them. We already pay a 5% tithe to fund them. If this discount is not passed on in full, then local itSMF chapters will be unable to compete with itSMFI selling direct - which they do now to Global members and it seems they might already be doing somehow via the itSMF UK - nor with all the big booksellers and ATOs who are no doubt already ringing TSO demanding their 40% too. If TSO are this promiscuous, it is only a matter of time before they do a deal with Amazon. itSMFI's margin will knock the local chapters out of the game.

As a consumer I think it is wonderful (well I would if I hadn't already bought my books at less than a 40% discount). As an itSMF member I'm less happy, both because of the lost revenue to the chapters and because of the ethics displayed by some of the major players.

...and this one went almost un-noticed by the ITIL world...

The month was marked mainly by a new flurry of itSMF silliness. I know I know. I'm as over it as you are, but when the guy who is the business partner of the person who wrote the book which didn't need IPESC review even though the other five did, gets elected chair of the same IPESC even though he only sits on IPESC as an invited representative of itSMF not as a nominated country member, just after his partner got elected chair of itSMF International in a hasty election by six sevenths of the Board who had been elected in an election where 42% of nominees were rejected ... well what am I to do? Ignore it? Now I'm not suggesting there is anything illegal, immoral or fattening in any of this, but it is silly. Such lack of good governance from an organisation like itSMF is farcical.

...as did this...

I don't see how OGC could have done anything else but accept bids from vendors for writing the books. Few others have both the qualifications and the willingness to commit the resources. Most of the authors have a commercial reason to be involved.

On the other hand, it will be interesting to see how well the concept of "Chinese walls" has been applied or enforced.

One ATO announced on this blog that they had already developed and piloted their initial (I assume Foundation) V3 training by the 1st of May (a couple of weeks after OGC released the materials) whereas another ATO is reported to have only received their V3 materials on 14th of May.

And I know of one IAG [ITIL Advisory Group – see the acknowledgements in any of the five ITIL V3 core books] member from a vendor organisation who has read all five books.

...and this...

This may not come as a surprise to you, but it does to me. I - along with The ITIL Imp - was under the misapprehension that the ITIL Live Portal was going to be free. Nope.

The money engine rumbles on. Now far be it for the IT Skeptic to suggest there is anything wrong in charging for web services. I would rather like to.

But this means the ITIL Live Portal will not be the long-hoped-for official community place for ITIL. It is just another ITIL commercial product. I for one won't be contributing any free content to a commercial site.

It also demonstrates how miserably out of touch with the 21st Century are OGC and the rest of the ITIL establishment. They need to get broadband up at the castle. Right after electricity.

...aaaaaand this...

itSMF International has announced that the ITSM Library (itSMFI's own product for must be about a year now) is a Good Thing. "Any concerns that itSMF International has expressed regarding these books have now been resolved".

It is nice to know that itSMF is about promoting ITSM, not about promoting OGC/TSO's products in particular. The fact that this was ever in doubt was a concern, and primarily revealed that itSMF's relationship with TSO and OGC was much too cosy, and contractual.

One day I'll get the full story of what went on with the transfer of the ITSM Library to itSMFI. It delivered several positive benefits for the ITSM/ITIL community:

- It forced itSMF to affirm that we are not OGC/TSO's lackeys even if we remain their free marketing division

- It allowed itSMF to demonstrate that we are not a one-string-fiddle based solely on ITIL

- It gave the ITSM Library the umbrella protection and IPESC stamp of approval of itSMF, ensuring an alternate voice on ITSM and ITIL into the future

- It revealed the contractual basis (if not the details) of itSMF's relationship with TSO, when most people did not realise the relationship was a commercial one

If anyone wants to fill me in, I'd love to know who was responsible for this brilliant political move. If I can never give credit on this blog, I'd just like to say: whoever you are, thanks from all of us.

High on the hill

There are a number of strongly established bodies of knowledge that ITIL bumps up against. COBIT especially and the Johnny-come-lately ISO20000, but also ASL, PMBOK, PRINCE2, CMMI, SPICE and several others. I think a big piece of work missed in ITIL V3 was working out the mapping, interfaces and role delineations between the BOKs and ITIL.

ITIL does a superb job of defining how its own processes interface: how incident and problem management work together or change and release. Why not change and project to the same level of detail? Or availability and project? It was in the too hard basket I suspect. "Not if we are ever going to get these books out".

But the people associated with those BOKs are in general busting to help integrate with ITIL. And it would have made implementation of ITIL a hundred times easier to have a little plug-and-play with other BOKs in the environment.

Acknowledging the existence of something is a long way from playing nicely with it. ITIL gives one patronising nod to the other systems, and then proceeds to totally ignore them in the detail.

- ITIL and ISO20000 use differing terminology and differing processes

- ITIL CSI 7-step is not even a process and not even consistent within itself which is why it bears no resemblance to any other pre-existing CSI process out there

- COBIT and ITIL are closely correlated (except that COBIT points up some embarrassing white space in ITIL) but ITIL makes no attempt to index that correlation

- ...etc...

ITIL goes its own stubborn way and cheerfully reinvents the wheel.

ASL

Everyone who is interested in ITIL V3's credibility in the Application Management space should read the recent OGC white paper[1] which shows how little ITIL used an existing respected on-hand body of knowledge. The conclusion of this paper is that ITIL and ASL are "Living Apart

---

[1] http://www.best-management-practice.com/gempdf/ITILV3_ASL_Sound_Guidance_White_Paper_Jan08.pdf

Together". The IT Skeptic's interpretation: they have divorced but stay in touch occasionally. The fundamental disconnect in how application maintenance is treated shows the irreconcilable differences

ASL positions Maintenance (including enhancement and renovation) within the scope of Application Management and defines Application Development as the function that produces new applications, not releases of existing applications. ASL sees advantages in clustering Operational Management of applications with Application Maintenance while ITIL prefers to separate them and cluster Application Maintenance with development of new applications.

Everyone is being very polite but reading between the lines I sense the frustration at how lightweight ITIL is in this domain:

> The ITIL publications give sufficient guidance for organizations that manage commercial-off-the-shelf applications but if an organization maintains the applications and therefore actually modifies the source code, then ASL provides additional and necessary guidance.

"...sufficient ... but..." Close but no cigar. What a shame that all this existing work has been done but not used, integrated or even referenced in ITIL V3. But then ASL is process-centric and process is out of favour in ITIL V3 so I guess it is no surprise. Can't have helped that it came out of the renegade Netherlands either.

ISO20000

ITIL 3, the "ITIL Refresh" is on its way. Like a Windows release it has been coming for a while, but we are assured it will be here soon. One issue with ITIL that we will examine in an upcoming blog is its rigidity: the revisions are few and far between. So ITIL can fall a little behind current thinking. ITIL 3 is positioned thus:

> ITIL was last updated in 2000. Our overwhelming driver for this refresh is to keep the guidance up-to-date such that ITIL continues to be 'fit for purpose' as the most widely accepted approach to IT service management in the world.

It may (just "may") be a case of too little too late. People are taking a broader perspective than ITIL: it is beginning to look a little narrow when compared to COBIT or ISO/IEC 20000.

ISO900x was the biggest load of crap ever foisted on the business community, but who would think of not being ISO900x certified in most business circles? In five years time most organisations will consider

ISO/IEC 20000 certification as a normal part of operating: a minimum benchmark.

ITIL3 will not be ISO/IEC 20000-compliant: there is much new territory in ISO/IEC 20000. ITIL 3 is taking at least six years. How long would an ITIL/20000 take, even if OGC choose to do one?

The horse has bolted with ISO/IEC 20000: the world sees it as "the ITIL standard" but OGC and itSMF have zero control of it. All we need is for someone credible (and probably American: they have the resources to do it quickly) to publish and certify ISO/IEC 20000-based guidance, and ITIL is stone dead.

Think about it: a set of books like the ITIL books but exactly aligned with ISO/IEC 20000. That means a more complete scope than ITIL, and it means an absolute ISO standard to back it up and certify against. And there would be good upward compatibility for existing ITIL shops. Who wouldn't go with it once the pressure to be ISO/IEC 20000-compliant ramps up?

Maybe the centre of the Service Management universe will move to the USA... Will we see [shudder] MOF/20k ...

Another strong contender to displace ITIL is COBIT, which is growing to be as meaty a body of knowledge as ITIL but across a wider range of IT. Not ISO20000 compliant ... yet.

Two years ago I asked "Is ITIL dead in the water?" One year ago, itsm_stephen asked me for an update. I did mean to respond, but to my shame I note today I never did. So, Stephen, here it is... a year late.

The thrust of that first post was that ISO20000 would capture the high ground from ITIL. ITIL V3 was "on its way" but was "too little too late". The coup de grace would come if/when someone released a set of guidance similar to ITIL but based on and compliant with ISO20000. Most likely someone with the deep pockets to do it, and I raised the ugly spectre of "MOF/20k".

So how does the landscape look two years on? I stand by my statements in that article. ISO20000 is finally gaining some traction as contracts start to ask for it in some parts of the world. So I still think "In five [three] years time most organisations will consider ISO/IEC 20000 certification as a normal part of operating: a minimum benchmark".

ITIL V3 is not ISO/IEC 20000-compliant, though closer than I expected. I still think V3 is "too little". You are all thinking "Au contraire! it is a big beast" (or something shorter and more Anglo-Saxon). ITIL V3 is too little in addressing the threat to ITIL from non-compliance with other frameworks, ISO20000 in particular.

With practical experience, the world will come to realise that doing ITIL might help get you to ISO20000 certification but only if you vigorously steer it that way - it doesn't come by default - and the reverse is not true: ISO20000 certification says very little about your ITIL state. It could be ITIL, it could be something else. The possibility still exists for someone to do "The ISO20000 Red Book" and then it's all over, Rover. IBM and Mickeysoft both remain remote from ITIL. Both have the loot to do it. One April 1st I suggested they had, together! Not a pretty thought.

The IT Swami foresaw one of ITIL's fates being kicked into irrelevance by one of the frameworks that ITIL aloofly ignored. ("aloofly"??? I doubt that is a word, but work with me here)

I believe Castle ITIL (the ITIL "inner circle") will come to regret snubbing ISO20000 in the ITIL V3 process (and COBIT and ASL and ...). They should have produced a compliant correlated document with ongoing compliance[1] baked in. They didn't, and maybe one day someone else will.

[It has been suggested that] had v3 been too explicit in supporting the current version of the standard it would be overtaken by events in the next couple of years.

So instead of OGC and ISO doing the work to keep the two coupled, we have to do it at the coalface. I don't buy that. This is a dynamic world. The coupling could be loose but it needs to be there. If I am ISO20000 certified what does that mean for my ITIL compliance? If I spend a million bucks on ITIL will that or will it not mean I can get ISO20000 certification?

If ISO20000 has a refresh coming that brings it into alignment, the books should say that, and describe where the gaps are that need to be addressed. Ignoring ISO20000 was not the solution

A new publication from OGC[2] highlights three good reasons why an ISO20000 certification of an organisation does not provide ITIL V3 certification (and the last one applies to ITIL V2 as well).

Studying this latest ISO20000 paper reveals three reasons why ISO20000 certification of an organisation is NOT ITIL certification:

---

[1] "Linkage" would have been a better word than "compliance"

[2] http://www.best-management-practice.com/gempdf/ITIL_and_ISO_20000_March08.pdf

- ISO20000 only recognises the management of financial assets, not assets which include "management, organization, process, knowledge, people, information, applications, infrastructure and financial capital", nor the concept of a "service asset". So ISO20000 certification says nothing about the management of 'assets' in an ITIL sense.

- ISO20000 does not recognise CMS or SKMS, and so does not certify anything beyond CMDB

- An organisation can obtain ISO20000 certification without recognising or implementing the ITIL concept of Known Error, usually considered essential ITIL.

  Certification is a precise process. Certification says you have done it right. In theory certification says your systems will work with the systems of your suppliers and customers, in a value chain.

  If you don't even acknowledge the existence of a Known Error then this is an issue. A pedantic issue but an issue nevertheless. Compliance auditing is all about pedantry

N.B. Yeah yeah, I know it is called ISO/IEC 20000. "Stop calling him Bert. His name is Engelbert".

COBIT/ISACA

ISACA and itSMF can do more together. There is a great deal of synergy between our organisations and very little overlap. The linkage between COBIT and ITIL is strong. We can work together to share knowledge and experience, and to present a united message to the IT community about good practice in governance and service. If it isn't happening in your area, get it together. How about a joint Christmas function to kick things off?

Perhaps if we start dating it might lead to something more serious. Being a member of both organisations I can tell you that they can learn from each other. ISACA can teach

- centralised international administration of membership, IP, certification etc by volunteers without privatisation

- development of free, open source bodies of knowledge

- professional registration, certification, and ongoing professional development

- support of new chapters and new members

- regional cooperation

- member-oriented service

...and of course itSMF can teach.... um....

itSMF exists as a marketing arm of the ITSM industry, by definition. An open market is a wonderfully self-levelling system: money flows where the potential money is. So itSMF forms a very good indicator of where the interest or 'action' is in ITSM at the time. Right now it is ITIL. But what about the future?

Right now all the attention of the community is on ITIL, so likewise itSMF. Once the community twigs to the potential of something else, watch itSMF switch horses with alacrity. On the other hand, marketing closes a feedback loop, driving the community's interest. So itSMF's marketing will maintain interest in ITIL after the potential has moved elsewhere - there will be a momentum ("hysteresis" actually, if I recall my engineering) caused by the positive feedback loop. itSMF did attempt to drive or lead the market by drumming up interest in ISO20000, though pretty half-heartedly and I think mostly in the UK. It could be argued it was more of a mindshare land grab of the lucrative certification market than a promotion. In general itSMF seems happy to stick with ITIL for now, and I suspect will tend to be market driven rather than a thought leader (although that depends entirely on who steps up for future elections).

Finally, I think the potential lies with COBIT (and maybe ISO20000), and I think there is a particular issue with COBIT and itSMF. COBIT already has an "owner" organisation: ISACA. It is hard to think of two more different organisations. If the community started to get all excited about COBIT, would itSMF cooperate or compete or just not go there?

The long awaited ITIL V3 - COBIT V4.1 mapping white paper[1] is available ... for a price. This is the final paper in a long-awaited series that answer the question left unanswered by the ITIL V3 books - how does ITIL relate to the standards and frameworks around it? The answer is that ITIL is very much a subset of COBIT's more comprehensive coverage.

Those of you who read Rob Stroud's blog (quite a few if his page rank of 5 is anything to go by) picked up this news back in early August. If ISACA told me I missed it. OGC/TSO or itSMFI haven't mentioned it as far as I

---

[1]
http://www.isaca.org/Template.cfm?Section=Downloads3&Template=/Tag gedPage/TaggedPageDisplay.cfm&TPLID=63&ContentID=13742

can tell. This is odd because it is at least as important as the ISO20000 paper. Perhaps they hesitate to mention that it is available for download free to ISACA members and the rest of you peasants will have to pony up $25.

More likely though it is because the paper once again reiterates just how much more complete COBIT is as a framework (although ITIL has advanced since Version 2), and more rigorous, even if ITIL does have a bit more meat on the bones (not as big a difference as people think). Compare the tables on pages 10 and 18 of the paper to see how COBIT more comprehensively addresses the audience, and see the chart on page 19 that highlights the holes in ITIL. For those of you who don't have a spare twenty-five bucks, the COBIT processes not at all covered by ITIL V3 are:

> PO2 Define Information architecture
>
> PO3 Determine Technological direction
>
> PO6 Communicate management aims and direction
>
> PO7 Manage IT human resources
>
> PO10 Manage projects
>
> DS7 Educate and train users
>
> ME2 Monitor and evaluate internal control
>
> ME3 Ensure compliance with external requirements
>
> ME4 Provide IT governance

Nothing important in that lot is there? And the COBIT processes only partially covered by ITIL V3 are:

...oh never mind. There are 17 - too many to list. (ITIL only scores a full coverage on 8 COBIT processes). No wonder Castle ITIL isn't making a noise about this. If you want to see the details, buy the paper. Better still join ISACA and tap into all this good stuff. Some organisations amply return the membership fee.

PRINCE2

Further to my remarks about the invisibility of Project Management in ITIL V3 (see p193), it is interesting to see that there is even less mention of PRINCE2 in particular, despite it being ITIL's stable-mate at OGC. Not much walking across the corridor here! Of course, the North Americans were in control of writing much of ITIL V3 and none of it is actually done at OGC any more.

Not counting the Glossaries and References in each book, according to Google Search, "PRINCE2" is only mentioned in *Service Design, Service Transition,* and *Service Operation* in the common text in the intro that refers to "Publicly available frameworks and standards such as ..." According to the index, the *Official Introduction* never mentions PRINCE2, but it does. Once. A token nod on page 146 in a locked cupboard behind a sign saying "beware of the leopard"[1].

Apparently ITIL and "many of these frameworks have a solid harmony". Oh that's alright then - no need to ever define the mappings, role divisions or interfaces in any detail eh? So long as PRINCE2 is one of the "many". It is definitely one of the list of "more commonly known frameworks and standards that have synergy with ITIL".

"Have synergy with" is such a delightfully meaningless term that it has been adopted by the *Introduction to Real ITSM*. I should have used "solid harmony" too. Solid Harmony is a framework mapping status that I was previously unaware of, but I think we will be using it extensively in future.

CSI [Continual Service Improvement] does refer to PRINCE2 in 3.11.1 (p36) as one of a list of frameworks that "fully support the concepts embodied in CSI". Oh that's alright then. Appendix A is called Complementary Guidance and is an expanded description of the usual list of ISO0000, COBIT, Six Sigma and CMMI, where PRINCE2 gets a very glancing reference in the last paragraph on p177, which also makes the startling assertion that "Project Management is discussed in great detail in the ITIL Service Transition volume". Project and Portfolio Management tools get a paragraph on p149.

There is zero mention of Project Management, PMBOK or PRINCE2 in the index of *Service Strategy*, but Google finds PRINCE2 on pages 7 and 246, the standard intro and the glossary respectively, and p190 where it gets a glancing mention in the context of analytical modelling.

---

[1] That's a reference to *Hitchhiker's Guide to the Galaxy*, for the few who don't know

Ponderous

It may come as a surprise to some readers that there is an OGC Change Log for errors in ITIL, Prince2, M-o-R etc. We have referred to it in the past, and it was through our frustration with it that the IT Skeptic launched BOKKED, the Body Of Knowledge Known Error Database[1]. A recent check shows that the OGC log now has quite a bit in it. They must have got the word out somehow. It certainly isn't through mentions in OGC publications and announcements, or prominent promotion on websites or - least of all - mention in the books. But there are now a good number of issues on there.

There is still no way to rate, vote, comment, debate or otherwise involve the community. The requests are taken away into the bowels of the castle to be submitted quarterly at the feet of those In Charge who decide their fate. The result is posted back on the log for the edification of the grateful masses. Still, building something to allow community involvement must be hard eh? After all look how long the ITIL Live™ Portal is taking. For reference, the BOKKED took three hours or so to build and Real ITSM has taken three whole days. [That's not fair! Coming from a technology-hater like the IT Skeptic! The technology is easy. The processes, the training, the approvals, the politics... that is the hard part as the IT Skeptic always says. Boy they must be hard. The ITIL Live Portal has been coming for way over a year and the change log has been there that long too. Funny how sites that sell books or training, or promote ITIL, never seem to take so long.]

OGC is celebrating the first year of ITIL V3 [June 2008]. What do we have to show after a year? I'm underwhelmed. Obviously ITIL is a large mammal, or perhaps a tortoise, because its growth rate does not match that of Astro the puppy. After a year ITIL is not much bigger and certainly not noticeably more mature.

Books

Not counting the five books released a year ago, the passing year has brought us two new books, Official Introduction to the ITIL Service Lifecycle and Passing the ITIL Foundation Exam, one revised book, ITIL Small Scale Implementation, [updated: not until Sept 08] and five small derivative books, the Key Element Guides.

Complementary guidance? None. Apparently we can look forward to two books in the coming year Building an ITIL based Service Management Department (any day now) and Delivering IT Services using ITIL,

---

[1] www.bokked.org

PRINCE2 and DSDM Atern (April 2009). Hands up who has heard of DSDM Atern?

Online resources? One glossary. A token effort at a process map.

Qualifications

One Foundations course (with changing syllabus) and two Bridging courses.

Several more Examination Institutes to compete with EXIN and ASEB.

No Practitioner/Intermediate courses. No Diploma/Expert. No indication of what the Advanced/Master course might even look like. Names, syllabi and sample exams keep changing all the time.

Organisational

A new Board on itSMF International.

No public bylaws, policy or code of conduct. No published accounts. No resources for supporting new chapters.

A new itSMFI site precipitated by the old one having its plug pulled.

No sign of the long-promised official ITIL portal.

Imperious

There were allegations on the IT Skeptic blog that ITIL training providers were not letting prospective customers know about ITIL version 3 looming, and the implications for certification...

Whilst there must be an element of caveat emptor in all this, it does raise some questions about what is the ethically correct position for vendors to take and who oversees that, and what advice should be given to prospective purchasers of certification training. The IT Skeptic will advise you: read on.

In a recent comment here, Ian Clayton of ITSMI said

> "Why do we still see ITIL Foundation class numbers rocket in the US when the certification scheme is likely to change? Folks who ring us are unaware ITIL is changing and no-one is telling them whilst they call with a request for training. Why are vendors NOT explaining this? Is it the money? Where are course provider ethics in all this?"

A fair question. Have any other readers had this experience or had direct reports of it?

To me, the questions it raises are:

> What are the implications of V3 for certification? Is there anything vendors need to be telling prospective customers? And are they?

> Who polices this? Is there any governance mechanism for certification providers?

> If so, what guidance are they giving to providers?

So, let us see what we can find out.

The implications of ITIL V3 for certification

According to OGC

> Existing ITIL qualifications will not be invalidated by the changes to ITIL because the core principles will not change. The Examination Institutes will ensure that training course content, exams and guidance remain in step with the development of the Library. Therefore any course or certification undertaken during this transition period will remain relevant and will be recognised by any new structure... As far as the Examination Institutes are

concerned any current qualifications will remain relevant. However it seems likely that course providers will offer 'refresh courses' or 'bridging days' to provide any new or updated knowledge... partaking of these will be a matter for the individual.

The same statement is repeated by EXIN

No existing qualifications will be invalidated by the changes, because the core principles are not changing.

The British Computer Society (who run ISEB) are a little less crisp about endorsing existing qualifications

V2 Qualifications will continue until at least December 2007, with transition plans being put in place as soon as the V3 books are available

So nothing much changes as far as qualifications are concerned then? Well not quite.

For a start there *will* be changes to qualifications. OGC says

Any qualification changes will be clearly explained when announced. The majority of ITIL examinations taken are at the Foundation level, and it is this material that will change the least

So all qualifications may change somewhat, and the advanced ones are expected to change more than the Foundation.

It is interesting to note that an earlier OGC statement included the phrase "Any qualification changes will be enhancements" but this seems to have been dropped. I conclude that OGC could not guarantee that all changes would be limited to just "enhancement".

...As it turned out, they changed a *lot*, including radical (and repeated) overhaul of the Foundation syllabus...

Pink Elephant also state that there will be changes:

[Pink Elephant is represented on] the international panel that will work towards creating new qualifications to support the next set of certification exams based on ITIL v3 ... The panel's main objective is to ensure the updated Foundation, Practitioner and Management level exams truly reflect the needs of IT Service Management practitioners in countries across the globe.

Also, there will be more official resources to support studying for qualifications. According to OGC

Third and fourth tranches [that is, phases of work that will follow the publication of the new five core ITIL books, which are the

> "second tranche" of work] address specific support for the qualification scheme by introducing study aids for the Foundation and other examinations

All these statements are in the future tense. The qualifications will change but nobody knows how (or nobody is saying just yet).

Certainly the changes to ITIL in the Refresh are extensive. As "dool" said on this blog "There is one thing for sure that no one has called out. V3 turned out to be far more than a refresh."

It certainly sounds to the IT Skeptic as if there is enough change looming in ITIL qualifications as a result of the ITIL Refresh that prospective purchasers of ITIL training and certification ought to be aware of it.

Now as I said above, caveat emptor – let the buyer beware. People have to take some responsibility for their own decisions and have an obligation to make themselves aware of what is going on in the market. The ITIL Refresh is hardly a secret (well, the existence of it is not a secret even if much of the process and content is). All the material quoted here is on the internet.

On the other hand, I think most reasonable people would say that there is an ethical obligation on the vendors to at least point out ITIL V3, even if they let people do their own research.

Now the claim has been made that this is not happening in all cases. I have heard that at least one major vendor of certification training did not even mention V3 to one or more prospects, let alone spell out the implications.

See, the problem here is of course sales people. They are measured by the dollars they deliver, and so are the management who govern them. They are hardly going to lose their 2007 bonus just because V3 is coming and their market takes a 'wait and see' position.

Policing the training providers

So whose role is it to independently oversee the industry and try to prevent collective V3 amnesia amongst ITIL training provider sales people?

Is it OGC?

Or the ITIL Certification Management Board (ICMB), which comprised OGC, itSMFI, EXIN and ISEB before the CAR tender awarded certification to APMG. Does this body still exist? Well your guess is as good as mine. Neither OGC nor itSMF International nor itSMF UK nor itSMF USA have updated their information in this area. Their websites indicate that it still exists and oversees ISEB and EXIN who in turn used to accredit training providers. No mention of APMG nor the changed playing field since CAR.

Or perhaps something that came out of the "Agreement reached between APMG, BCS-ISEB & EXIN for the benefit of the ITSM community"? Well, so far there is no information we can find about what the agreement actually is. Read the announcement. One of the finest examples of vendor bullshit doubletalk you could ever hope to find. It does a magnificent job of saying exactly nothing.

Or APMG's ITIL V3 Exam board? No: their role is only to "develop a set of qualifications to support ITIL v3"

Or APMG's Chief Examiner for ITIL v2 examinations? No: his role is only "setting consistent examination questions which conform to the stringent standards adhered to by APMG"

Or the itSMF Qualifications & Certification committee?

Or the UK Accreditation Service who certify APMG as "impartial"?

I believe it falls to APMG as part of their new role of accreditation. They would most likely argue that this is one of the issues they want to address by getting tighter control over the training industry, as they are moving to do amidst much protest.

But right now the whole area seems to be a dog's breakfast, left in complete disarray by OGC and ICMB.

Advice for people seeking certification

Of the five main players in this question of what certification providers should be saying to prospects – OGC, ICMB, EXIN, BCS-ISEB and APMG – what advice are they giving?

ICMB has gone to ground.

OGC and APMG are saying nothing that we can find in the public domain.

ISEB's code of practice requires training providers to agree that they will "Specify in our advertising and promotional material the prior knowledge that students require".

And what advice are the players giving to the poor confused or ignorant marketplace? If you look at the OGC FAQ, the answer is neither 'yes' nor 'no': no advice is being provided.

The IT Skeptic concludes that ITIL V3 is a significant change to the structure and content of ITIL. There is clear evidence that qualifications will change as a result. The content taught will change. The structure of the practitioner certificates may well change extensively to reflect the new ITIL book structure and new roles introduced.

While all parties involved are making disingenuous statements that existing qualifications will still be recognised, nobody is saying whether they will be superseded, and it is almost certain they will be updated.

If you are considering buying ITIL certification training at this time, you need to weigh up how urgently you need the IP versus how long you want it to stay current. Since the "second tranche" – the books – is due in June, one would presume that the qualifications structure will follow later. According to ASEB "V2 Qualifications will continue until at least December 2007, with transition plans being put in place as soon as the V3 books are available".

I suggest that in almost all cases, prospective purchasers will need training before V3 training is available, so you need to purchase ITIL V2 training and certification. You will almost certainly need further training when V3 training is available to stay current and retain the value of the certification you have purchased. So negotiate with your training vendor for a package deal which includes both V2 training now and V3 training later. And if at all possible, defer training until V3 is available.

Which is the advice the governing bodies and vendors should be giving to the public, but it seems they are not.

Call of a crow!![1] What is going on in Castle ITIL? Is there a battle royal between vendor factions? The whole V3 Certification thing is lurching around like a pantomime donkey where the front guy has flatulence. e-learning is now in the syllabus (I am told but cannot confirm that it was not explicitly specified previously). This leads to a dire prediction for ATOs if Castle ITIL decides to cut out the middleman...

Contact hours for certification are now defined as "(hours of instruction, excluding breaks, with an Accredited Training Organization (ATO) or an accredited e-learning solution)". So the online training providers can compete. Good. That is nearly what the IT Skeptic raved about. But not quite.

1) APMG are still running a closed monopolistic shop by requiring contact time before certification and requiring accreditation of contact providers.

---

[1] "Call of a crow"? Years ago I worked in an Aussie bar which had a bottle of red wine on the shelf called "Call of The Crow". It was called that because nine out of ten people on first tasting it exclaimed "FARRRK!"

You can bet that the low-cost online providers will struggle to get accreditation from an organisation that answers to the high-cost providers. There is zero independence or transparency about the accreditation process.

2) I think certification should be unbundled from training. You should be free to train anywhere you want and still sit the exam from an examination provider.

If I want to buy training I should be able to buy training (online or classroom, accredited or not, should be my choice as a consumer). If I want to sit certification I should be able to sit certification. And if I want a package of certification plus training entirely focused on passing it I should be able to buy that too.

Right now the market only offers the third option because the ITIL industry uses the copyright and trademark of ITIL to force a monopolistic position where alternative providers are threatened with legal action.

If accreditation of an ATO genuinely provides a superior training product then I will buy it. If it is NOT just a revenue-raising rubber stamp then it should not need to force a monopolistic position - the market will seek it out. It is argued by APMG and the ITIL Qualifications Board that Intermediate level certification requires classroom time as well as an exam. I don't agree with this. Either the exam proves proficiency or it doesn't. In this case they are admitting it doesn't and that somehow classroom time is essential as well. This is patronising in the extreme; many attendees will be more experienced and knowledgeable than the kids-in-suits training them. Any suggestion that those trainers are qualified to sit in assessment of the trainees will go down very badly. So why couple them? See point 1 above.

If multi-choice online exams are a defective mechanism for proving intermediate (or expert) level competence then contact time is not going to fix that. They should change the certification mechanism to written exams or interviews or peer assessment or whatever (but they won't because multi-choice is so cheap and efficient).

At least we are one step closer. Now the earth-bound training providers must deliver some additional value, such as teaching skills or experience, and those without the money or access to (or need for) classroom training have an option. All good.

But a friend has pointed out to me that if you combine this subtle change of policy with the emergence of the ITIL Live website then two plus two equals an ugly scenario for many ATOs if Castle ITIL decides to cut out the middleman. A link from the official ITIL website to official online training from the official publisher combined with official online certification from the official accreditation organisation would be a compelling formula to the majority of buyers, who are after all spending somebody else's money.

Once upon a time IT Service Management was a movement dedicated to improving the levels of service delivered by IT. And ITIL was a body of knowledge put together by the government as a public service and released into the public domain. The books weren't free simply because costs had to be covered.

This rosy view of the past conveniently overlooks the fact, or at least allegation, that the original driver for ITIL was to facilitate the outsourcing of British government computing to private enterprise.

Nevertheless the intent of ITIL V1 and even V2 is clear. Quoting from the earlier editions of V2 before it was quietly expunged by an unseen hand:

> 1.1.1 Public domain framework
>
> From the beginning, ITIL has been publicly available. This means that any organisation can use the framework described by OGC in its numerous books. Because of this, the IT Infrastructure Library guidance has been used by such a disparate range of organisations, local and central government, energy, public utilities, retail, finance, and manufacturing. Very large organisations, very small organisations and everything in between have implemented ITIL processes.

Then the government was reportedly forced by EC regulation to outsource to private enterprise. The Government printer, TSO, got sold off. And OGC handed the keys to APMG.

...In late 2008 TSO launched ITIL Live® with eye-popping subscription charges to provide content and a service that was originally promised by the Chief Architect to be free. The ITIL Imp said on the blog...

> There is no way that I will be paying £2500 per year for content as an individual person. Who came up with that pricing model?

I'll tell you who. Someone who is charging the maximum the market will bear in order to maximise profits to a private enterprise, that's who. Somebody who doesn't give a flying fox about improving IT. Someone who might as well be selling office furniture as intellectual property. Somebody who exploits to the hilt a monopolistic hold on copyright and a dominant brand.

I want to get rich too. But I hope I won't do it by screwing people. (I'm beginning to think that's not possible, but that is another discussion). In fact the reason I'm not being terribly successful at it is partly because I'm a crappy businessman but also because I'd rather like to make the world a better place in the process. By eliminating porn and spam from my product options I've severely limited my internet possibilities.

But how much do you think the product managers and marketing people at TSO care or even know about improving IT professionalism or integrating IT with the business? ["aligning" is so last year] They've all shed their cardigans and they're paid on quarterly profit targets now.

It already happened to certification and training and now it is happening to content.

The original ideals of ITIL have been lost, along with its down-home feel. It may be that ITIL can survive and continue to prosper. After all no-one thinks Microsoft make Windows or Office in order to improve desktop productivity. And the product is in fact real - the snake oil is actually good for what ails you. Or it may be that people will get sick of being screwed. It is like being sold medicine by salesmen instead of doctors; fat men in ornate suits on the back of wagons flogging potions for exorbitant prices because they can. Snake oil salesmen don't give a toss whether the product actually works. They couldn't care less for the welfare of their customers. They aren't out to improve the health of the community - they are out to make as much money as they can as fast as they can.

It is also like buying operating systems that cost ten times too much because of almost-monopolistic market dominance. Castle ITIL should look at the rise of Linux and Mozilla and Google Apps and think twice before they bleed us.

But they won't. They'll milk this for all it is worth then move on; to governance, risk, business integration, information engineering, cloud/grid, whatever comes next.

I feel for those who really want to improve things - and there are lots of you, including in the higher echelons of Castle ITIL. It must be distasteful and frustrating for you too to see the money engine taking over. I predicted it a while ago: the gorilla is choking the pig. Or perhaps more precisely, many monkeys are choking many pigs. There isn't one big commercial entity at work here: there are a number of them all going for their slice of the action.

Those of you whose boss is paying will be less affected - it is someone else's money - but for those of us out in the cold on our own resources, this is going to get worse. The response is simple: I have no intention of getting ITIL V3 certifications and I use COBIT content more than I do ITIL now. I don't think I am alone and I don't expect to get lonely.

All this British public service "you'll know when we decide it is time to tell you" stuff is not how new versions of all standards/frameworks are developed, and I don't think it is best practice.

The British civil service has always had a terror of open debate. [You could say that is explained by the vigorous, nay: fanatical, way the British debate things. I'd say it has bred that approach]. It is the castle as opposed to the commons.

I was in sales long enough to know that perception will substitute nicely for reality, but OGC (and their lieutenant the itSMF) don't even pretend to an inclusive approach. To follow the metaphor, the OGC model of consultation is:

The king's method of writing a new decree

First send the chancellor out round the villages once to get opinions from whoever is there at the time. Go through the results back at the castle and form an opinion of what they meant.

From there on "consultation" is with the knights feasting at the royal table, who hopefully talk to commoners occasionally and can represent their views.

Send the town crier out twice a year to tell them what colour the paper is, who is writing, and how long the scroll is so far. When the clamour gets really loud, tell them what the headings are.

Then when the work is almost finished, herd a couple hundred more into the castle courtyard, read them the scrolls, ask them what they think (as if there was time to make any big changes), then threaten to put their head on a pike if they tell anyone what they have heard.

Ignore the wailing in the villages. Ignore the rogue knights roaming the land exploiting the old laws before the new decree comes out. The solstice is the time for decrees and the decree can wait for the solstice.

It is not exactly a parliamentary approach is it? let alone an Icelandic Allthing, or an autonomous people's collective.

The IT Skeptic is not a rabid socialist (to put it mildly) but I don't like hammering on cold stone walls either.

Represents the establishment

The penny dropped. Finally I understand the gap between the behaviour of itSMF at the International level (and sometimes at the Chapter level), and the expectations of its members. Even though we are called "members", we aren't. We are shareholders.

Most professional organisations exist to serve the members or to at least control and certify the members. itSMF does not. We have discussed in the past how the constitutions of the Chapters and of International do not mention representing the voice of members. They seldom talk much about providing a service to members other than networking. Conferences, newsletters, local forums etc are actually more to do with promoting ITSM than they are to do with serving members.

itSMF is not the "ITIL User Group" either. itSMF only cares if you use ITIL in a statistical sense not an individual one. Apart from the almost accidental effect of local networking, itSMF has no interest in your personal relationship with ITIL.

Looking at another model, cooperative investment society "members" are actually customers. We aren't that either (except one step removed when we buy ITIL books, training or consulting from someone). We do not join itSMF so we can band together for some mutual benefit (other than book discounts, but itSMF is hardly the ITIL Book of the Month Club).

No, we are shareholders. itSMF exists to serve the industry. itSMF's customers are the owner (OGC), the primary vendors (TSO, APMG), the secondary vendors (EXIN, ISEB, Pink, Fox, HP, CA, IBM, BMC, Marval...), and perhaps the small local and independent consultants like me, though in practice we can be safely ignored.

We invest our annual subscription to be owners of a not-for-profit (no really) company that employs our funds and our volunteer labour to advance the industry from which we derive our income. Nothing wrong with that, once we understand it. itSMF is owned by the "members" but it does not exist to serve them, only to have a common interest with them in promoting ITSM in general and (right now) ITIL in particular.

So itSMF does not need to care about democratic representation of members beyond the letter of the law regarding its obligations to shareholders. itSMF doesn't need to care about vendor domination because vendors are the engines which grow the ITIL industry. Of course itSMF does not criticise its biggest customers even if they do not act in the interests of the end consumer. itSMF can be as deeply commercially entrenched in ITIL as it wishes because it is all part of making a buck from

ITSM which is what itSMF is all about. No conflicts there for an organisation which exists to promote the industry.

itSMF doesn't even need to get on board the current fad for "shareholder value" since there are no transferable shares and hence no shareprice or dividend. We shareholders have no right to any return on our investment in membership other than to see ITSM grow as an industry.

To me a user group is a grass-roots bunch of people who draw together based on their common usage of something, so that they can exchange information with each other and speak with a common voice, often to the supplier of the thing.

itSMF members put money into itSMF but itSMF does not exist for the purpose of giving them something back directly, individually. itSMF exists to "promote service management". Hypothetically, if a butcher happened to think it was time IT adopted service management so paid his money to help see that happen, itSMF would take his money even though itSMF has nothing to offer him directly.

itSMF publicly states that this is its purpose for existence. Ian and I have both pointed this out in the past. And itSMF behaviour bears it out. Members are not the customers of itSMF, just bystanders. Important: I'm not saying itSMF acts as if this is the case. I'm saying it IS the case.

Shareholders may not be the right word (as you say there is no equity stake) so I'm happy to go with stakeholders. The key point is that while we have a stake in itSMF's success, itSMF does not have a stake in ours individually. itSMF is solely interested in the success of the ITSM movement/industry as a whole. Right now ITSM = ITIL.

It is fair to say itSMF is the volunteer marketing arm of ITIL, but not the user group.

Once this is understood, then itSMF becomes a lot less disappointing and puzzling.

N.B. The Institute of Service Management is NOT part of itSMF. It is a distinct organisation. If IoSM was part of itSMF we would have rolled it out worldwide using the existing infrastructure instead of a local project in the UK and a disputed one in the USA. IoSM *should* have been part of itSMF.

Plenty of activity is directed at helping the industry which INDIRECTLY helps members. But the focus of itSMF is to promote industry.

Learn to live with the fact that itSMF serves the ITSM industry not the practitioner community. Consider whether you also need to be a member of another organisation committed to representing your interests and developing your profession.

A reader asked

> ...what will it take for you to change your view? What would the itSMFI have to do to demonstrate that it is, in fact, acting in member's interests?

itSMF - as I understand/perceive it - current does none of the following:

1) constitutionally commit to member's interests and write that into goals/objectives/vision

2) get ratification of members for rules, policy, strategy and major decisions

3) report to members in a meaningful fashion: WHAT is policy and strategy, WHY decisions are taken, HOW money is spent. Since itSMF is a not-for-profit and since members are a diverse and scattered group, I believe the simplest way to report to members is to do so publicly. I see no reason for secrecy.

4) adopt a community approach: forums, feedback, councils and consultation

5) support and create member development and certification initiatives instead of spinning them off (IoSM) or allowing them to be run by vendors unrestrained (APMG)

6) implement effective governance to restrain commercial influence on itSMF

7) speak up publicly on behalf of - as the voice of - members, even where that conflicts with itSMF's commercial interests

8) encourage members to participate e.g. publish calls for nomination publicly and far in advance instead of one month ahead to chapter heads, make the rules public, advertise

I don't believe itSMF will do these things simply because that is not the purpose of itSMF any more than representing the interests of shareholders is the purpose of Shell Oil, or representing the interests of subscribers is the purpose of National geographic. itSMF does not exist to represent members; it exists to represent ITSM. So long as we are all clear on that we won't be disappointed.

Now here's my thought for today: I'm not sure I want itSMF to change to meet these "desiderata".

Readers may have noticed in my recent posts that I am accepting of the fact that itSMF represents ITSM not members.

I feel more comfortable about many itSMF behaviours as a result. It is like coming to terms one day with the fact that your boss is a complete asshole (not - I hasten to add - my current situation but one I have known several times in the past).

Once you accept the fact and stop getting mad about it, things get simpler. I once asked my friend Alan what it was like reporting directly to one of the most horrid bosses I've ever known. "The easiest boss I ever had" he replied. "I always knew what to expect. Whatever happened, I knew Adam wasn't going to like it". [Incidentally in private Adam was quite a nice guy. He was a professional asshole]

Likewise, if you know itSMF is always going to act to further the interests of the ITIL industry not those of it's paying members (unless they happen to coincide) then you won't be disappointed or upset.

Promoting ITIL is a good thing (despite my best efforts it still pays my family's bills). Perhaps we should leave itSMF to do what it does best, and look to some other organisation to represent, develop and accredit ITSM practitioners as a community.

There are any number of candidates in the wings[1]:

- **ISACA: Information Systems Audit and Control Association** A nice organisation I am enjoying being a member of
- **ITIMA: IT Infrastructure Management Association** A bit too CA-centric for my tastes but at least committed to the professional
- **SM-I: Service Management Institute** Renegade and born of a consulting vendor, but committed to presenting an alternative
- **HDI: HelpDesk Institute** Been around for ever and fading a bit. If only they'd rebrand from "helpdesk"
- **IOSM: Institute of IT Service Management/ICSM: Institute of Certified Service Managers** There to do exactly what we want but not getting far
- **Society for Information Management**
- **Association for Information Technology Professionals**
- **IEEE** A bit left-field for ITSM but as professional as all get out
- A notable peer (and sometimes competitor) of IEEE, is **Association for Computing Machinery**
- Even **AFSMI: Association For Services Management International** Given that they have been around for 30 years (apparently) it is fair to say that they have grown slowly. There is a

---

[1] Thanks to Charles Betz for some of this list

good list of international chapters, so it's not just some guy in a garage. But the Board details are not there. The only major sponsor is Oracle. The emphasis seems to be heavily on helpdesk. And they've apparently never heard of ITIL.

Sadly there is a popular misconception amongst members that itSMF exists for them. itSMF should either clear up the misunderstanding and let those people go join a member organisation if they wish, or it should change its official purpose and de facto purpose to serve the members better.

There is much talk right now from a number of senior office holders to suggest itSMF wants to do the latter.

This makes a great change from the "let them eat the books" attitude of the previous regime. We shall see.

For the overall health of ITIL we need both industry and user representation, from itSMF and/or somewhere else.

Now that OGC have outsourced ITIL certification and trainer accreditation to APMG, a private for-profit company, let us look at the people who influence the shape of ITIL V3's slowly emerging qualifications system.

The governing body advising APMG, the "senior examiners", is mostly made up of the biggest vendors. Check out the names:

HP x 2	Pink Elephant
Fox IT	BMC
CA	EMC
IBM (ex Guillemont Rock)	ITpreneurs
Itilics	Aspect Group
Itilligence	Gartner (ex Carnegie Mellon)
Det Norske Veritas	Wardown Consulting
UBS Investment Bank	

The foxes aren't just in the henhouse. They are managing it and designing the new henhouse. And equally interesting is the country mix:

Canada	Canada
USA	USA

USA	USA
UK	UK
UK	UK
Singapore / Australia	Norway
Brazil	Denmark
Hong Kong	Japan
India??*	

* (I can't see anything in this person's LinkedIn profile that suggests India for any reason but - one assumes - country of birth)

So if you are a software, consulting or training vendor from North America or the UK you'd be feeling pretty good that your interests are well represented in shaping the direction of ITIL qualifications.

Perhaps that is why the shape of things suits the training vendors so nicely: large class numbers, only one instructor required, five days of content wedged into a more saleable three-day format, exam on the third day to get them out the door (why would they need to absorb what they have learnt?), multiple choice format even for the higher-level exams...

I don't see much emphasis on the importance of principles of adult learning, quality of practitioners, value of the training product delivered, or perception of the ITIL industry (unless "rapacious" is a perception we aspire to).

I respect (and like) all the people on that list who I know. I could think of worse people to be on it. And yes I agree they earned their place there. That is why I didn't get personal about it. It is what they represent that troubles me, not the individuals. The fact remains they sold their soul to rock'n'roll: just about everyone now represents the money engine.

I like to think "best practice" governance requires steering bodies to represent the constituency. This one doesn't.

As for we foreigners "showing up at the table", I think you will find it is the other way around. You bloody Poms and Yanks want to make a buck selling us ITIL without a say in what is pushed at us ☺

With the release of the new format for ITIL V3 Intermediate exams, once again APMG and the ITIL Qualifications Board have opted for maximising profitability and saleability of product for the ITIL Version 3 training industry over maximising the quality of the resulting trainee.

I enjoyed reading ITSM View commenting on the new exams for Intermediate level ITIL V3 qualifications:

> 8 multiple choice questions! ...if you consider that the exam is 90 minutes long you get the idea that these are not simple questions. In fact the questions are scenario based, each with 4 possible answers and (get this) there are varying degrees of "correctness" for each of the 4 answers...Now there is a really right one that is worth 5 marks, a not quite so right one that is worth 3 marks, a answer that earns 1 mark and a "distracter" worth 0... Having a gradient scoring system is very subjective. In real life there are multiple ways to achieve a result, so in this regard it makes sense to have different "correct" answers. However, my view of what is the right way to deal with a situation will be different from someone else and the choice is dependant on many more factors than can be documented in an exam (e.g. emotions, experiences).

What the ITIL Qualifications Board is saying is you can have your own view and now we'll mark you down for it instead of marking you wrong for it. What it shows is that the Intermediate courses really need to have written answers so people can argue their alternate point and demonstrate whether they actually know what they are talking about or just guessed the wrong answer. But written answers would reduce EI profitability, interfere with instant gratification of the buyer, and favour those who are literate. We all know being literate isn't a requisite for people who own processes. Ponder this: what does a manager think who paid x thousand dollars for an employee to go on a course which will qualify them for a process management position, and finds out the course was three days and the only test of the trainee was a multi-choice quiz?

The itSMF USA Bylaws are good, but one phrase describing its Purpose caused me (and others) to double-take and may need some re-work. In my version of the Bylaws (April 2008) the very first clause under "the specific objectives of the Corporation" is

> To provide for commercial organizations and vendors of products and services a forum in which to exchange and share experiences which will assist organizations to manage their IT services in accordance with the best practices embodied in the Office of Government Commerce IT Infrastructure Library.

Firstly, is it just me or does "commercial organizations and vendors of products and services" sound a bit narrow? How about public bodies? Academics interested in ITSM? Annoying little bloggers from some goddam island that doesn't allow our nuke warships? One would hope itSMF is a happy family for anyone with an interest in ITSM and the membership fee.

Secondly, since when did itSMF explicitly link itself to ITIL? There are other BOKs, frameworks and standards around.

So the IT Skeptic thinks that bit needs some re-work. As if that matters. "ooh ooh quick Ken, the IT Skeptic says we need to fix the bylaws. Let's work all weekend to get it right". I don't think so.

BTW, the IT Skeptic holds that all membership organisations such as itSMF should publish their bylaws (and accounts and business rules and processes and minutes and...) on a public website. Why not?

[A comment responded:]

> Paragraph (a) of Article 3 is not superior to the other 8 paragraphs. The issue of concern is addressed in (h). And it would be hey Sallie, the President elect and chair of the Governance committee, or hey David, President of itSMF USA, not ooh Ken, he's one of those international folks these days.

Ah yes thanks Mike. I had forgotten that HP have been passing the itSMFUSA baton amongst themselves. The two Kens' names were on the April version of the Bylaws that I have seen. There may indeed be another clause that broadens the scope of the organisation. I'm just saying that having the first clause launch into discussion of the money-engine may not be the impression the itSMFUSA seeks to give. Or it might.

...and so nice that the little people get a mention in paragraph (h) which brings us to...

Ignores the peasants

Just how does itSMF involve the members? What does itSMF International do for international communications? How did the ITIL Qualifications Board survey the ITIL "community"?

According to a Statement from the ITIL Qualifications Board published Friday, May 23, 2008 by APMG:

> The ITIL Qualification Board is pleased to make the following announcements regarding ITIL V3 qualifications.
>
> Official Qualification Titles:
>
> The Qualification Board involved the ITSM community by surveying itSMF members and Accredited Training Organisations (ATOs) on their preference for the formal titles of ITIL Qualifications. The results of the survey were reviewed and endorsed by the Board...

This sounds pretty good. The IT Skeptic has been critical of the ITIL establishment not involving the ITSM community. But the IT Skeptic mixes in ITIL/itSMF circles worldwide and had heard nothing of any such survey. I am notoriously absent-minded so that could mean several things. So we had a survey of our own [on the blog]. Here are the results:

> To itSMF members: were you surveyed by ITIL Qualifications Board on your preference for the formal titles of ITIL Qualifications
>
> Yes 8%
>
> No 92%
>
> Total votes: 47

So as at today, 43 out of 47 itSMF members who responded were not surveyed. I'd be interested to know what "surveyed" means. It could mean someone asked the members at a local itSMF meeting. Or the pub. Since the Qualifications Board are almost certainly all members themselves, perhaps they just asked each other? Or since the ATOs are probably all members too, perhaps they thought that asking the money-machine is the same thing as asking the ITSM community. At least one of the four "yes" was I believe in the capacity as an ATO. An email to the Chief Examiner and to the CEO of APMG asking the question has not yielded any response a week later. They are busy folk.

The IT Skeptic welcomes further information on the process involved in getting ITSM community involvement in APMG decision-making. The four readers who voted yes, please respond. What was the context of the survey email? i.e. why was it addressed to you, because of some role you play in itSMF?

The fact is no mechanism exists for itSMF to effectively survey all members. Every country has its own mailing list. The itSMFI website uses Drupal which means the results can be centrally collated using a voting mechanism exactly like the one used here. (Voters can be required to be registered.) But they aren't ... yet.

Branches are spending money setting up 50-odd islands of infrastructure for services such as email, newsletters and membership because itSMFI still has not moved to provide a central platform. This is financially inefficient, inconsistent, unreliable, and unprofessional.

What is all that itSMFI money for then? It is nice to see Sharon has implemented videoconferencing for the Board, which will hopefully reduce the excessive travel expenses of old. Perhaps this will free up funds for itSMFI to make a useful contribution to the local chapters that fund them, such as a common member register and emailing engine.

In the meantime I hope the ITIL Qualifications Board will stop sounding like a vendor with wild marketing-speak about how they "involved the ITSM community by surveying itSMF members" when over 90% of our itSMF readers don't know what they are on about.

...We later found out the process...

From the itSMFI Forum

> The survey was conducted via all of the Examination Institutes who sent out a questionnaire asking their Training Providers to respond and also itSMFI who asked the respective Q&C committees within each country's chapters to respond.
>
> A variety of options were put forward for each level however all responders were also free to suggest alternatives.
>
> The itSMF UK Q&C committee responded, these results were collated and discussed by the Qualifications Board and their decision has now been published.

So the "itSMF community" is in fact the "itSMF UK Q&C committee", one Aussie (see the forum thread) and possibly a few others.

..And so on...

The latest ITIL Refresh newsletter reveals that OGC sees keeping the community informed as the same thing as keeping the community involved. This is an elitist patronising attitude so typical of British government in general and OGC in particular. It is time ITIL went from a closed to an open community.

The usual rah-rah remarks from Pippa Bass (OGC Director) warrant closer study than these things usually do. The message is headlined "Keeping the Community Involved", and says

> Keeping the ITIL user community up-to-date with the progress of the Refresh project is essential to ensuring the continued success of this well-established service management guidance.

As I write, a public review of the new version of ITIL is currently underway and this will be complete by the time you read this.

So keeping the community "involved" consists of sending them newsletters; and releasing the books in secrecy to a hand-picked list of reviewers is a "public review".

Perhaps the IT Skeptic is over-sensitive and reading too much into a subtle distinction between words, and poor Ms Bass meant "informed" rather than "involved", but I am a believer in the Freudian slip: that people's simple mistakes with words reveal a lot about inner thoughts, attitudes and beliefs.

I have said in an ITSM Watch article[1] how OGC has failed to build any sort of community mechanism for ITIL (nor has the itSMF). These recent remarks just serve to reinforce my perception that the OGC attitude is that ITIL consists of carved tablets of wisdom to be handed down from an enlightened priest-hood when they are good and ready, for the edification and improvement of the grateful masses receiving them.

There is no need for feedback mechanisms for the "Great Unwashed" to have their say because the content and quality of ITIL is safely in the hands of the elite. We involve them by occasionally giving them a peek behind the curtains to see what the anointed ones are up to in the inner sanctum.

I will be accused of a backflip when I do my blog entry questioning the validity of the Web 2.0 "wisdom of the commons" in the near future, but there is a spectrum of positions from the Cathedral to the Bazaar, and OGC are firmly wedged off the Cathedral end of the scale.

It is high time the owners and hangers-on of ITIL got off their high horses and opened ITIL up to the community collaboration so easy in this

---

[1] http://www.itsmwatch.com/itil/article.phpr/3640461

millennium (and described in my article). If I may continue the analogy: not to the extent of letting the money changers and hookers into the temple, just some sort of protestant reformation.

..And so on...

APMG [ran] an anonymous public survey for "your valuable feedback" on the ITIL V3 Foundation Syllabus. Who knew? Oh, come on! You had a whole five days to hear about it and respond.

How many readers heard about APMG's review of the ITIL V3 Foundation syllabus within the five day window between it being announced by itSMFI on September 12th and submissions closing on September 17th? A five day window is one way to ensure you hear from those you want to hear from.

It was also on the Official Site (which has no RSS feed) from 1st September. It may have been on the APMG website but not that I can tell...

...Until it was all too much...

Yet another unhappy camper prompted me to hammer on the cold stone walls of Castle ITIL once again, right over the blood-stains of last time I tried. But I won't. I give up. ITIL training and certification isn't going to change. It has been taken over by the money engine and is lost. The real experts are elsewhere. We've banged away here long enough. We've pounded on the walls of Castle ITIL. The training vendors own the design and management of ITIL certification and they show zero sign of even acknowledging the dissent publicly let alone changing course.

It's all about the money now. ITIL is too big and too successful for it to be anything else. I don't see this changing (though I guess I will keep on trying). The vendors will feed off the creature until it is dead, and then move on (watch out COBIT). We users need to come to terms with this and go our own ways. If you want to work within the ITIL establishment, then you have to play by their rules now.

If you choose to use ITIL without feeding the parasites, you can with a little difficulty (I am V2 Foundation certified and I still get consulting work, at least for now until Castle ITIL figure out a way to force people like me out. Ironically they will probably do this with the very professional accreditation I think this industry needs). If you want to seek and promote and work with alternatives to ITIL then you can. The comment said

> I'm not embarrassed to say that I've taken the exam twice now and failed both times. I'm almost proud of the fact as it proves my point.

I'd say you are following the right course by being proud to have failed the ITIL Expert exam. You should be judged by your results delivered and your experience, not by a debased certification. Let newbies pay the money to get in to the industry, and the vendors use ITIL Expert to try to show they have in-house expertise. The real experts are elsewhere.

Crumbling

The Pillars of ITIL are crumbling. Is it time for OGC to hand over the reins? This discussion was first published as an internet article on ITSMWatch in 2007, but was updated on the blog in January 2009. We slightly overstep this book's 2008 cut-off and present here the more recent version...

ITIL started out as just the books, but it is much more today: it is a movement, a professional group, and an industry. A great deal of activity goes on in promotion and support of ITIL worldwide. Much of it is ungoverned and ad-hoc. There are many pillars of the house of ITIL and OGC governs and manages only four.

OGC's own part of ITIL isn't growing at all. With v3, OGC is maturing what they have — documentation — but where is the surrounding infrastructure? As ITIL has grown in adoption it has also grown in scope to match. ITIL isn't just books anymore and hasn't been for some years. The growth that is happening is ad-hoc and outside the control of OGC or any one body.

OGC (the U.K.'s Office of Government Commerce) is providing an essential public service by creating and owning ITIL for which we are all grateful. It is hard to think of a better owner than a government body. But it is time the OGC either hand over the reins to someone that can control all the pillars, or take it to that level themselves.

There are several components that make up the scope of ITIL, my "Pillars of ITIL." You may name a few more.

Core content

The tangible part of ITIL is a set of books. Owned by OGC and tightly controlled through copyright. Good stuff.

Individual certification

Other than the content, certification is the other Pillar of ITIL that OGC did well: establishing the ITIL Certification Management Board (ICMB) and accrediting the trainers and examiners. In late 2006, OGC outsourced accreditation and examination to a private company, APM Group or APMG.

Brand

The ITIL brand is wrapped up by trademark in the UK and USA.

Complementary content

The official complementary publications are well regulated and quality assured. The independent – and hence unregulated - ITIL book industry (of which this book is an example) is of course a mixed bag.

Those are the four pillars that OGC has some control over. But there is so much more that constitutes "ITIL":

Governing body

There isn't one. There is no über-body that represents all the stakeholders, has elected members, sets policy and strategy, and provides governance, for all the Pillars of ITIL. As one vendor says "The ITIL market is still predominantly a market guided by customers but dependent on a delicate coalition of interests (OGC, itSMF, APMG, ISO, TSO, EXIN, ISEB, education companies, consulting companies, and tool suppliers). For the market to work effectively, the players need to collaborate."

The Combined Strategy Board (CSB), chaired by OGC, may provide this function – it remains to be seen but it is unlikely. APMG says said [link no longer active] the Board has "responsibility for global marketing and overall product development" which is a promotional role rather than governance one. Moreover there is no transparency of this body: it publishes little, its membership is appointed not elected, and it has no accountability.

Professional body

There was nothing until recently that provided registration or a college for practicing professionals. Now we have the Institute of Service Management in the UK and the Institute of Certified Service Managers in the USA. Or the ITSM Institute. Or the Service Management Society. Or the IT Infrastructure Management Association. Or the Association for Services Management International. Or the AITP or IEEE or ... None of these have the official recognition or charter of OGC, and OGC provides no governance over their activities or standards.

User group

The itSMF, the IT Service Management Forum, arose from ITIL and regards itself as the unofficial guardian of the "integrity" of ITIL (although the OGC is not consistent in seeing them that way). It is often presumed to be the user group for ITIL practitioners and users. But it isn't. According to its aims, itSMF is a body dedicated to the promotion of service management standards and practices, including ITIL. itSMF's purpose is to promote the service management industry not the interests of the user community (unless they happen to coincide).

In practice it varies from country to country: in some it is an ITIL networking club; in others it is the public face of ITIL, serving the theoretical aims; in others it veers close to being the captive body of vendors. Sometimes it presents itself as the voice of members, but how does it derive its understanding of what members want? There is now an official online forum, but feedback mechanisms into OGC are primitive or nonexistent. There is no voting, no surveys. Try suggesting additional or better content for a book. It would be more accurate to say itSMF represents the voice of the senior network of the ITIL "elite".

OGC has done nothing to create or control a community of ITIL practitioners and users (see ITIL Must Embrace the Collective). We hope it will address the whole issue of creating an online community and embracing 21st century collective technologies.

Industry regulation and governance

There is no control over the ITIL industry other than exam certification of trainers. When vendors of products or services are given the right to use the trademarked term ITIL, no body governs what they do to ensure they do not misrepresent the concepts of ITIL or their capabilities to deliver them. In theory it is OGC, but there is no mechanism to effect this in practice.

Product certification

One of the leading ITIL consulting firms, Pink Elephant (a brand nobody forgets) stepped up to provide PinkVerify as a commercial offering to certify ITIL products because OGC consciously backed away from the whole issue of product certification.

Nor does ISO20000 appear to address it (yet – there are rumours of a "part four" that will).

There needs to be an open transparent non-commercial product certification mechanism run by an independent body and we needed it about ten years ago.

Organisational certification

The world's many consulting firms all had to (re-)invent their own ITIL maturity measurement methods and scales for assessing where their clients are at.

ITIL emphasises the Deming cycle, and assessing As-Is status. But it provides no standard mechanism to measure ITIL status within an organisation. ITIL refers to CMM maturity levels but provides no guidance as to how to assess them. This was forgivable in the first version. It has been an obvious crying need ever since. Perhaps with ITIL3's emphasis on a lifecycle we can hope for an assessment standard (though early indications are not good).

A standard

We waited a long time for BS15000, and now ISO20000, service management standard. An ITIL standard would have addressed the organisational certification issue and possibly the product one too, and given ITIL additional credibility in business. The result is that BS15000 and now ISO20000 came out so long after ITIL2 that the evolution of the industry meant the new standards are well in advance of what is in ITIL V2.

We all hoped that ITIL3 would bring them back closer. While ISO20000, (and other important bodies of knowledge such as COBIT), are acknowledged in the books, there has been no systematic work done in the books to bring them all into alignment, or even to point out the links along the way, and ITIL V3 persists in going its own way. Whilst the two have drawn closer there is still a gap.

The theorists offer the rationale that ITIL is not absolute (it is only guidance: "adopt and adapt") so there cannot be a standard, and/or that following a standard would constrain ITIL somehow. The fact that just about every consulting vendor manages to define their own assessment "standard" undermines this argument.

Above embarrassment

At the IT Skeptic website we try to maintain the highest standards of decency and decorum but this one, entitled "OGC rebranding comes apart, so to speak", was irresistible. For your amusement, the less easily offended readers should read on...

The Register reported last month that OGC's proposed new logo had run into problems [see the logo at www.ogc.gov.uk].

Printed on a mouse-pad, the logo can be viewed from different angles, which is where the problem came up, as it were.

Slower readers may find this link[1] of assistance in grabbing the concept.

OGC haven't rebranded yet. The web is abuzz with the story and the mouse-pads are predicted to be hot items on eBay.

While everyone is mocking OGC, it is the marketing firm that "came up" with the logo who should be embarrassed. What dick-heads.

Remarkably, all though this all came out before it was launched, OGC has gone ahead with this logo. They show a stiff resolve and a firm grip.

---

[1] www.hein.org.uk/ogclogo.gif

Analyst Claptrap and Crap Factoids

The IT Skeptic introduced the concept of Crap Factoids. Crap Factoids are pure bull-excrement that almost sound like a fact, and will be presented so often that everyone will think it true. The worst perpetrators of Crap Factoids are analysts (closely followed by vendors and consulting firms).

Chokey the Chimp is the public spokesman for The IT Skeptic's Crap Factoid Early Warning Service.

Chokey the Chimp hates Crap Factoids.

Poor Research

"...% of Fortune 500 companies reported that..."

"...% of CIOs confirm that their decision to adopt..."

"...with an estimated average annual saving of $..."

Asking people how well something works has been used to justify astrology, tarot, homeopathy, acupuncture, Lysenkoism, ITIL...

My concerns are that research is

- commissioned to prove a point, like cancer research paid for by the tobacco industry but with less observers ready to scream "foul"

- created as a revenue generating exercise, therefore the results need to be useful, attention getting and self-serving (grow the market)

- often anecdotal and opinion-based

- Often asked of the wrong person: "How brilliant were you..." "Did you make the right decision to..." "what ROI have you had from your spending..."

- lacking transparency (and hence impossible to reproduce): what was the methodology? what questions were actually asked? how was the sample derived? what controls were there (generally none)? what were the raw results?

- lacking peer review ('cept blogs like this). Where are the professional journals and conferences with real review boards?

I think IT should be renamed Information Engineering, and should be held up in comparison with the traditional engineering disciplines, where it compares very badly. If a bunch of post-grad engineers set themselves up as self-appointed experts and wrote a paper on how 86% of Chief Engineers surveyed agreed that bamboo is the material of choice for bridges in 2008 (and sold it for $3000 a copy), they'd be torn to ribbons by peer review.

My issue is that business cases are floated that quote all sorts of Crap Factoids about the positive returns of ITIL. And ITIL is sold as this magic pixie dust that makes IT work better.

Let us look at a case study: "66% of organisations surveyed around the globe have engaged with the Information Technology Infrastructure Library (ITIL)", according to a survey released in February 2008 by

DimensionData[1]. This survey was the subject of a previous Crap Factoid Alert. It is neither the best nor the worst around, but seems nicely typical to use as an example of what to look for when detecting Crap Factoids.

Dimension Data commissioned the survey from Datamonitor. These are not professional scientific researchers, they are professional market researchers, which is not the same thing. But at least they know how to construct questions and analyse results.

"The research surveyed over 370 CIOs from 14 countries across five continents." But how did it select them? As DD customers? How did it bias the sample? Not stated, but see below.

Look at the spin put on the press release: "Two-thirds of Enterprises Engage with ITIL – Is Your Company an IT Service Management Laggard?" The intent of the exercise is evident, which puts the credibility of the research into question. Scientists set up a hypothesis but they try to be impartial about its veracity.

Look at what the survey measured: people's opinions. "What do you believe to be ...?" "In your opinion, what is the potential impact..."

At least the ITPI research that we have been debating on this website actually measures some hard metrics from the sites. This opinion-based 'research' is not worth the self-aggrandising wind of the respondents who produced it. They might as well ask "How clever were you..."

Then we get graphs like "What do you believe to be the primary inhibitors to adoption of ITIL / ITSM best practices?" Well what were the options they chose from? We only get told the "Six strongest". My local Resident's Association recently surveyed the village and asked something like:

> Which would you least like to see in The Bay?
>
> cycleways
>
> walking paths
>
> playgrounds
>
> beach improvements
>
> big ugly housing developments
>
> gambolling unicorns
>
> fairies in the dell
>
> "99% of residents agree the last thing they want to see..." (1% = me)

---

[1] www.dimensiondata.com/NR/rdonlyres/DF7A4A99-CA40-40B4-9951-FFFE637FFA79/8876/AreyouanITILlaggard2.pdf

Note all the way through the Datamonitor paper they are arguing strongly from a pre-assumed position. The intent is clear: to talk up ITSM frameworks in general and ITIL in particular. Remember that analysts are parasites on an industry: they sell information and opinion on it. If the industry grows they grow. If the industry withers they have to go start again somewhere else - expensive. Analysts have a clearly defined motivation to pump up an industry that they have invested in.

And now the doozy from the results document itself from Datamonitor:

> "Admittedly, this Datamonitor study deals with a somewhat self-selecting sample, as the screener question probed for those that have evaluated, although not necessarily adopted, ITSM frameworks. Methodological nuances notwithstanding, the survey results indicate that over two-thirds of the enterprises interviewed claim that they have engaged with ITIL".

"screener question"? to select the 370 or to select the responses that made it into the results? The graphs show "n=372" so I'd say the 372 were deliberately selected to be already predisposed to ITIL. Either way Datamonitor are freely admitting the results were deliberately skewed. Then they cavalierly brush this aside as "Methodological nuances". Deliberate distortion of data, I'd call it.

This jaunty approach to statistical science is repeated elsewhere, such as this one on p11: "Granted, the statistical significance of a 10 percentage point differential could be the subject of further scrutiny. Nevertheless, the swing testifies to the positive experience of those that have implemented ITIL and corroborates qualitative evidence in favour of ITSM approaches in general and the ITIL best practice framework in particular... Those that have engaged with ITIL are more optimistic regarding its actual impact"

Since the survey questions, the methodology, and the raw data are not published we cannot draw proper conclusions. This is a classic attribute of pop-knowledge Crap-Factoid fluff like this that strongly distinguishes it from scientific research: you can't check it out for yourself.

The IT Skeptic said some time ago that the IT analyst industry badly needs a code of practice to reduce this kind of pop-knowledge crap. Please spread this article around, get the word out, and put some pressure on them.

The analysts survive on their credibility. Based on the bilge they produce, they don't deserve it. If we undermine it, they'll have to do something to improve, to deliver real scientific research. If we don't, they'll keep shovelling this stuff into our managers and you'll live with the results.

Really bad statistics

The IT Skeptic's Crap Factoid Early Warning Service lists the following Crap Factoid[1] as mild, so Chokey the Chimp is staying at "high" risk, but watch out you don't step in this one. Relatively harmless but still smells bad on your shoe.

> "In a recent INS survey completed by 130 IT organizations either currently using or planning to use ITIL [so this is a consultant-solicited survey from a self-selecting sample]... Once ITIL has been adopted, its impact becomes obvious. Of the 76 respondents to the INS survey who are currently using ITIL, nearly half consider it very critical to achieving their goals for managing IT processes, and another 40% deem it somewhat critical."

Well duh! How many people will answer:"We spent all that time and resources implementing it but we don't consider it critical". What is not in the data is how many organisations didn't consider it critical and therefore didn't do it, but they are not part of the sample. The real data might show that 90% of organisations consider ITIL not critical but INS managed to find most of the 10% who do.

By the way the article also said

> "One of the best pieces of news about ITIL is that the cost of implementation is relatively low because ITIL concepts are in the public domain. To get started, a minimal investment in documentation (which is copyrighted) and training is all that's required, although many organizations decide to go with a third-party consultancy to jump-start the process. "

They should go to jail for that.

...or this one from EMA...

Dodgy stats and talk-up-the-market hype mar two otherwise interesting articles on CMDB. Here are two good articles worth reading on CIO Update from Dennis Drogseth of EMA: *Why IT Management is at a Tipping Point* and *Riding the CMDB Tidal Wave, Part One: Understanding.* I've not always been kind to Dennis, but I generally agree with him here and found some new ideas in the articles. Only one bit made the skeptical radar bleep loudly, a typical piece of analyst's talking-up-the-market: the "CMDB Tidal Wave". The stats are dodgy:

1

http://www.computerworld.com/action/article.do?command=viewArticleBa
sic&articleId=98872

> Our data shows that about 30% of our respondents were not interested in CMDBs, and the other 70% divided almost equally between those who had specific plans or deployments in place and those who had interest but no specific plans.
>
> This year's research has targeted actual adopters and we see a parallel ratio where about 50% are in active planning and 50% are in deployment. Most are in relatively early stages with about 15% showing two-to-three year deployments.
>
> Given the fact that just four years ago the acronym CMDB would have been affiliated only with ITIL with far fewer than 10% in planning or deployment, I would say what we're seeing is indeed a tidal wave.

Sounds good eh? Now be a critical reader and take that apart. Last time EMA surveyed a wide audience and found 1 in 3 interested and 1 in 3 planning or doing. This time they surveyed only those actually doing. So don't make any comparison between the two sets of numbers.

Of that unknown proportion of the total population who were selected for the latest survey based on the fact that they have actually adopted CMDB, only half had actually got around to doing anything and only 15% (of the total adopters or of the 50% who have roused themselves to action??) have multi-year deployments under their belts. Last year 33% were planning-or-doing. We don't know how many this year - let's say there is a big wave and we'll guess as much as 50%. So somewhere between 3% and 8% of the industry have "done" CMDB (3% = 15% x 50% x 50%, 8% = 15% x 50%) and 25% (25% = 50% x 50%) are doing (something). Not bad, but a Tidal Wave?

Planning-and-doing has gone from 10% to 33% in four years. An increase indeed, and the term "CMDB" is indeed the leading keyword and search word at the moment, but a Tidal Wave? "Definitely observable ripples" I would have said. And one wonders how many of those ripples of interest are caused by people (analysts and vendors) calling CMDB things like a tidal wave.

All this ignores the fact that most vendors' and analysts' "research" is methodologically suspect. One wonders how many people "doing" CMDB are in fact putting in an asset database, or license management, or some other user-defined version of CMDB. Or how many are there where "doing" means Fred has been told to come up with something in his spare time with no budget. Or where "doing" means we bought a tool that says CMDB on the brochure but we haven't got past implementing network alerting or incident tickets yet.

The idea of CMDB is making quite a splash but I still don't see too many people swept away.

Re-inventing language

The IT Skeptic's Crap Factoid Early Warning Service has detected another Crap Factoid emerging. silicon.com reported[1] that

> Two-thirds (66 per cent) of companies around the globe are using IT infrastructure library (Itil) - the IT service delivery framework - to help manage their IT infrastructure.

Nice of them to help the mathematically challenged there with the percentage. Statistics always make crap factoids more credible. Strangely, PR Newswire which came to me via the famous Ajax World reported the same survey as showing:

> Fifty-nine percent of U.S. organizations have engaged with Information Technology Infrastructure Library (ITIL), a best practice framework for IT service delivery... However, only 8% of respondents deemed themselves aligned to the ITIL framework.

Then things become clearer as we read on and find

> ITIL and other IT Service Management (ITSM) frameworks seem to have broader acceptance in other parts of the world, with 66% of organizations outside the U.S. engaging with -- i.e., evaluating, partially implementing or fully practicing -- ITIL and 17% dubbing themselves practitioners.

So silicon.com's "using" turns out to mean "evaluating, partially implementing or fully practicing", whereas what the reasonable man in the IT shop might expect "using" to mean turns out to be 17%. Lies, damn lies and statistics eh? The problem is that the absence of any objective certification or assessment of ITIL adoption means anyone can be classed as an ITIL shop, including apparently those "evaluating" it. Shame, silicom.com, shame. But you can bet this Crap Factoid will gain a life of its own. It will be an unstoppable meme infecting PowerPoints and webpages across the planet.

---

[1]

The greatest CF (so far)

Re-reading this now, I am still left aghast by it...

This is a CATEGORY 1 Crap Factoid alert from Chokey the Chimp at the IT Skeptic's Crap Factoid Warning Service. THIS IS NOT A DRILL. Be on EXTREME danger alert for CF "CMDB savings of more than $1 million per year"[1]. BMC and Forrester are shovelling it. This Crap Factoid has all the attributes of a very severe one:

- "millions dollars save"

- "CMDB"

- well known analyst [Forrester. Just be grateful it wasn't Gartner, or Chokey would be recommending evacuation]

Most readers and quoters of this paper will overlook the fact that it is commissioned by a vendor of CMDBs (BMC), and that the sample is 26 clients "provided by BMC":

> a Forrester representative conducted in-person, roundtable interviews with 35 key individuals (e.g., IT directors/managers or more senior representatives) from 26 organizations to better understand the value of the BMC Atrium CMDB. Seventy percent of the interviewed organizations had been using the BMC Atrium CMDB for seven to 30 months; 30% had been using it for six months or less.

The IT Skeptic has blogged before about the validity of asking the decision-makers "just how much have you saved on your investment in this technology?" and calling that research.

But there is worse hidden in the paper. The million-dollar number being crowed about is "the net present value (NPV) of savings the sample composite organization realized over a three-year period" yet the organisations interviewed had been using the tool for a maximum of 30 months, so this number has to be projected not actual dollars. [A bean-counter among you might like to comment on the validity of a discount rate of 12% to calculate PV and NPV - seems high to me].

We also know it is a projection because the figure being trumpeted is a "best case" and the "risk adjusted" figure is less than a million which won't cause anywhere near the same excitement (marketers need the m-word).

---

[1] www.bmc.com/USA/Corporate/attachments/TEI_CMDB_FINAL_version_2-21-08_V3.pdf

And the figure is over three years but is already being quoted as per year.

The crap gets even deeper when you look at the costs: $263k over three years. A hundred k a year to install, configure and populate and maintain a CMDB? **** off! The only in-house costs is "12 senior IT and business stakeholders spending 33% of their time over three months planning the implementation".

Then there is $100k for BMC to do "design, discovery, and population of CIs". In an existing BMC environment. No money for integration/federation/reconciliation. No money for processes. No money for staff training other than the ITIL sheep-dip. No money for ongoing ownership or maintenance.

But it gets worse. Take a close look in the paper at page 12: license costs ZERO because they got the CMDB with the cornflakes of their much larger investment in BMC tools. This is at the very least obfuscation and possibly worse. How many readers think this is a fair presentation of the costs of the CMDB?

The icing on the crap-cake is the suggestion that "the BMC Atrium CMDB could facilitate and accelerate the adoption of ITIL standards". BMC just can't resist this silver-bullet, technology-fix-to-a-process-problem bullshit that they have peddled before. I'm appalled that any company that considers itself a fair trader can produce this bull. And I'll be shocked by any BMC employee who looks me in the eye and quotes it. Despite all that, this CF is going to spread widely and do serious damage. Be aware.

...so then the IT Skeptic ran the numbers for himself...

Several readers argue well that ROI is not the right measure for a CMDB, but nevertheless management wants to know what they get for their money, and BMC's own research suggests "not much".

BMC got Forrester to do an analysis of 26 BMC clients. Their research waved around these numbers:

> Best case Present Value of "savings [real money] and benefits [B.S. money]" over three years $1.48M
>
> "Risk adjusted" case $1.26M

Looks impressive huh? But wait, there's less.

The IT Skeptic had a go at them because their numbers are obtained by asking those who spent the money (duh!), are those people's future projected estimates not a measured figure (naughty), and didn't factor in TCO (very naughty), or even the cost of the software (very VERY naughty).

So let's do a rough re-analysis of the data for ourselves shall we?

Forrester's PV of costs $263k included ZERO allocation for software purchase.

If you bought Atrium... say $100k conservatively [anyone know? BMC aren't saying. "If you have to ask..."] then costs would be $363k.

If your environment was not pure BMC [imagine that! but you know what? I'm betting they only ~~sell~~ give Atrium to wall-to-wall BMC shops and they clearly say they only interviewed pure ones] so that you had to pay for integration/federation/reconciliation... say VERY conservatively another $100k, total costs of $463k

If you accounted for the TCO instead of just the setup (only fair if you are going to measure the payback over time)... say another $100k per annum (it is that very same Forrester that says we need a CMDB manager over and above change and config managers, not to mention hardware, monitoring, maintenance of software and database....) so TCO costs of $300k over three years, Present Value at 12% = $265k (?? check this somebody, I'm a hopeless bean-counter), gives us total costs of $728k

If you apply a discount for asking those with their career at stake how well they did ... say 30% discount (your own views on how conservative that is) then the risk adjusted PV of the "savings and benefits" is about $900k or best case $1M , against costs of $700k++.

I'd say using BMC's own numbers more reasonably, you end up with a line ball of BMC Atrium CMDB just about maybe paying for itself after two or three years in a favourable case, if you can get them to give it to you for $100k.

It also assumes you are willing to accept Forrester's "benefits" in your business case. This is not an idle question. Forrester created a hypothetical composite organisation based on interviews with the 26 then assumed various numbers about that hypothetical composite. Fully half the total "savings and benefits" identified by Forrester is based on the assumption that "the BMC Atrium CMDB helps the service desk get information about recent changes to CIs that will help improve first-time fix rates, reducing failed changes from 20% to 10%" leading to "saving $330,000 annually ($990,000 over three years) in reduced labor costs".

Likewise they guesstimated "reducing time and effort involved by an average of 25% per [Service Desk] call" thanks to the wondrous Atrium, "saving the organization $187,500 annually or $562,500 over the three years of this analysis".

These are postulated numbers for a made-up "sample composite" organisation that might hypothetically exist based on the optimistic forecasts of 26 hand-picked BMC clients.

I can smell the bullshit from New Zealand.

...Sadly this was not an isolated instance, nor was it a sweet innocent vendor being led astray by nasty analysts...

Chokey the Chimp warns of a moderate Crap Factoid in the wild, with our old friends at BMC claiming a 370 percent ROI over 30 months on implementation of BMC's ITSM v7. One would struggle to swallow that kind of number from any business case, but given BMC's recent high-level bullshitting, Chokey definitely calls "CRAP!"

The happy client basking in this result is Telvent. According to the press release[1]:

> Telvent estimates that BMC ITSM will deliver a total $5.5 million (370 percent) return on investment as well as improved service quality to its customers worldwide over the 30 month project lifecycle.

We have no source of data other than the press release. A search of BMC's site for "Telvent" returns nothing else.

Reading the release, we learn that Telvent are rolling out BMC's tool across seven data-centres in 30 months (CRAP!). And it is costing $5.5M/370% = $1.5M in total (CRAP!) I'm betting the software alone is costing that.

> This ROI is calculated as follows: 193 percent attributed to improved IT management and 177 percent coming from new customer revenues and expanded orders from existing customers.

$2.65M in "new customer revenues and expanded orders" over 2.5 years actually sounds like a very modest claim for a company based in 17 countries. In fact it sounds very much to me like the old business case trick of "if we can just increase by 1%..."

As usual the tool is getting the credit for the results of extensive process and culture changes going on, and it is pretty obvious it is getting billed with none of the costs for those changes.

> ...we changed from an unstructured, siloed IT model to one that provisions predictive, organised, and efficient services...

1

www.bmc.com/BMC/News/CDA/hou_PressRelease_detail/0,3519,857374
0_0_124124273,00.html

consolidated change management processes across Telvent's seven data centers in Europe and North America... reduced the time needed to plan, schedule and deploy changes from three weeks to one week. With better risk management processes in place, Telvent also reduced system outages by 25 percent... ability to deliver high quality managed services was instrumental in enabling Telvent to conform to Information Technology Infrastructure Library (ITIL) best practices and achieving the international recognition of ISO 20000 certification

Did that with a tool? CRAP!

There really isn't enough to go on here, but nevertheless this one stinks. Which is getting to be a familiar odour in BMC statistics.

1.8.6   ParasITSM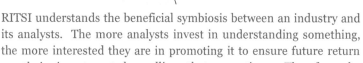

RITSI understands the beneficial symbiosis between an industry and its analysts. The more analysts invest in understanding something, the more interested they are in promoting it to ensure future return on their investment by selling that expertise. Therefore the ParasITSM program provides support for analysts, such as:

- Crash introductions to Real ITSM, usually over lunch, known as "Talk the Talk"

- References customers from the happy customer base

- Recognised industry experts available for interview

- Boilerplate text for white papers, guaranteed unique and untraceable

- List of vendors willing to be reviewed, and a table of recommended charges

- Keynote slots at all conferences

The IT Skeptic's own CF

On a back-of-a-napkin calculation, I reckon the ITIL industry is worth about $2 BILLION to $5 BILLION per year. I was triggered in these musings by noticing that LCS, the new Examination Institute, has processed 100,000 exams.

What proportion of North Americans are employed in IT? I couldn't find the figures, but I think it would be a conservative estimate that 1/300 Yanks will be trained in ITIL in the next 5-10 years, i.e. a million people. Since LSC have done 100k already on behalf of EXIN (and ASEB have done who knows how many more, say 50k) in a market that is just blossoming, a million people looks pretty real to me.

Now remember that many people do the Foundation exam with no formal training these days (it is easy enough - the training industry's dirty little secret), so that isn't $2k per person. On the other hand a certain proportion of them will go on to do practitioner and diploma training. So assume that all averages out to $2k per head, there's $2 BILLION right there.

Now what proportion of total ITIL costs is training? According to Bruton's 2004 survey "ITIL: has it been worth it?" it is about a sixth of external spend. So that gives us a total estimate for the USA of $12 billion in consulting, tools and training. The USA is about 1/3 of the world's economy, so that would suggest a worldwide spend of $36 BILLION. Europe has already spent some of that but Asia is only getting started so that balances out.

On these numbers I'm pretty comfortable with my original estimate of $20 billion to $50 billion over ten years, call it $2 billion to $5 billion a year. No wonder the industry is getting commercialised, and even at times corrupt.

Why Crap Factoids spread

We had an interesting discussion thread going on the suspension of critical faculties in the face of analyst research, and especially on the desire for it to be true. Cognitive dissonance and denial were suggested as two causes. The IT Skeptic explored some ideas...

Yes cognitive dissonance and denial happen once people are in the drek. To get there involves other factors:

Recommenders

(Those asking for ITIL spending)

ITIL advocates may have joined the cult. They've been "sheep dipped" on Foundation training and seen the light: ITIL is the way. Like any faith (non-rational) decision, evidence is then selectively believed to support it

In a milder case of the same syndrome, people just want it to be true. The numbers offer hope that they can fix systemic problems in their organisation with whatever snake oil the analyst is peddling: they grasp on to that hope.

We've bred several generations of suckers. Critical analysis and objective debate haven't been taught for years. Post-modernists have captured the education systems of most countries and now teach people anything can be true if they want it to be. Magic happens in the New Age.

People just don't think any more.

Or in a Dilbertesque move, they don't fall for it but they are cynical enough to try it on the boss.

Approvers

(Those approving ITIL spending)

Managers can often be sociopathic (or even entirely psychopathic) and the probability increases with rank. They don't give a toss, if they think the consequences will not stick to them personally. Others are just trying to keep the family fed, and survive on the old "yes up, no down" strategy. They don't have the guts to tell the boss. Still more are, as the thread discussed, deluded by their own self-image, usually as a result of arrested development I say: teens know no fear. Over-confidence is a strong contributing factor to promotion.

In parts of Asia I saw a wide-spread strategy of "Assume it won't go wrong until it does. A problem is not a problem until you can no longer ignore it. Planning for it is a waste of resources" - the opposite of the Anglo "be prepared". Many people think like this and not just in that part of the world.

There are a couple of fundamental causes underlying the success of analyst Crap Factoids as memes [a meme is an idea that propagates through the species like a gene]. As a comment said, one fundamental cause is "People Want it to be True". You've joined the ITIL cult and you are evangelising new members. If somebody says 86% of sites use ITIL, they reduce costs by 48% and an average of 76 little boys in Montana get cured of leukaemia with every implementation, then you grab that and wave it without a lot of critical analysis.

Another fundamental cause is "Nobody Thinks Any More" (much of the present company excepted of course, as there is plenty of evidence of critical analysis in the comments on this blog). The piles on my desk and the bursting "must read that one day" folders in my email attest to the fact that there is far more information than anyone can process into knowledge. Someone said the last person to know everything was the Librarian of Alexandria [Comments suggested it was Leonardo da Vinci or Thomas Young. One can argue that the internet (or perhaps Google?) is the first repository of all knowledge since the Library of Alexandria]. Since then either all knowledge has not been accessible in one place or, since it has been again, it has been practically impossible for one person to get across it all. Most people deal with this by consuming as much as they can. As a result they consume in 30-second sound bites. The media have trained them to do this. The media serves pre-digested pap for quick easy consumption. Analysts are part of the media (so is this blog). Not enough people read past the analyst's press release to even look at the actual "research", let alone stop and think about it for a while.

Me, I read no daily papers or news websites; read no regular magazines except for my hobby, for pleasure; watch zero TV except the occasional dinner with my son if my wife is out; read no websites on a regular basis; scan and delete 98% of my email without reading it. I do scan Wired and Computerworld feeds semi-regularly if I have an idle moment. If it is important enough, then people will be talking about it - it will be a meme. I found out about 9/11 because my neighbour told me. I read books and magazines that interest me. I read about 5% of the headlines that come up on my ITIL news Feed. Most of all, I read some of the stuff that is personally recommended to me. And what I do read, I may speed read but I think about it, critically. I wish more people would read less and read better by thinking. Then maybe Crap Factoids would spread less effectively.

Vendors

On the blog I once said "For many more, their interest is entirely commercial and I don't have a problem with that. ITIL isn't sacred, to be kept pure and unsullied by venal motives. It's business." I need to remind myself of that sometimes when I see the ITSM sales industry at its venal worst. Often they get to me: "they" being vendors of software, services, books, training and opinion (analysts).

Analysts? Yes, analysts are vendors. Analysts should call themselves what they are, marketing outsourcers, instead of dressing themselves up in a cloak of respectability by pretending to make impartial assessments in the best interests of their readers. At least the other vendors are overt about it.

The influence and behaviour of vendors is a worry. There are not a lot of controls. Some very ugly stuff seems to have been going on, that I sincerely hope everyone will know about some day. Where I'm convinced by the evidence, and more importantly where I think I can withstand the assaults of the vendors' lawyers, I'll be telling you. Fortunately several vendors are a little sensitive about governance which might incline their executive and board to be less aggressive and more effective in responding to revelations. Otherwise if this blog disappears one day, you know what happened.

ITIL started off with simple aims and an informal culture based on individual professionalism and decency. Unfortunately the ITIL movement has grown far beyond that approach being able to cope with governance or control.

I have never taken the position that the monolithic single-vendor solutions are inherently wrong. Caveat emptor: buyers should go in realising that the vendor will want to lock them in, and that they will probably be locked in. On the other hand, they will lock in with a big user base, which means a big revenue stream, which means better odds that the products will still be around in 3-5 years despite acquisitions and bankruptcies - which can not always be said of niche products.

Usually niche products are acquired and integrated, but sometimes they are acquired and just rubbed out, and occasionally they just sink without trace. The big vendors also have services (of varying quality) in most countries, and a third-party services industry following them around. Most of all, big vendors fund R&D out of revenues, not out of capital investment, so assuming the product is successful development of the next version is under way as this one comes to market. The advantage of going with a multiple-tool vendor is that one is effectively outsourcing the integration problem to them, which allows them to charge the premium they do. If two of their tools don't play nicely it is their problem under the support contract. If your product does not work with my systems monitoring tool then which vendor do I turn to? Heaven forbid that the two vendors would get into a finger-pointing war!

This software salesman dies and, by some bookkeeping error, goes to Heaven. He gets issued with his halo and harp and assigned a cloud. He sits for a few days strumming the harp, perfect weather every day, constant peace and tranquillity. After day four, he gets up and walks back to St Peter at the gates. "Hey buddy, does anything ever happen here?"

"Happen? This is Heaven. Nothing happens in Heaven".

"I hate to say it but I'm bored. I could use a little action, you know what I mean? Some fun."

"Fun? Why don't you try Hell? They specialise in that sort of stuff".

"Hell? I dunno about that..."

"Look, you can go down, try it, come back up. Let me know what you think, then if you want I'll damn you for all time or you can go back to your cloud".

The salesman figures he's got nothing to lose, so St Peter rings down on the red phone, the salesman gets in the express elevator, and comes out in Hell. It's a bit smelly with the smoke of cigars, and definitely the heating is too high, but there is a smooth blues band playing on a stage up back, low tables with candlelight, free drinks, and cute women everywhere. He stays for a couple of whiskeys, watches two songs, chats up an attractive brunette at the next table, and heads back up to see St Peter.

"Yup, that's for me".

"OK if you are sure, I damn you to Hell for eternity" says St Peter, takes his halo and harp back, and sends him back down. The salesman steps out of the lift and is thrust straight into a vat of boiling oil. As he comes up for air, a goblin stabs him in the forehead with a red-hot pitchfork, pushing him under. The second time he comes up, he dodges the fork long enough to scream "Hey! Where's the babes? The booze? The blues?"

The goblin stops and looks mystified. "Babes? Booze? Blues?"

Then his face clears, he smiles, and pushes the salesman back under with the fork, saying "Aaah, you were here for the demo".

In the ITSM community

Vendors are an essential part of the ITIL community. But we lack the governance to ensure that presence is a healthy one.

I'm not sure I would say vendors are the only ones with sufficient time and resource to be thought leaders, nor should they be. Vendors get a good broad holistic view of what is going on. They are often weak on deep solid experience. Some of them know as much about running IT as a hammer manufacturer knows about building houses.

Some of our best "independent" thinkers have recently been hoovered up by the big vendors but many remain.

In addition, the majority of the leaders of the ITIL community do NOT represent (at least officially) the big vendors. Look at the Boards of itSMF International or itSMF USA or itSMF UK or IPESC or even the ITIL3 authors (a line ball): most are practitioners not vendors. For all that I heap criticism on Brian Jennings [Sharon Taylor's predecessor as Chair] and his Board at itSMFI, I've never questioned his or their vendor independence.

Vendor influence is strong in ITIL but it need not be too strong, if we have the right governance in place to moderate vendor influence. Do we have it now? I don't think so. Is it too late? I don't think so either.

The whole area of governance is a dog's breakfast in itSMF internationally and locally. Some reform now will go a long way towards ensuring a healthy organisation to come, and vendor moderation will be a key element.

Governance is something itSMF should be demonstrating expertise in, but the cobbler's children have no shoes.

Vendors are people too (I was one). There are plenty of crooked non-vendors around and plenty of nice vendors... well some anyway :-D Any demarcation is arbitrary and discriminatory.

Vendors DO have a right - the same right as any other member of the ITIL community. They also have the same obligations and responsibilities as any other member of the ITIL community and should be subject to the same governance (OK *more* governance, they have more of their own $$$ at stake).

I strongly disagree with any policy that says vendors are subhuman. First I think it is arbitrary to define a vendor, therefore it is discriminatory to do so. Second I think it is insulting to the decent vendors out there to suggest that they are incapable of conducting themselves like civilised human beings.

I'm the first to pile it on them when they come out with crap. I'll also be the first to defend their right to equal treatment. There is a fine line OGC must walk between finding the experienced qualified people to author the books and reinforcing the established cliques.

We should police the officers of itSMF wherever they come from. Have a code of conduct and enforce it.

Perhaps I have been associating with the cult for too long, but I don't think that there is something fundamentally wrong with ITIL content.

I have always disagreed with the term "best practice" for ITIL, much preferring "generally accepted practice" or "good practice", because the use of the term "best practice" leads with the chin.

But beyond that, I feel the ITIL authors know what is going on and mostly write up the generally accepted practice of the day. They make mistakes sure. And sometimes they try to lead: I think CMDB in version 2 was a spectacular example of that going wrong. In V3 they are trying even harder to lead, to create a core that will be current for years. This could be great or it could backfire - I think it'll be great just because service lifecycle is well supported in the industry and I happen to agree with it.

But do the books lead us down a destructive path in order to further the evil designs of the grubby vendors? I'd be delighted to plaster it all over this blog if you have evidence they do :-D but I think not.

The motivation of most of these people is to be seen as an expert. For some it is ego, for others it is commercial. For that strategy to be successful, they need to be as close to "best" as they can get, otherwise someone else - like me - is going to knock them off the tower. So pushing some secret vendor agenda would be a very high risk strategy for an author.

It is not about whether we should have vendors, it is about how good the policing is (I can't use the word "governance" here any more). itSMF must have good policy on conduct and disclosure (for general members and for office holders), and then enforce it well. Neither of these things exists now.

Vendors can be good or bad, all depending on how itSMF harnesses and uses the energy.

References

Let's talk about references, shall we? Any vendor who cannot rustle up one positive reference is so inept they are out of business anyway. References can be obtained by four main mechanisms:

Love them.

This requires far more vendor resource than could ever be sustained in more than 2 or 3 clients, but no-one seems to notice this, least of all analysts.

Appeal to ego.

Make them look a hero. Put their face on full page ads in magazines where their peers will see. Give them a poster-size framed version of the ad for their office wall.

Bribe them.

I am sure research on the number of reference sites whose CIO went to the world conference at the vendor's expense as a speaker or regularly appears on speaking tours to warm sunny countries would yield interesting results. This works particularly well with a CIO about two years from retirement: apply #1 and #2 above so they look like a hero, then once they retire employ them on contract to be an overseas superstar keynote speaker at conferences in exotic places.

In the face of defeat, declare victory.

This was an old British military tactic when faced with unshakeable guerrilla insurgence: walk away and hold a victory parade. What CIO will admit the half-million-dollar project is a failure when they can bluff their way out of it? Tell everyone how successful it was for long enough and even your own staff might start to believe it, especially if they start getting invited to conferences in exotic places.

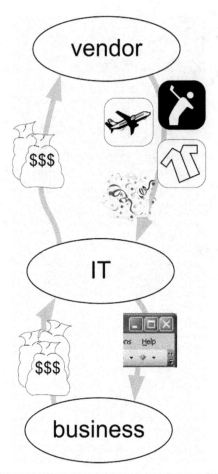

The illustration, The Vendor/IT Value Chain, is from the author's first book, *Introduction to Real ITSM*.

It is worth seeking to be a reference site. Being a reference site will bring love and attention. This requires far more vendor resource than could ever be sustained in more than a few clients, so be one of them.

Branding

What is it about these big software companies and their inability to come up with decent branding of their products (and companies)?

Taaadah! Microsoft enter the service desk market (the Fat ITSM Four just became the Fat Five). We've known it was coming for quite a while, but the wraps are starting to come off. Fresh off the news wire from Redmond:

> SAN DIEGO, March 27 /PRNewswire-FirstCall/ -- At the Microsoft Management Summit 2007 (MMS 2007) today, Bob Muglia, senior vice president of Server and Tools Business at Microsoft Corp. (Nasdaq: MSFT), outlined how Microsoft is delivering on its Dynamic Systems Initiative (DSI) through investments and partnerships that blah blah blah blah blah blah blah blah blah blah blah blah blah blah blah blah blah blah blah blah blah blah blah ... the first public beta of Microsoft System Center Service Manager offering (formerly code named "Service Desk") available in 30 days blah blah blah blah blah blah blah blah blah blah blah blah blah blah blah blah blah blah blah blah

So the product is to be known as MS System Center Service Manager, much as HP is merging OpenView Service Center and OpenView Service Desk together into HP Service Manager.

I'm sure all these marketing guys drink in the same pub. Apparently it is trendy to drop brands: CA are burying the Unicenter brand too. The IT Swami says Remedy is next. I never cease to marvel at these branding gurus. I thought the re-branding of Computer Associates to CA was genius. Cut loose all that negative baggage of the old name. Completely changed my perception of them overnight. Was worth whatever millions CA paid to work that one out.

Seriously, these companies spend a decade building good solid brand recognition like Unicenter and OpenView then chuck it out like last year's shoes while on the other hand their CEOs drag the company name through the mud and the courts (both companies) and they decide to keep it. Meanwhile, the worst ops software brand of them all, Tivoli, hangs on like the smell of old pizza. Go figure.

And now the company that is only marginally less rich than Magrathea deploys their finest branding talent to come up with [drum roll] Microsoft System Center Service Manager. Catchy. Succinct. Iconic. Lilting, even. And not to be confused with Microsoft Service Manager, which we all own already (Start>>Programs>>Administrative tools).

At least they haven't changed "Microsoft": the irony of the "micro" got left behind long ago. And of course "IBM" must be one of the best brands on earth. But there is something special about operational software that attracts some of the world's worst marketing.

I guess it is hardly glamorous. It can't be easy to come up with automobile names either, but I don't drive a Toyota Propulsion Systems Sedan Transporter. Even Boeing 747 is catchy. The niche guys do better with Heat and Marval and Infra, but the Fat Five are locked in some vortex of corporate numb-speak that honours the bland and the clumsy.

Roll-call

Many vendors have been on the receiving end of an IT Skeptic post at some time. Here is a roll-call...

APMG

The APM Group had their accreditation by the UK Accreditation Service suspended. APMG are the accreditor of all examination bodies for ITIL (and Prince2 and ...). This blog is (currently) ITIL-centric, so most readers will be interested that I believe ITIL is not covered by the suspension. The information on the UKAS site that would confirm this is replaced by a suspension notice. I am told, by someone who knows, that UKAS accreditation of APMG actually only covered the other, older, services of APMG: Prince2, M_o_R etc... APMG had not yet sought UKAS coverage of their ITIL services. Some might argue that this is a bit like saying it's lucky they didn't buy new driving lights because they just ran into a tree. Certainly APMG made much of their UKAS accreditation in the ITIL market, as their website still attests.

Why are the UKAS references still on the site? I guess APMG would argue that seeking accreditation and audit is as much the point whether they pass the audit or not. I think that is a fair argument so long as they get the accreditation back promptly. I hope for their sake that OGC see it the same way, given that OGC's decision to out-source ITIL certification to APMG was not exactly met with universal acclaim.

This is going to mean APMG walking a tight-rope in the near future; on the one hand there are auditors pressing them to tighten process; on the other they are entering a new market already squealing about the tough new cop on the block. I don't envy them the position, but I look forward to enjoying some spectacular corporate high-wire acrobatics.

And what does it mean to readers? For the majority, not much. Hardly any purchasers of ITIL training even know of APMG's existence, let alone care if they are accredited. In the short-term I don't see it affecting sales of ITIL training. But in the longer term, it is yet another embarrassment in the ITIL governance world. One wonders how many more there can be before the general public start to get restless.

I remember seeing an Aussie comedy TV show once (*The Games* as I recall?) where it suggested that a public statement by the Prime Minister that "So-and-so has our full support" meant they would be out within days. This memory came to me as I wondered why it was necessary for Keith Aldis, CEO itSMF, to come out with a press release to tell the world that "Real progress is being made in the development and implementation of ITIL V3 qualifications". A year and a half after go-live one would bloody hope so.

"itSMF is pleased to see real progress being made by APMG and its partners... APMG ...is proving a very useful ally..."

Shades of "has our full support" eh?

How long is it since planning started for ITIL V3? I think it is fair to say that most of the planet thought qualifications would all be done and dusted by now, so one has to wonder why "real progress" is something worthy of positive note. As compared to what has been happening until recently, perhaps? Is it in order to hose down some back-room power struggle to oust APMG? Conversely could it be a warning shot over APMG's bows? Or just for the hell of it?

We may never know, but it is a strange noise coming from Castle ITIL.

BMC

People want to believe that "magic happens" (why is that bumper sticker so often on cars that look like not much magic happened to them?). Vendors know this and exploit it by selling magic.

BMC's Ken Turbitt recently put out a paper "can you really get ITIL out of the box?"[1], also available in podcast for those who have nothing better to do.

Basically it is that old vendor trick of blatant denial in the face of the facts: saying my product isn't one of those nasty things you fear then calmly listing all the attributes that say it is ... as evidence that it isn't (but buried in the paper away from the exec summary where no-one who matters will read it). If I may offer my synopsis of the 10 pages:

Apparently "some industry experts are skeptical" that you can have a fantasy easy way out of the ITIL problem: a magic out-of-the-box solution (I did not find this paper because it contained the word 'skeptic' and I would have addressed it anyway even if it didn't - it is far too good to pass up). These sceptical spoilsports suggest that some products may not be as simple as advertised; that they may not play nicely with what you have; that training may not magically produce effective ITIL people; and that you might have to think about how processes will work in your organisation. Imagine that. Trouble makers.

---

[1] www.bmc.com/USA/Communities/attachments/BMC_BPWP_ITIL.pdf

Then in a quick three-thimble trick, Ken pops in a paragraph that makes the disclaimer (and in the exec summ too: this guy is a risk-taker), but as an off-hand aside:

> "Of course, technology alone cannot bring you the entire distance. There are still tasks left up to you. For example, you need to bring about the necessary organizational changes to transition your staff to a more business-oriented approach to IT service. You also have to determine the implementation sequence best suited to your particular environment by deciding which ITIL processes to begin with, based on your most pressing needs. And you will have to personalize the solution to your particular environment."

Oh, is that all? That sounds remarkably like the skeptics' list. This is immediately followed by:

> "So if you want to implement ITIL, but are put off by the skepticism, this paper should help relieve your concerns. It describes the extensive capabilities you can gain from today's advanced IT service management solutions and how they can propel you forward in your journey to ITIL implementation. The paper also provides a step-by-step approach to planning, selecting, and implementing an ITIL out-of-the box solution. Finally, it presents a real-world example of how one organization is taking advantage of out-of-the-box technology in implementing ITIL."

Get their eyes back on the girl in the sequins.

The body of the paper makes the claim that definition of roles, process flow, process integration, and a CMDB are "advances" in the available technology "available today". Elsewhere on this blog we have debated whether CMDB is even possible, but the rest of it sounds pretty bog-standard service desk technology, as implemented by hundreds of projects that failed because they tried to do a technology-led out-of-the-box solution for ITIL.

BMC's paper maintains the approach of dismissing skeptical concerns as old-woman worrying:

> "For example, a comprehensive out-of-the-box solution defines the roles of the groups involved in ITIL processes. All that remains for you to do is to supply the actual people's names within the groups."

Wow, it is that easy! Every modern manager knows that once you get the org-chart right the rest takes care of itself. Down about page 8, where no decision maker will ever venture, reality begins to loom its ugly head.

> "Although IT service management solutions are available that accelerate ITIL implementation with substantial out-of-the-box capability, implementing ITIL is still by no means a trivial task.

"That's why you should approach it in a disciplined manner. This section provides a three-phase, step-by-step approach to implementation. Each phase consists of five steps for a total of 15 steps."

What follows is a good description of the huge task involved in any proper ITIL project, except in a technology-driven order rather than a people-driven order, and with the whole process analysis and design phase buried away as "gap analysis... software needs analysis... software localization... tailor the solution...personalization... rules unique to your specific organisation... fine tuning" (apparently, raising a process from one CMM maturity level to another requires only "fine tuning" - how easy is that?). Having described the typical large ITIL project, the paper wraps up by again claiming the opposite: "viable IT service management solutions are available which ... make it possible to implement ITIL processes out of the box... these solutions significantly reduce the effort required to implement ITIL." Compared to what? No tool at all?

The final duck-and-weave is: "BMC offers solutions that help IT organizations facilitate ITIL implementation out of the box" which may or may not be the same as saying BMC products provide ITIL out of the box. Hands up all those who feel that BMC Remedy (or any tool) provides an out-of-the-box ITIL implementation?

Butler Group

This line in a Butler Group white paper synopsis[1] pressed a button for me: "Service Configuration Management enables quick establishment of Configuration Management Database (CMDB) through auto discovery". I respect the Butler Group more than most analysts, and I am too tight to buy the full text from them, so I hope the synopsis is a bit misleading. Though from the tone of the rest I fear it isn't. This pernicious idea turns up regularly, mostly from software vendors. It must be stamped out. Read my lips: CMDB CANNOT BE AUTO-DISCOVERED.

Tools auto-discover almost all the physical assets in the environment, and plot their network inter-relationships. From the same page: "Configuration management involves the identification and definition of the assets within the IT infrastructure such as switches, software, and servers, and the relationship between the various components". No it doesn't. That is only the bottom layer of a CMDB. Most tools cannot auto-

---

[1] No longer online

discover the software layer and the inter-relationships of software components across nodes. Web Services is making this almost impossible because it is so loosely coupled. No tools can auto-discover the logical functions. And no tools can automatically relate those functions to processes. And no tools can automatically relate those processes to ITIL services. And no tools can automatically relate those services to business units and stakeholders. And no tools can autodiscover and relate SLAs or UCs or.... It is all manual, dammit. And that is why it can't, practically, be done.

When will people stop muddling asset databases and CMDBs? Vendors play this game all the time. They offer an asset database, call it a CMDB, and promise the benefits of a CMDB: how does discovering my network diagram help me understand what business service is impacted? Unmitigated bullshit. I expect better from Butler Group.

CA

CA has never had a good enough bollocking from the IT Skeptic to fill this space. It has nothing to do with my having worked there for 17 years. Just maybe CA really have pulled their collective head in since their CEO went to jail but I am of course skeptical. In fact I find it hard to think of a more deserving organisation. I view their having missed out as one of the major oversights of the blog to date, and I will be doing my best to rectify it in future. There have been a few gentle swipes...

Life imitates art, twice. A NetworkWorld article quotes two surveys, both of which link beautifully - the less skeptical would say spookily - with two items published by the IT Skeptic on the same day!

The very same April Fools Day the IT Skeptic was trying to wind you up by saying...

> ...systems will all be under the control of the new infrastructure uniting networks, servers and storage into a self-managing, self-healing unified whole. Neural logic systems will predict and respond to eliminate all need for human intervention...will employ state of the art best practice in the form of ITIL Version 3 and Prince 2 processes to ensure nothing can go wrong with the design, implementation or deployment of the technology

...NetworkWorld quoted Enterprise Strategy Group (ESG) as saying

36% of those polled considered "highly effective IT organizations" are deploying IT management workflow automation across multiple technology layers, such as servers, storage, applications and user devices...ESG also found that IT service management best practices, such as ITIL -- as well as automated IT asset management tools and automated event monitoring, correlation and root-cause analysis tools -- contribute to highly effective IT environments...

Wooo, spooky. Even spookier: April 1st or not, I think they were serious.

Ignoring for the moment the usual crap about "36% of those polled", it gets even spookier when the same NetworkWorld article quotes CA as having YAFDS (Yet Another Dodgy Survey):

...Sixty-five percent of those polled by CA said many of their data center tasks are automated, 31% of which are under centralized governance...

...which links in remarkably with the Skeptical Informer newsletter I just sent which said

the IT industry is in the process of debasing the word "governance" to the point of meaninglessness... by analysts, commentators, journalists and of course vendors. ..."governing" is coming to mean "measuring or monitoring or checking". Which it isn't.

"Centralised management" if you must, now that "management" has been debased to mean "doing". "Centralised control" would be better. But, hey CA! Software never does governance.

EDS

You would think all the early work by Computer Professionals for Social Responsibility to counter-act plans for a fully-automated nuclear response on the grounds, basically, that computers are stupid might have taught technocrats something, but it seems not...

PLANO, TEXAS, April 1st. Today the National Astronautics and Space Administration announced a project to implement a fully automated IT operations capability for all future space projects.

Both the onboard systems and the ground-based systems will all be under the control of the new infrastructure uniting networks, servers and storage into a self-managing, self-healing unified whole. Neural logic systems will predict and respond to eliminate all need for human intervention. All events in the environment will be handled, as well as almost all maintenance tasks including operating system upgrades and server farm extensions.

EDS has been given the contract for combining technology from BMC, CA, HP, IBM and seven other vendors into a fully integrated package that will drive off a single CMDB to fully automate control centres in Houston and every one of the five other NASA data centres around the planet, bringing them to lights-out status for the first time.

"The staff savings alone in having zero operators, reduced support staff and almost no network or server engineers will go a long way to paying for the $2 billion cost of the project" said NASA spokesperson April Witling.

"We expect to greatly enhance the stability of the on-board systems of all future spacecraft, including the Space Shuttle after a retrofit this fall, by managing their systems remotely and automatically by the ground-based autonomous event manager being created for us from leading-edge systems management technology by the team at EDS.

"They have drawn people from all the vendor organisations onto the team, giving us levels of cooperation never before seen in the industry. We expect the cross-vendor committee structures we are putting in place will allow us to fast-track the development of these systems while the combined expertise of these companies will ensure the reliability of the result" said Ms Witling.

EDS will employ state of the art best practice in the form of ITIL Version 3 and Prince 2 processes to ensure nothing can go wrong with the design, implementation or deployment of the technology.

The new system is to be known as the Ground/On-board Total Control Holistic Automation, expected to go live in just twelve months from today so note this date.

This mindless faith in technology and now process will be the end of us all. Rise up people! Speak out against this foolery before the skies are raining space junk! Let April 1st 2008 be the day IT professionals everywhere cried enough!

EMA

Recent "research" (in the analyst sense of the word) from EMA shows that even amongst those who say they are working on a CMDB [which other numbers indicate is 10%-30% of the ITIL population], those with functional CMDBs remain a minority. This confirms our recent assertion that CMS and SKMS and CMDB represent best practice blue sky. There is nothing "generally accepted" about CMDB practice: about 2%-5% of IT shops I reckon. In true market-hyping fashion Dennis Drogseth of EMA is fond of referring to the "CMDB tidal wave". Based on their own numbers I gotta ask: where's the wave Dennis?

The paper[1] says

> "Our new research reveals that CMDB deployments are at a fundamentally different stage than just two years ago, as they move from the planning stage to value-driven initiatives," explained Dennis Drogseth, vice president at EMA... Drogseth and his team gathered 174 quantitative survey responses and conducted more than 15 in-depth focal interviews with IT professionals actively involved in the planning or deployment of their organization's CMDB.

(As an aside: What is with this modern thing for "more than"? "more than 15 interviews". They don't know how many "in-depth focal interviews" they did? Some might or might not count? Was it 16? Go on, say "16". I'm a grownup: I can handle numbers that aren't a multiple of 5.)

> The respondents were 90 percent from North America, but focal interviews reached out to deployments ranging from Australia to the U.K.

90% of "more than 15" = about 2. So all the interviewees were from North America except one Pom and one Skippy.

> Key study findings include:
>
> -- Most CMDB deployments are less than two years underway, with 43 percent less than a year underway and 68 percent not yet in full production.

I'll resist the temptation to do the usual demolition of analyst "research" and use of statistics. I'll just take these numbers at face value.

Recall that these numbers apply to those "actively involved in the planning or deployment of their organization's CMDB". So even if we take the more optimistic numbers of say 30% of sites working on a CMDB, then 68% of them haven't got one yet. That means, best case about 10% of sites have something working that they are willing to label a CMDB.

What proportion would meet the ITIL definition of a CMDB? Less than half I bet.

---

[1] www.earthtimes.org/articles/show/enterprise-management-associates-offers-new-set-of-cmdb-research-and-services,504201.shtml

Furthermore, allow for the fact that the population analysts talk to tends to be skewed towards larger sites (read: MONEY), and those who are active with vendors, and those willing to talk to analysts (read: more successful at implementing).

Add all that up and I reckon you have to go a LOOOOONG way to find a working example of an "ITILly-correct" CMDB - I reckon 2%-5% of IT shops - which confirms our experience when we asked for anecdotes of any seen in the wild. Once again, a "tidal ripple" I'd say.

...Even analysts suffer from the same marketing departments as other vendors...

Chokey the Chimp was happy we weren't seeing any CFs in May, but I knew something would come along, and I might have guessed EMA would oblige. I might also have guessed it would be CMDB-related.

For once this Crap Factoid isn't based on what passes for "research" amongst analysts like EMA. It started as a prediction[1]:

> EMA predicts that over 50% of all current CMDB implementations will fail because of inadequate planning.

...but by the time the EMA marketing department was done with it, it had built up into a category 1 Crap Factoid[2]

> Fifty percent of all CMDB projects fail due to inadequate planning.

Watch this one blow across the Itilsphere. All sightings welcomed.

Forrester

See page 309. Enough said.

No not enough said. I love Forrester – they provide me with so much material...

---

[1] http://www.emausa.com/ema_lead.php?ls=cmdbreqwebpr0608&bs=cmdb reqweb0608

[2] http://www.earthtimes.org/articles/show/ema-announces-it-management-webinars-for-june,415887.shtml

In my country, the broadcast industry and the advertising industry both adhere to a voluntary code of practice to police the more extreme behaviours of their members. I wish the software vendor industry and their parasitic analysts would do the same.

There are a thousand examples of where it was needed. The one that has me wound up today is this one: The Forrester Wave: Application Mapping For The CMDB Q1 2006[1].

Nineteen pages of the benefits of application-to-infrastructure-mapping-tools ("better understanding of how applications are deployed in production ... better control of infrastructure and application changes ... possibility of controlling spiraling [sic] application costs ... better way to consolidate infrastructure ... better planning of backup sites" ... heal warts ... make her love you ... reconcile East and West ....) and comparison of eight tools, and NOT ONE WORD about whether the tools are actually useful or what the limitations of the concept are.

Forrester's research into the effectiveness of this mapping in general or the tools in particular consisted of "customer success", which appears to have been measured via references.

For the part of the actual research that looked at functionality

> "Forrester looked at the product architecture for its real-time capabilities in building maps and detecting changes. We considered key issues such as time to collect data, the need for manual intervention, the depth of data collected, and the security and maintenance of the resulting CMDB."

How about the usefulness of the data for managing a business service?

And they did this by (a) asking the vendors and (b) asking "three companies that had conducted independent evaluations of the vendors' products". There is no info on whether these three companies had actually installed the products and to what level they tested the practicality of the results, but if I were a betting man... Anyway there is no evidence that Forrester actually saw any of these products in action, let alone installed and tested them themselves.

For the uncritical reader - and as you will all know most IT people are far too busy to be critical readers - a 19-page analyst white paper with pretty graphs and lists and tables looks very authoritative. Most will thumb through to the chart that shows nLayers at the front and CA at the back (to save you all downloading it), and just accept the premise that this must be

---

[1]http://www.cnetdirectintl.com/direct/bmc/Q3_2006/ebook/Service_Mana gement/UK/registration.htm

a good idea else these people would not be selling tools and analyses to help select those tools.

Now I've never seen one of these tools successfully deployed (who has?) but I've worked at selling one and talked to the geeks who made it work. I suspect these tools are DUMB. They all detect some concept of "same" to link CIs together and they are easily misled. So if you are ever evaluating one of these things, test these:

Have two different (apps that provide) business services

- use the same email server to send automated emails

- share a common code routine

- share a common database table

- share a common app server and/or web server

...and see if it can tell them apart.

Then see how it handles:

- A load-balanced web-server or Citrix-server farm

- any EAI middleware

- Citrix, VMWare or any other virtualisation technology

- Web Services dynamically accessed from a UDDI

The IT Swami predicts: while some automation of CMDB service-to-infrastructure-mapping may result, it will be at an expense in money and resources wildly beyond the benefit derived, especially once you factor in the cost of constantly checking and fixing its dumb misunderstandings.

But you will look in vain in the Forrester paper for any discussion of how far the technology has progressed, how far it has to go (the gap), what industry pundits (e.g. itSMF) have to say about the current usefulness, or - heaven forbid - whether any of these tools actually WORK.

Gartner

Everybody is piling into the CMDB frenzy now, including dodgy journos and madly re-inventing software companies... and this blog. ITIL may not be a fad but the IT Skeptic thinks CMDB now is one.

I can't believe someone from Gartner said this[1]:

> Companies — with the exception of BMC Software, which has been in the market for a few years — began offering commercial CMDB solutions only about six months ago, said Ronni Colville, a vice president at IT research firm Gartner

They may speculate wildly, they may pump up markets, but normally Gartner have their facts pretty straight. I suspect this was a mis-quote. The same article goes on to say

> Organizations can invest in CMDB software from companies such as IBM, BMC, Hewlett-Packard, CA or Managed Objects to get started.

which either means that all those others have piled into the market in the last few months or the reporter has a little to learn about both CMDB and facts checking. But it fits the pattern: everyone is sniffing around CMDB, even those who know very little about it. The very title of the article suggests someone who hasn't a firm grasp:

> A prescription for preventing service outages
>
> Configuration management databases can alert managers to dangerous interactions

and this one later on

> CMDBs are like the software that alerts pharmacists to dangerous drug interactions.

and, like, you know, no way.

The media keeps pumping ITIL but the public is losing interest, according to one of my favourite barometers[2]. Not so CMDB which is definitely the hot topic.

Some would have us believe this is because the advent of virtualisation is the tipping point driving everyone to discover CMDB. That draws a long bow. If there is any tipping point it is of course the take-off of ITIL in the USA, but even more I think the CMDB hype wave has reached critical mass and is now exploding. The vendor/analyst machine is well experienced in whipping up these frenzies.

I had hoped we got wise to their games after Y2K but IT seems hopelessly vulnerable to promises of silver-bullet technology solutions to process problems. To create solutions, think of people, process and technology in

---

[1] http://www.fcw.com/article97849-03-12-07-Print
[2] http://www.google.com/trends?q=ITIL

equal parts and in that order. Read the blog entry predicting top data centre trends for 2007[1] and the associated 10 top stories for 2006[2] for a beautiful example of technology-centric thinking. Remember my crude linguistic test for process orientation or technology orientation: do they talk about verbs/actions or nouns/things? ITIL is mentioned only in the context of metrics; disaster recovery is fixed by tape transport; big iron; liquid cooling; site selection etc etc etc

So IT gets more complex and unstable every day and the solution is not to look at how we do things and the quality and culture of the people doing them. Oh no, it is to introduce yet more technology: federating, synchronising, reconciling, singing, dancing CMDB.

The vendors are piling in. The established ones are spending millions to re-invent, graft on or acquire anything that can be labelled a CMDB. CMDB startups sprout like mushrooms.

For a moment there I thought there was hope when the first article mentioned above asked "What comes first — setting up a CMDB tool or defining processes for configuration management?" But look at the answers!

> "A lot of people get enamored with starting with the tool first," Lithgo said, adding that "it's a big mistake." [Good! Good!] Irvine said he agreed that people can easily misuse the tool. "A CMDB is thought of as something technical when in many ways it shouldn't be," he said. [great!] "It should be treated as more of a services-based project that identifies first and foremost all the services you want to map in the CMDB." [Nooooooo we're back to things! What about the Configuration Management processes?? Shouldn't we start with them first??]
>
> A service-oriented approach is the way to proceed, said Andy Atencio, manager of information and technology for Greenwood Village, Colo. The city will be using a hosted CMDB to supplement its ITIL best practices. [So service-oriented means paying for someone else's CMDB-thing instead of having your own thing] If a technology component isn't directly connected to the provision of a specific IT service or business process, it doesn't warrant being tracked in the CMDB, Atencio said. "You have to be smart because otherwise you are tracking everything," he said. [Things] Other experts offer similar advice. "The big key is process first, and let the tool serve the process," Lithgo said. [ooh yeah, looking good...] "Historically, IT organizations have been about heroics, secret knowledge and the select few. That's hard to give up," he said. But

---

[1] http://searchdatacenter.blogspot.com/2006/12/top-data-center-trends-and.html

[2] http://searchdatacenter.blogspot.com/2006/12/top-data-center-trends-and.html

all secrets about how things work must be shared via the CMDB [oh no, we're back to processes as things to be stored!!] if the organization expects to achieve repeatable processes and replace anecdotes [Things] from the IT trenches with tangible metrics [Things], he added.

Is it just me? Am I being over-sensitive? Or are the vast majority of IT people incapable of thinking in terms of process and people as well as stuff/things/artifacts/technology?

[Deep breath] Aaaanyways, they seem to get us all worked up over things like CMDB in ways they can't over far more useful concepts like ITIL (though they tried). ITIL is showing steady growth commensurate with sensible adoption. CMDB is going nuts. Irrational exuberance ends in lost money.

As was noted at Microsoft's 2004 IT Forum Conference, "Recent studies are showing that an IT service organization could achieve up to a 48 percent cost reduction by applying ITSM principles." [1]

This is one of those factoids that's gonna stick, I just know it. A little Googling reveals it originates from ... come on you know this one, all together ... Gartner!

Not 50% Not 45% 48% Bullshit sounds less like bullshit when it is exact bullshit. And "up to". Just like the "up to 50% off" sale.

One thing Google couldn't find for me was the Gartner paper in question. I'd love to check out their data, and their methodology. Anybody help me out here? See my recent blog entry for a discussion on how this analyst twaddle is typically generated.

At the end of the day, though, it doesn't matter how they came up with the number. (I know how they came up with it: they pulled it out of their ... um ... analyst). 48% has a nice authorative ring to it and we will never stop hearing it. How do people keep falling for this bilge and how can someone call themselves a credible source while repeating it?

Helpdesk Institute

So Ron Muns has cashed in his HelpDesk Institute, also known as ThinkHDI, also known as Think Service Inc, for a cool $30 million, give or

---

[1] http://www.infoworld.com/article/06/10/20/43FEitil_1.html

take small change. What does this mean for the Service Management community?

Think Service has been acquired by United Business Media for its subsidiary(?) CMP Technology. This will give them all something to talk about at the next HDI conference in March in Dallas (most of you have probably had the multiple brochures in the mail). And the nice fat cheque will inspire the likes of the IT Service Management Institute. Well done Ron!

The IT Skeptic had wondered in the past whether HDI represented a potential competitor to itSMF to provide a professional organisation for ITSM practitioners, or even an alternate BOK to ITIL. To date they have skittered around the edge of ITSM, preferring to focus on the call centre side of the service market. The name change to Think Service showed signs of trying to align more closely with ITSM. The CMP acquisition means one of two things:

(1) CMP wants to go that way

(2) CMP will bring it back to call centres

A search of the CMP website for the word "ITIL" does not indicate high levels of attention to ITSM right now. Nor are media companies noted for taking conference organisations in new and innovative directions. The IT Skeptic suggests CMP will be more interested in running the existing formula for as long as the conferences pay.

So as far as the ITSM community is concerned, I think this means HDI will continue to operate at the periphery - no impact on status quo.

HP

Given their dominance within Castle ITIL, HP should have come in for more flak on the blog but they seem to have got off lightly. This may be another oversight that needs rectifying, or maybe they are just nice guys...

When I was at CA, they were pretty good at acquisition of companies. HP struggles. Look how the Compaq name/brand/image/culture/entity lives on within HP.

The comparison is perhaps unfair: CA was much smaller and more focused - software only. HP is this big sprawling giant that tries to sell everything from printers to IT consulting. On the other hand IBM tries to do the same and I think manages to project a clearer, more unified culture and image - not much more but they do better at it. (...nowadays. They had similar challenges in the past).

William Vambenepe[1] triggered my musing with this gem:

> Two months ago, HP announced the acquisition of EDS...One month later ..."EDS Asia Pacific Standardises on BMC Software Atrium CMDB to Improve Service Delivery".

CA was brutal. On day 1 of the acquisition, you had a job or you didn't. For those who did, the uncompromising message was "You are CA now. Here's how we do things". Over the next 3-6 months another tranche would leave when they found they didn't fit that culture. It was quick, it was clean, and it preserved a consistent cohesive culture. CA didn't do so well with later (larger) acquisitions, and they lost that culture later but not through acquisition.

Many criticised it. Me, I prefer that to six months or a year of uncertainty, wandering around after the acquisition wondering if you have a job or not.

HP needs to put its stamp on EDS and get control soon. Someone in EDS Asia isn't on board yet.

...and later...

Don't expect laser focus from your HP providers over the next three years, they'll all be wondering if they have a job. 24,600 don't. And that's the official number starting out.

I like HP. They helped convince the Yanks that ITIL is a good idea. But I've previously commented on how their acquisition process needs work. How can it possibly be good business to take three years to tell people if they are in or out? If they think it will ginger them up, they are wrong. It is a great de-motivator. I've seen a company gut itself that way (not my previous employer - they were pretty good at acquisition :)

I wonder if they shovel the "staff are our most valued asset" stuff at HP. Dilbert decided they actually come ninth, after paperclips. If you really value your people you get the ugly stuff over with as fast as you can.

---

[1] http://stage.vambenepe.com/archives/227

IBM

Is it just me or does anyone else think it is a bit rich IBM lecturing ITIL vendors?[1]

After all, this is the company with such a firm grasp of ITIL strategic issues that they sold their service desk product to Peregrine, abandoned to an inevitable brutal death. That's a bit like GM getting out of making engines and then telling other auto makers what they need to make cars. Listen to IBM's understanding of how important a service desk is to service management:

> "It would be wrong to assume that it was a non-performing product," insists Dean Verhaege, VP strategy at Tivoli's enterprise solutions group. "It generated a consistent cash flow and delivered a satisfactory return on investment. The reasons for selling it are primarily due to the refocusing of Tivoli's business."
>
> Or, as Mike Twomey, senior VP at Tivoli's small-to-medium business management solutions group, put it at the time of the sell-off: "The question was does this fit strategically as a product set? The conclusion was no. It's still a strong product, considered one of the leaders in the space."[2]

I have a lot of respect for Big Blue. I was aghast when the sale happened and the mystique of IBM died for me that day. To this day that move mystifies me. I actually agree with the main thrust of the article: the vendors have been slack in documenting how to do ITIL using their tools: "the onus is on IT management vendors, not customers alone, to figure out how to do that". But people who live in glass houses shouldn't throw advice.

It also begs the bigger question of why ITIL does not address some of this. As the vendors work their way up from the technology, OGC should be working their way down from the processes. But that is a blog for another day...

This isn't a beat-up-IBM blog, really it isn't, BUT....

Someone (presumably IBM or ex-IBM) has gone to a lot of trouble to make sure Wikipedia credits IBM with providing "key inputs to the original set of ITIL books" and "the ongoing involvement of IBM ...in ITIL authorship is a matter of record".

---

[1] *IT Vendors Need to Make ITIL Actionable*, John Long, ITSMWatch
http://www.itsmwatch.com/itil/article.php/3618271
[2] http://www.cbronline.com/article_cbr.asp?guid=5B038A1E-81E2-40CD-9201-67A4B2737FEC

Well, yeah. But I think they "do protesteth too much". Malcolm Fry of BMC claims a similar thing. (Rumour has it he has described the "creator of ITIL" line as a mis-quote).

You won't find many authorship credits for either of them, so while I'm sure their contribution is real, in neither case was it quite to the extent they'd have you believe.

The difference is that Malcolm Fry has real credibility and a proven record of commitment to ITIL over decades. I question the same for IBM. And nobody else sees the need to claim credit on Wikipedia.

...This was hotly debated especially by Charles Betz who wrote the Wikipedia entry, but I feel the weight of evidence from a number of ITIL pioneers who commented on the blog [1]supports the contention that IBM (and in particular Ed van Schaik) was only one of a number of sources of ITIL, not the main source and certainly not *the* source. I summarised my views later...

Just when I say that all the hype is in CMDB and that ITIL in general is ticking along fairly soberly, along comes someone to prove me wrong. Two people actually: someone hyping their own significance; and what passes for a journalist on the web these days uncritically lapping it up. I refer to a recent article *Expert offers roadmap for the ITIL data center*[2] about how "Alasdair Meldrum ... literally wrote the book on the IT Infrastructure Library (ITIL)." The reaction from those I spoke to in the ITIL world was WTF[3] is Alistair Meldrum? Apparently

> Alasdair Meldrum [is] European Program Director for the Uptime Institute and an independent consultant... Meldrum was manager of the U.K.-based team at IBM Global Services that wrote the ITIL framework for data center best practices. Almost 20 years ago, the U.K. government approached IBM for the best practices document and the rest is ITIL history.

While the significant input from IBM into ITIL Version 1 is generally acknowledged:

- it is also established that "significant" does not mean they were anywhere near the sole contributor, though one might be led to think

---

so at times. Given that there were 40 books in ITIL version 1, one might better focus on who didn't contribute.

- it might come as a shock to all those who contributed to the original IBM material that there was only one author - their manager.

- that was version 1 of ITIL, back in the mid 1980s with content that dated from even earlier. Back from when there were only "eight practices" apparently.

- I have my own views on IBM's commitment to ITIL in the intervening years. Somewhere within the vast IBM empire I have no doubt the ITIL flame has been kept alive all these years. I am referring to the organisational focus, which until recently compares poorly with arch rival HP. Most vendors were absent through the early days of ITIL but most vendors aren't now loudly claiming paternity.

- the OGC have made their own call on IBM's potential contribution to version 3: they didn't get picked as an author.

We can only hope this was a misquote like the unfortunate Malcolm Fry incident. Given the current state of web journalism it is all too possible. After all my years of criticising print journalists, I now realise they were not as bad as it can get. Also clear to me is the essential role that sub-editors perform. Of course it could also be that Mr Stansberry is very clever and subtle, and has given Alasdair enough rope to hang himself. Maybe.

...And a final shot...

IBM just can't get over the fact they dropped the ball on ITIL, can they? Here is yet another claim[1] that stretches the truth to the point of distortion (my old friends EMA had a hand in this one too):

> IBM is a founding member of the ITIL research committee and still actively involved in the support and creation of new library materials including ITIL, Version 3.

From what we know about the history of V1 and the authors of V3 this statement to me implies a much greater role in both ITIL V1 and ITIL V3 than IBM can rightly claim. Even though both claims are strictly correct, any reader not knowing any better would be lead to believe that (a) this constituted a major part of both versions and (b) IBM was equally active in the intervening twenty-five years. Neither is the case. Puffery.

---

[1] ftp://ftp.software.ibm.com/software/tivoli/whitepapers/EMA-ITUP.pdf

Interfacing Technologies

No me neither. But Scott Armstrong of Interfacing Technologies was kind enough to draw attention to his product with a comment on this blog, so we will took look at its capabilities. [Vendors take note: spam comments will be responded to mercilessly] ...

We can start with Scott's helpful comment

> Agreed too many companies try to ride the ITIL buzz hype. Best support I found for ITIL implementations is at a company called Interfacing Technologies [link removed]), they have built out the entire list of ITIL volumes into a comprehensive process hierarchy (including roles, documents, interactions between processes at multiple levels, etc.). I recommend it for anyone who is struggling with a costly & lenghty[sic] ITIL initiative.

I can imagine this really is the best support Scott has found, as he works there, as the Sales Manager. So his recommendation might need to be taken with the tiniest pinch of salt, especially as he didn't disclose that connection when making it.

But I bet the product is great anyway - that's why we have all heard of it.

So I went to look.

Warning: visit the site with your PC on mute, as it drones at you immediately on landing. Wading through the frankly nauseating hype (sample: "By implementing a Service Oriented Architercture (SOA) through Business Process Management, your company will flourish beyond all expectations") I worked out that IT sell a process modelling tool.

The IT site is a quintessential example of the "silver bullet" marketing technique: technology as a solution to a business problem.

"By building effective flowcharts ...your business process reengineering project will be effective". So that's why so many BPR projects struggle! Not enough flowcharts!

They've built four sets of process:

- ISO Quality Assurance

- Service Oriented Architecture (SOA)

- Enterprise Risk Management

- ITIL Process Framework

Our interest in this context is the last one, since Scott commended it as "the entire list of ITIL volumes into a comprehensive process hiearchy (including roles, documents, interactions between processes at multiple levels, etc.)". Since it is "for anyone who is struggling with a costly & lenghty[sic] ITIL initiative" I'm sure it can solve the ITIL problem as easily as it did the BPR one. And sure enough "Implementing the ITIL framework is easy with Interfacing Technologies". Great news!

On a page headed "What's new in ITIL v3?" IT inform us that

> The ITIL v3 core volumes are:
>
> Service strategy
>
> Service design
>
> Service operation
>
> Continual service improvement

Well it's close enough, right? Show the punter you know your subject.

After much discussion of ITIL V3 we learn that...

> Interfacing Technologies' ITIL Process templates provide guidance in the following areas:
>
> Service support
>
> Change management
>
> Configuration management
>
> Incident management
>
> Problem management
>
> Release management
>
> Service delivery
>
> Service level management
>
> Financial management
>
> Capacity management
>
> IT service continuity
>
> Availability management
>
> Security management
>
> Business perspective

Yup, ITIL V2. It's that old bait-and-switch trick again. They talk about V3 long enough that the less ITIL-educated reader is not going to notice this is a V2 product, they hope. Of course it never once actually says explicitly that Interfacing Technologies' product is ITIL V3 compliant. That exercise is left for the reader. Just the kind of people one wants to do business with.

When we get to the nub of it (at long last)...

> With Interfacing and as your partner [sic] in implementing the ITIL framework, our process clarity can help fill in the gaps and make it easy for you to reap the benefits of the guidelines. We provide the ITIL Process Templates that tie all ITIL requirements together.

...Interfacing Technologies sell process templates. They have the bells and whistles of "our comprehensive Enterprise Process Center™ BPM package for superior ease of use". They have some integration with Unicenter TNG and - of course - with Visio.

As far as I can ascertain the tool provides workflow management to drive ITIL process, which is probably the useful part of the solution but not that you could tell from the marketing crud. For a site doing V2 ITIL, this tool might actually have some use.

Now I'm the first to enjoy a good process diagram, but I venture to say that Interfacing Technologies' claims of a new dawn with all our ITIL problems solved and implementation as easy as anything might just be a bit overstated.

In fact I'd go so far as to say Scott had a damn gall agreeing "too many companies try to ride the ITIL buzz hype" then claiming to solve the ITIL world's problems with a BPM tool. A V2 tool at that.

The spiel ends (at last) with some startling statements:

> You can rely on the fact that
>
> ITIL will continue as a single, consistent standard worldwide,
>
> ITIL is clearly distinguished from unofficial, unapproved course providers,
>
> ITIL is in accordance with international best practices, endorsed at the highest level by the G8 Summit at Gleneagles in July 2005.

No I don't know what any of that means either. ITIL isn't a standard and there are two of them right now. The training waters are murky with unapproved providers and what has that to do with the Interfacing Technologies tool? And most of all what the freak has G8 got to do with ITIL? I googled away but I can't get a match. As far as I can tell the Gleneagles Summit was more absorbed with AIDS and global warming than ITIL. Anyone?

So sadly we are left with the conclusion that Interfacing Technology's solution is yet another technology solution to a culture problem, that it is unbelievably over-hyped, that it is outdated, and only peripherally addresses the ITIL world - a world that Interfacing Technologies seem to have only a tenuous grasp of.

Managed Objects

Antonio gave us an interesting link[1] in a recent comment. Excuse me folks, but what a load of crap it is.

> A just-enough CMDB should provide a full picture of the following:
>
> All technology components related to the specific service.
>
> The relationships and interdependencies among those components, including relationships between logical and physical components.
>
> Context from a service perspective -- role-based views of the technology that consider the requirements of the audience.
>
> State, in terms of availability, business performance and technology performance.
>
> Governance -- automated management of what is currently running versus what should be running and was last approved.
>
> Management of service through defined, monitored and automatically managed service levels.
>
> It is important to note that a just-enough CMDB must include definitions of services and information on state and automated governance/management, all frequently updated."

Dear God, what isn't in there? How does "just-enough" differ from "everything"? This is "top-down" alright: "top-right-down-to-the-bottom".

This is the kind of platitudinous claptrap peddled by vendors and their analyst sycophants to lull people into adopting their lunatic ideas (and buying their products and consulting). Make it sound easy, obvious and do-able.

"less is more ", "top down", "just enough", "relationship-discovery tools", "design and implementation can be made much easier", "critical services".... Crap.

---

[1]
www.computerworld.com/action/article.do?command=viewArticleBasic&tax
onomyName=it_management&articleId=9001306&taxonomyId=14

If you drill down far enough to find everything listed here for just one service, the complexities and inter-dependencies of a modern IT environment mean you will have found a fair proportion of your entire environment. And wasted plenty of time and money doing it... if you ever get there.

What is happening with the vendors and analysts with CMDB as represented by this article is interesting.

What is being left out of this proposed "just enough" CMDB? The whole concept of the CMDB as the Change Management repository, that's what. Presumably the JECMDB does not include desktop devices and their software. It does not include objects that support only a "non critical service".

It has all the functional complexity of a full CMDB, just less data, which confirms my thesis that scale of data is the fatal flaw of the CMDB concept.

They see CMDB is too hard, so they are trying to come up with methodological approaches that will lessen the problem, by breaking off bits and calling that a good-enough CMDB. But they are addressing the symptom not the problem.

The problem is that CMDB is an inappropriate underlying concept for ITIL. It is fundamentally at odds with the basic principles of ITIL: pragmatic and conservative use of existing environments in better ways; fixing processes not technologies. It can't be done practically but people are busting themselves trying and they are living with half-baked compromises like this one.

We need to come to terms with the fact that CMDB is an alien intrusion in the ITIL world. It is a nice-to-have peripheral technologist's fantasy that we can do without.

Which is what this article was saying without them realising it, which is why Antonio drew it to our attention. "You can [have to?] do without a full CMDB to get the job done". So before I went off my head over vendor sweet-talk I should have realised that this article is actually wholeheartedly supporting me, and I am supporting it.

...Then a couple of years later...

CMDB vendor proponents are often full of wind but this one is blowing a gale. What are they smokin' over at Managed Objects?

The IT Skeptic is immune to most vendors by now but three strikes in a row from MO are too much for me.

One, a recent blog post[1] got me going.

> As a manager, your ... [blah blah generalisations about management]...there are a number of similarities between effective business management and effective IT management – particularly, as it relates to the CMDB.

Draw that long bow almost to breaking point Siki, but OK I'll stay with you.

> the CMDB provides a central focal point -- an accurate and complete view of the IT infrastructure

Oh really? In how many organisations? This is presumably an idealised view.

> And yet, CMDB data inaccuracy is the number one cause for CMDB project failures -- followed closely by a lack of broad adoption of the CMDB across a broad set of constituents within both IT and the business.

Ah yes it was an idealised view. We are back to the real world now.

> Going forward, the CMDB must be an absolutely accurate, trusted source of IT infrastructure information. In addition, the CMDB must be widely accepted and adopted across a broad set of IT and business users within the enterprise. IT organizations will each need to address both of these challenges for CMDB projects to be successful over the long-haul.

"Must" eh? And just how exactly?

> Don't think Managed Objects hasn't noticed.

Innat nice? I feel better already. That folks is the end of Siki's post. Some platitudinous claptrap about CEOs, the most tenuous segue of the year to get us somehow to CMDB, admissions that CMDB doesn't work, wrapped up by a vague indication that Managed Objects are going to make it all better. Sounds like Siki was at CA too long.

Then I found this New Age woo-woo[2]

---

[1] http://www.wearebsm.com/managed_objects/2008/06/ceo-impressions-because-its-ca-1.html

[2] http://www.wearebsm.com/managed_objects/2008/06/ceo-impressions-cmdb-cult-or-c.html

If I had a crystal ball, I'd look to see the IT of the future. The flow of data, streamlined communications and an accurate map of the relationships between applications, technology, and the business -- the IT future would be clear, in fact, so crystal clear even the line of business would enjoy the view into IT.

This sounds more like the IT Swami than the CEO of a software company. There will be aromatherapy pyramid crystals in the CMDB next. Are you sure Managed Objects aren't a California firm? The post also contains a Crap Factoid gem but I'll issue an alert for that separately. There's more where that came from. I especially like the way the blog's headlines don't relate to the posts. "We Are BSM" [the name of the blog]: I think the "M" in "BSM" should in this case be dropped.

But the final straw is of course "MyCMDB", a social networking CMDB. Read the press release[1] closely. It is an exquisite piece of vendor double-talk. The problem is presented in the second to fourth paragraphs: keeping a monolithic federated database up-to-date. Then the answer to a different problem is presented: a "new visualization paradigm" [!retch] - a buzzword-rich environment which if you read closely is a bucket of bells and whistles for viewing only.

And fair enough too. Even if they are smokin' Acapulco's finest they wouldn't suggest letting end users update CMDB data. "Built-in governance lets users publish proposed CMDB changes while ensuring that actual CMDB updates are performed only by authorized personnel." i.e. we haven't eased the workload any, we just let end users raise RFCs to point out errors. Not a bad thing but hardly a nooo paradime in CMDB data maintenance.

So what we have here with MyCMDB is YAFI, Yet Another Interface. Doesn't Siki remember how successful slapping a portal on Unicenter wasn't? That was the buzzword-du-jour then too.

> "Social networking techniques are going to revolutionize IT management, by changing the way operations users interface with both the IT infrastructure, and each other," said Siki Giunta, President and CEO of Managed Objects. "myCMDB is not only the first-ever social networking application designed for IT, it represents the first delivery of the clearest, most concise strategic vision in the IT management industry today."

I'll have an ounce of what she's having.

Our industry has enough inept managers that vendors can actually survive by shovelling this stuff. Pile on the buzzwords, jump on the "2.0" bandwagon, make it new new NEW and there are enough idiots out there

---

[1] http://www.managedobjects.com/company/pressrelease.jsp?id=435

to fall for this crap. I guess it is appropriate that it was released at a Gartner Summit: an audience weighted towards the rich and gullible. Meanwhile Managed Objects' shiny new toy hasn't done jack about solving the original problem. Granted there aren't many vendors around who actually make sense. As far as I can tell, you should add Managed Objects to the list of those who don't.

Last post on MyCMDB: Scott Wilson on CIO Weblog said[1]

> this sort of software [MyCMDB] depends primarily on the implementation and culture at the business which installs it. You can't buy a social network in a box; you can put software in place which may facilitate it, but you can't expect it to grow up magically around it

IT has an appalling track record for cultural change. We are bad enough at addressing Process with the Technology, let alone People too. Managed Objects are to be commended for giving people the tools to try, but the tools are not the problem. In other words they are trying to solve an IT culture problem with yet more technology - a typical IT software vendor response.

The other telling point Scott made is that people don't need more networks. I already ignore my Naymes and Plaxo and MySpace and Facebook profiles and focus on LinkedIn.

Wikis and other social collaborations attract the attention of an anally obsessive tiny minority. When the watershed population is enormous, as in Wikipedia, this works. When the pool is a few hundred people you get one or two do all the work just as they would have anyway. It buys you nothing and throws out all the security and quality controls at the same time.

...and finally (because Managed Objects has since been acquired) ...

Dang, they're doing it again! Managed Objects' people linking the real problem (capturing and maintaining accurate and consistent data across federated CMDBs) with an irrelevant solution, MyCMDB, a shiny new way of looking at the data, rich in Web 2.0 buzzwords. MyCMDB may indeed improve non-technical people's ability to walk the CMDB data and to chatter about it, and maybe even to tell the tech folk about it, but it does nothing to address the maintenance of the data: control, validation,

---

[1] http://www.cio-weblog.com/50226711/mycmdb_the_cool_bsm_software_with_the_funny_name.php

reconciliation, audit... i.e. to solve the problem being raised as a bogie-man. Even if the full MO suite does this stuff, MyCMDB doesn't (far as I can tell). This is one of the oldest vendor tricks there is, and is closely related to the old bait-and-switch.

> the biggest barriers to a successful CMDB implementation is the accuracy, currency, and usability of the data – especially across federated sources...The key elements that are missing include an easy way to populate the missing information (which isn't stored in any uniform fashion) such as relationships between IT elements, applications, and business services...We built myCMDB to address these challenges in the CMDB market. [1]

What the world needs is a better screwdriver which is why we have designed our hammer with such a comfy handle.

But enough picking on Managed Objects. [We see plenty of] examples of the bait-and-switch from other vendors. There are two popular formats:

- They invoke FUD (fear uncertainty and doubt) of a problem and then segue to a solution to a different problem (or to no problem at all)

- They invoke FUD of a problem then talk loosely about their overall capabilities across their product suite that may actually address the problem, allowing the prospect to assume these capabilities are in the specific offered solution

McKinsey

McKinsey are an analyst firm whose crap factoids are less crap than most, but they did produce this one, demonstrating that "Well, duh!" must be one of my favourite phrases...

Most analysts produce a combination of insight and gibberish, none more so than McKinsey.

A recent pronouncement from them had this to say

> CIOs must be more attuned to the way technology is being applied throughout their industry and related markets if their companies are to use innovation to create a competitive edge. In addition, IT

---

[1] http://dougmcclure.net/blog/2008/07/guest-sme-author-abbas-haider-ali-burning-questions-mycmdb/

executives should take advantage of their vendors' investment in innovation, looking for early opportunities to add more value by incorporating innovative products and services into their strategies faster and better than competitors do.

This shift to the next level of IT strategy will require changes in management and budget priorities, as well as multiyear planning,

...which I thought was quite good. It certainly highlights the importance of ITIL V3's Service Strategy book.

But what is it about analysts' inability to understand basic statistics?

"only 34 percent say that they are more effective at introducing new technologies than their competitors are" is like saying "only 34% are tall". Well, duh! It's a bit sad when supposed business gurus can't grasp the concept of a bell curve.

Microsoft

A recent patent application appears to indicate that Microsoft is applying to patent CMDB. This issue is not attracting the outrage that it ought to. Next time you see your Microsoft rep, ask him/her WTF they are up to. And if you get anything like a rational answer, post it here so we can all understand.

I find this so hard to believe that I am putting it out there for you readers to help confirm or deny. Perhaps I should find it easy to accept given Microsoft's history in the patent arena.

A reader drew my attention to a recent patent application (20060004875) for "CMDB schema" by Anthony Baron and others. The assignee for the patent is Microsoft, their employer.

The same guys are responsible for attempting to patent (20060080656) patch management on behalf of Microsoft too.

And finally, as far as I can discern through the blizzard of legalese, Microsoft (via Baron and others) are also busily attempting to patent (20060064486) the ITIL ICT Operations book or normal ICT operations with a standard Deming cycle. Just amazing.

If Microsoft gets sick of being called the source of all evil, they should stop behaving like it. (Of course Microsoft are not the only ones playing these silly games. Take a look what BMC are up to.)

Reading these patent applications, they look to me to be vexatious and disingenuous. They are worded so as to seem a precise and complicated definition to one not understanding the details of the subject, but are in fact pretty broad ambit claims.

The patch management one sounds to me like every patch or software install packaging mechanism I ever saw, but let's focus on the CMDB one. Once again it is hidden in complex wording but the claim seems pretty simple. They are patenting:

- the idea that the CIs are in one table and their attributes are in another: sounds like every implementation of an object model in a relational database to me

- the idea that relationships are in a separate table to the CIs: when I started out, we called this "third normal form" and it was pretty standard database design. Apparently now it is a radically new concept deserving of patent

- the idea that another table stores "a default list of approvers for changes": this is less clear but it sounds to me like they want to patent aspects of ordinary change workflow

- the idea that another table stores "dependencies between requested changes": likewise more opaque but sounds like normal release management

Now I am not a lawyer (said with pride) but this sounds like any CMDB schema that stores data in multiple tables according to normal object-to-relational and relational-normalisation principles is infringing patent, as is any change workflow that assigns default approvers or release tool that stores change dependencies.

Remember you read it here first that Mickeysoft are ideally placed to "invade Poland": they could blitzkrieg in and take ISO20000 and ITIL out in one fell swoop simply by upgrading the MOF documentation to ISO20000 and doing a deal with itSMF USA to back it. They don't have to make it open content. [Note: Microsoft later DID make MOF open content!] ITIL isn't open content. Microsoft can keep a MOF documentation of ISO20000 practices as locked up as OGC does ITIL. Having a patent on CMDB wouldn't hurt. It would be like France having already surrendered. And they already have MOF gaining ground, which is akin to having the king of your main opponent on your side[1].

---

[1] If you don't get this snide historical allusion, find out what Edward, Duke of Windsor and briefly King Edward VIII was saying and doing before and during WW2.

One would hope that "prior art" will kill all this nonsense stone dead, but the US patent system is in such a parlous state (mostly by allowing patents on methods, but more generally by the meddling of the US's prime pestilence: lawyers) that anything could happen. My best-case hope is that Microsoft employees get bonused on patent applications and these guys are just busy "writing themselves a Winnebago"[1], but I doubt it.

...A comment asked, tongue-in-cheek I suspect "Where would we be if Microsoft didn't step in and help standardize things?"...

Oh puhhleeese!!! The only thing Microsoft standardise is their technique for corrupting public standards. Name one "standard" that Microsoft is responsible for that isn't a proprietary product of Microsoft: Windows, VB, .NET. Name one public standard that Microsoft have adopted without subtly bastardising it so theirs is incompatible: MS-SQL, LDAP, ITIL....

...And then a comment said

> Microsoft is worse than ITIL?
>
> The Vendor and British ITIL cabal are busy redefining their closed, theoretical "framework" to include everything under the sun. And, they seem to be doing it for the express purpose of advancing the vendors sales performance. Why would Microsoft be more challenging than are they? Your comment implies that Microsoft is more avaricious than HP, IBM, CA or BMC. You don't really believe that, do you? I would submit that any such suggestion is either astoundingly naive or indicates an anti-Microsoft bias.
>
> ITIL went from ignoring the two-thirds of the IT budget that is purchased from vendors, and a pitiful financial mini-note, to, with v.3, taking over procurement and all negotiations. Poorly, of course.
>
> What next? CRM and ERP are soon to be part of ITIL because these same vendors sell that software too?

...That comment sat me back...

First I don't believe I have an anti-Microsoft bias. I see the positives in what it has achieved (and I develop and run my business on a Windows/Office platform even if my host chooses Linux). I do think I have an anti-vendor bias: as we say on the important hemisphere, I like to keep the bastards honest. But I'd hope I hand that out fairly evenly. I

---

[1] from a Dilbert comic (before I hear from Scott's lawyers) [...or I thought it was but I have since re-read the comic in question and the punch-line is entirely different to my recollection. Whatever.]

certainly wouldn't count naivety amongst my many weaknesses, so I have to conclude that I don't agree :-)

The comment refers to "ITIL" as a political entity, then seems to refer to "HP, IBM, CA or BMC" as the same thing. I don't think the Fat ITSM Four have captured ITIL yet, though one of them is giving it a go and all make sure they have an influence, as they should.

If pressed, yes I probably do think Microsoft are more avaricious than the Fat Four, by a nose. Not that they wouldn't behave the same way in the same situation, but I feel that Microsoft's dominance inclines it to a taste for monopoly. Several times it has corrupted a standard to its own version in the hope that it would drive the open version under (MS-SQL, COM, LDAP, MOF, OpenDoc...). They haven't pulled it off yet but they keep trying. More successful, of course, is the ploy of bundling stuff with Windows to kill off competitors. None of the Fat Four have the capability for these kinds of tricks. And none of them seem to be going after patents on the obvious in quite the same way as MS.

I did point out that BMC seem to be playing the same dirty game, but MS are taking the lead. The IT Swami tells me Microsoft are about to make a big push into the whole ITSM space. I reckon they are laying legal landmines before the assault. The other members of the CMDB Consortium better watch their backs (and don't think they aren't: I bet some of the management meetings are like a poker game in 19th Century Promontory or Carson City).

I do agree ITIL is shaped by the ITIL industry in their own image, but I think that power bloc is wider than just the Four (or Five... or One if MS have their way). And I firmly believe the four couldn't actively collude on anything for long. Skeptic that I am, I don't see a conspiracy in Version 3 (at least not this conspiracy). It does seem to me to be a natural and reasonable evolution to address a big deficiency in the earlier books: the lifecycle of the service. But it is a really interesting point: to what extent is the evolution of ITIL driven by the vendors' (and consultants') desire to expand their sales?

Windows Vista makes the claim of "faster boot times". Faster than what? Tectonics? I upgraded from a single-processor 1.5GHz machine running XP Pro to a dual core 2.3GHz with 256MB graphics accelerator and bloody Vista, and the dang thing runs slower! It boots slower, it shuts down slower, it copies files slower. I don't have the time, skills or inclination to do a scratch XP build on this machine [later I did]. Sigh. No wonder Mickeysoft fell on its face with this one: it is bloated crap. As the saying goes: like a sick slug crawling up a wet nudist.

A couple more pet hates about Vista:

- staring at a totally black screen during startup - seriously stressful, the first few times. "Is it ever coming back?"

- watching a screen that says "0 seconds remaining" for extended periods

One more thing: the Economist had an article recently (can't find it right now) on how IT accounts for several otherwise inexplicable percentage points in world annual GDP growth over the last decade. If my experience of Vista is being repeated in millions of homes and offices across the planet then Microsoft may well cause a measurable reduction in world GDP growth with this dog. Lucky for them the recession came along just in time to mask any measurable effect. Hey! you don't suppose.....

I'm sure I'm not the first to reflect on the evil genius of .docx document format but I feel the need to vent a little spleen. Only the Evil Empire of MickeySoft could be this twisted.

The ITSM community should ponder this for two reasons: (1) just how much do we trust Microsoft's 'free' MOF 4.0? (2) ITIL's inability to play nicely with COBIT or other de-facto standards might result in eventual convergence or it might not - watch the scrap between OOXML and ODF for clues.

After years of resisting open standards, Microsoft suddenly sees the light and embraces open standards. Most were suspicious from the start and quite rightly so.

First they promote an alternate "open" standard of their own so as to provoke a standards war with their competitors.

Then they indulge in suspect shenanigans to gerrymander adoption of the standard.

And when they finally release a version of MS-Word that uses the new standard, they make it the default save format, so that early adopters start emailing .docx files to those who have yet to upgrade.

They even start publishing some of their own support documents in the new format.

Pure evil genius.

You can now get the Microsoft add-on to Office 2003 here[1] (thanks to Digital Inspiration). I installed it - it works. And there are a few file convertors around for those who don't have Office.

Until now I've said I am too far over the Word learning curve to go back (I did try Open Office), but there are days... Must go look at Google Apps. [Google *Docs* actually, and my first experiences are pretty good.]

Pink Elephant

A little clarification is in order after my recent article on ITSMWatch[2], re my position on PinkVerify. Bill Irvine of Pink Elephant published a response on ITSMWatch clarifying that PinkVerify does not claim that certified products are ITIL compliant. "In order to comply with something you need a standard".

Funny, that's what I thought "certification" required too.

Never mind: strictly speaking I never actually said that PinkVerify claims to certify compliance. The line was "PinkVerify ... in my experience ...is not a good indicator of compliance to some of the criteria that follows". This may sound like now it's my turn to play with moot semantics, but let me explain why this hair is being split: while PinkVerify never claims ITIL compliance, I doubt Pink are so naive as to really believe that vendors will not make the implication.

So a vendor can pay to have their product tested to obtain a licence to put the distinctive logo on their brochureware ... and say what to their prospects? Well perish the thought that a vendor salesman would ever use the word "compliant" when drawing an executive's attention to their certification. And I'm sure all product buyers are savvy enough to make the clear distinction between compliant and "verifies" "certification" that the product is "compatible with ... Service Support processes" "to ensure ITIL processes are effectively supported to at least a minimum level ... to help ...identify some of the products that at least meet ITIL's guidance".

So it is quite true that PinkVerify does not claim "compliance". But it certainly does assert assessment, validation, verification, certification, compatibility, comparison against criteria, explicit demonstration of commitment, reassurance, diligence, support for definition and

---

[1] http://www.microsoft.com/downloads/details.aspx?familyid=941B3470-3AE9-4AEE-8F43-C6BB74CD1466&displaylang=en
[2] http://www.itsmwatch.com/itil/article.php/3644451

requirements, and guidance met, which does not leave much else in the thesaurus.

The second time I mentioned PinkVerify in the article was to suggest some questions for buyers to ask vendors about "their supposedly ITIL-compliant or ITIL-supporting tool (including some PinkVerified ones)" [See page 130]. So I assert that some PinkVerified products do not meet all of the criteria I listed for what I believe is a reasonable standard for ITIL compliance. Obviously therefore I am setting a higher benchmark than the "minimum level" used by Pink Elephant. This is not to say that PinkVerified products do not meet the PinkVerify standard, only that they don't all meet mine. And of course the main point of the article was that in the absence of any lead from OGC or itSMF I'm as free as Pink Elephant to set my own standards for ITIL compliance   ...   er   ...   I mean   ... compatibility.

Finally, let me repeat what I said on the ITSMWatch forum: I like and respect Pink Elephant and their people (of whom I have met quite a few). They do good work and they are always very generous with sharing their IP publicly. I am not suggesting any dishonesty on their part. I do believe there is more marketing and less value in PinkVerify than in their other services and offerings, but I don't allow that to influence my broader view of the organisation and nor should you.

Plaxo

Who else thinks Plaxo is an unethically intrusive piece of malware? Recently I started using this thing again after ripping it out years ago as a dangerously intrusive invasion of my privacy. Plaxo apologised back then for being worms.

It is no better now. As far as I am aware I gave no permission to Plaxo to upload my email contacts, nor to email them all inviting them to Plaxo. But it did. Including my dead father.

Somehow I invited my aunt in Australia. She accidentally invited a friend of hers. Now, I know I get busy and I get dumb but the pattern to me is too obvious. This thing is deliberately viral and deliberately misleading in its interface. I don't doubt that Plaxo has successfully socially engineered me into doing this and that they would be able to point to something I clicked to make it happen. But guess how easy it is to unravel this stuff. Not. Every single one of my Outlook contacts needs to be manually deleted, one by one.

I don't like the way these people operate and I don't trust them. They aren't evil but they play fast and loose. I have ceased use of Plaxo. I had to wade through help text to find out how. For anyone else who wants this creepy thing out of their lives, go here[1]. I'll stick to LinkedIn and Facebook. Two's enough.

If it was only me, OK. I screw up all the time. But the only thing my aunt did was respond to an invite from me by registering on Plaxo. She does not have the toolbar installed and there is no software on her machine identified as "plaxo", yet it emailed her contacts. They lost my trust when they crawled all over my machine in the past and now they're out of it forever.

Stratavia

Submitted by Manny (not verified) on Tue, 2008-02-26 15:53.

ITIL V3 can indeed be complicated and the implementation process can be equally challenging. My employer recently made the decision to implement such things and is going down a heavy automation road. Though both our IT team and it's leaders are competent and educated we watched them have plenty of issues with itil. It eventually got to a point where the company decided to bring on an outside company, one that specializes in itil service management (www.stratavia.com/itilstandards.php). Once this third party stepped in and worked their magic, everything fell into place.

Wow Manny! That must have been miraculous to see! I was always a bit skeptical about magic especially in the context of ITIL services, but if you saw it then that's good enough for me. Those Stratavia guys sure seem to do magic alright. Anyone who can solve ITIL problems by automation coming from a database and data modelling perspective is certainly doing magic.

Quick everyone, stop wrestling with nasty problems like people and culture and process. Go buy some of the Stratavia magic and you can automagically implement a database-driven IT automation solution for ITIL! What a relief! Even those readers who are "competent and educated" (both of you) will benefit. Now we can all relax and stop worrying.

...What an idiot. Most spammers are an insult to my readers' intelligence.

---

[1] http://help.plaxo.com/al/12/1/article.asp?aid=1218&tab=atr&bt=4

Tideway

Here at the IT Skeptic we are not above picking on organisations, so let me use an example drawn to my attention today: Tideway. I don't doubt their product, Foundation, "takes auto-discovery to the next level of embedded intelligence", to try to unravel the service dependencies. I do doubt that they have removed the manual element from the process: there are plenty of clues that they haven't: "Reduces manual effort of building business service views by up to 80%". There ought to be a law defining use of the term "up to" as an illegal business practice. I have already discussed how I'm skeptical of the ability of these tools not to be excruciatingly stupid.

And most of all I do doubt that, except in the most complex of organisations, there will be a solid business case for replacing "up to 80%" of the manual effort with an expensive, complex, high-learning-curve tool that still requires a manual effort to check it, work out what it did, tell it when it got it wrong, add the really interesting data that it simply doesn't understand, and keep it correct in a dynamically changing environment.

Auto-discovery is very useful where initial data is rubbish: it is good for helping get a baseline set of CIs. If your Change processes are any good then you don't need it after that, though you can use it to audit data quality and detect non-compliance. And if your processes are no good, then it is not a substitute.

TSO

Another vendor that has got off fairly lightly on the blog so far is The Stationery office, TSO, the privatised British Government printer and publisher. Well, they have been one of several organisations jointly on the receiving end, as you will have noticed elsewhere in the book.

But their ITIL Live™ website, the possibility that OGC will sub-contract the management of the next version of ITIL to them, and a number of their commercial practices are bound to attract the attention of the IT Skeptic in future.

Look for a more substantial entry if there is a future edition of this book.

Speaking of which, I hope you have enjoyed this book. Whether you did or not, please write to me at skeptic@itskeptic.org and let me know your thoughts.

About the author:

The IT Skeptic is the pseudonym of Rob England, an IT consultant and commentator. Although he works around the ITIL industry, he is self-employed and his future is not dependant on ITIL – he has nothing to sell you but the ideas in this book.

He has twenty years experience mapping business requirements to IT solutions, ten of them in service management. (Some readers will be relieved to learn that this book reveals what "service management" means). He is active in the itSMF (the professional body for ITIL). He is the author of a popular blog www.itskeptic.org and a number of internet articles taking a critical look at IT's absurdities, especially those relating to ITIL. He is also a paid-up Skeptic. He lives with his wife and son in a small house in a small village.

Introduction to Real ITSM

It is not often that ITSM books are funny, but - according to readers - this one is funny.

This book is not about ITIL®. Really. Real ITSM is a tongue-in-cheek satirical look at what the real-life processes of IT Service Management might be, as compared to the "official" defined processes published in the authorised books of frameworks like ITIL. Find out what the Service Desk are really up to. The Introduction to Real ITSM is not all lampooning the status quo in IT. It also promotes a number of alternate ideas to stimulate discussion.

See more Realitsm at www.realitsm.com

Owning ITIL

This book is essential reading for **all decision makers** (IT-literate or not) who are presented with an ITIL® proposal or asked to oversee an ITIL project, or find something called "ITIL" or "Service Management" in their budget. It tells you what the ITIL industry won't. For **everyone else involved in ITIL** projects, this book will help you stay grounded and safe.

The book explains, in lay-manager's terms, **what ITIL is**. It reveals what ITIL is **good** for, what it is **bad** at, what to **expect** from it. It describes how to ensure an ITIL project **succeeds**, what to look for in the **business case**, and how to measure the **results**.

See www.itskeptic.org/owningitil